Meta-translation

Lao Zi's

Dao De Jing

(1-37)

The Physics of Psychology

Dr. Auke Schade

nemonik-thinking.org

Copyright

First Edition 25 December 2016

Second Edition 20 February 2017

Third Edition 2 January 2018

@ nemonik-thinking.org

ISBN 978-0-473-42678-1

Abstract

The title of Lao Zi's ancient book *Dao De Jing* means literally—*A Classic about the Way of Nature and the Way of People*. *Dao De Jing* aims to maximize your success, which is to obtain what you seek and escape what you suffer. Success is maximized by aligning the *Way of People* with the *Way of Nature* (Schade, Stunning Revelations about Lao Zi's Dao De Jing, 2017). Despite the great efforts, previous translations of *Dao De Jing* do not present an adequate understanding of that mysterious manuscript. In order to take optimal advantage of the expertise accumulated in such earlier studies, this meta-translation is based on an English meta-analysis and a Chinese meta-analysis. The English meta-analysis is based on the following English translations— (Chan Wing-Tsit, 1988); (Cheng Gia-Fu and English, J, 1972); (Henricks, 1993); (Land, 1990); (Lau, 1985); (Lin, J. P., 1977); (Man-ho Kwok; Palmer, M.; & Ramsay, J., 1997); (Waley, 1968); and (Wing, 1986). The Chinese meta-analysis is based on the following Chinese versions of *Dao De Jing*— (Wang Bi, 226-249 AD); (He-Shang Gong, 179-157 BC); (Fu Yi, 555-639 AD); (Mawangdui-A, ~200 BC); (Mawangdui-B, ~200 BC); and (Guodian, ~300 BC). This meta-translation of Dao (Chapters 1-37) is based on a special dictionary (Schade, Dictionary Lao Zi's Dao De Jing, 2018), while it is the foundation for (Schade, Lao Zi's Dao De Jing Demystified, 2017).

Free eBook @
nemonik-thinking.org

Dr. Auke Schade

My life started during the devastation of World War II. As a teenager, I worked as a carpenter and studied building engineering at night school. During the seventies, I became a financial manager for a multinational corporation, ran my own business, and studied economics in my spare time. My interest in the psychology of management extended to the interaction between the mind, body, and reality. In 1980, I immigrated to New Zealand where I obtained a doctorate in psychology from the University of Auckland. My mission is to make people the smartest thinkers they can be, which has led me to the development of nemonik thinking (Schade, Think Smarter with Nemonik Thinking, 2016).

Download free eBooks and videos
@ http://nemonik-thinking.org

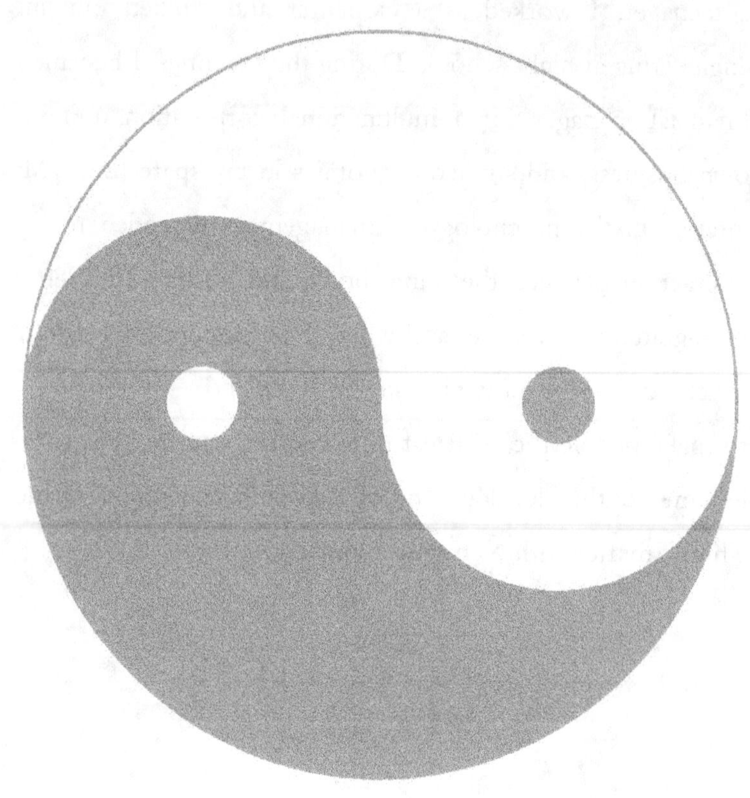

Yin-Yang

CONTENTS

LAO ZI'S DAO DE JING 11

Introduction 12

Dao—Way of Nature 23

Legend 24

Chapter 01 25

Chapter 02 31

Chapter 03 41

Chapter 04 48

Chapter 05 54

Chapter 06 59

Chapter 07 61

Chapter 08 66

Chapter 09 73

Chapter 10 78

Chapter 11 85

Chapter 12 89

Chapter 13 93

Chapter 14 101

Chapter 15 112

Chapter 16 121

Chapter 17 131

Chapter 18 136

Chapter 19 140

Chapter 20 146

Chapter 21 160

Chapter 22 167

Chapter 23 175

Chapter 24 182

Chapter 25 187

Chapter 26 197

Chapter 27 203

Chapter 28 212

Chapter 29 223

Chapter 30 229

Chapter 31 237

Chapter 32 249

Chapter 33 256

Chapter 34 260

Chapter 35 267

Chapter 36 271

Chapter 37 277

APPENDIX 283

Index 284

Bibliography 297

Secular versus Sacred 306

The Ways of *Dao* 319

Chinese versions of *Dao De Jing* 327

My other books 341

Website 358

Endnotes.. 359

老子之

道德經

Lao Zi's

Dao De Jing

nemonik-thinking.org

META-TRANSLATION

LAO ZI'S DAO DE JING

(1-37)

Dao—Way of Nature

INTRODUCTION

Title *Dao De Jing*

After more than two-and-halve thousand years, Lao Zi's *Dao De Jing* (老子之道德經) is still the most intriguing literary and philosophical legacy received from ancient China. Despite the great efforts of many brilliant scholars, *Dao De Jing* has been hiding crucial information about the universe and humanity behind a veil of simple aphorisms and poetic beauty (Schade, Stunning Revelations about Lao Zi's Dao De Jing, 2017).

Mystery surrounds the person of Lao Zi, who allegedly lived from about 570 to 490 BC. His biography was initially written by the historian Ssu-ma-Ch'ien (145-90 BC) who compiled the first comprehensive history of China. He reported that Lao Zi's real name was Li Erh who was a historian in the state of Chu. Legend has it that Lao Zi left Chu because of the corruption in that state. Travelling through a narrow mountain pass, the keeper of that pass asked him to write down his wisdom. However, some scholars have raised serious questions about Lao Zi's identity and his authorship of *Dao De Jing* (Schade, Stunning Revelations about Lao Zi's Dao De Jing, 2017, pp. 170-171).

Even the title of Lao Zi's manuscript is enigmatic. The pictograph 道 *Dao* means literally *road, path, way, or pathway.*

However, most scholars agree that in the context of Lao Zi's philosophy, 道 *Dao* is short for the 天之道 *Way of Nature* *[09.05b, 73.06a, 77.01a, 77.04a, and 81.10a]*. In Lao Zi's philosophy, *Dao* is the origin, principle, substance, and force of the universe. On the other hand, 德 *De* could be translated as *virtue*, which stands for the 人之道 *Way of People* *[77.05 and 81.11a]*. Furthermore, 經 *Jing* was later added to the title denoting that Lao Zi's manuscript had become a *Classic* book. Hence, *Dao De Jing* means *A Classic about the Way of Nature and the Way of People*. It is emphasized that 道 *Dao* has an entirely different meaning in Confucius' philosophy.[i]

Nowadays, the *Way of Nature* is called *Physics*, while the *Way of People* has become *Psychology*. Therefore, the modern meaning of 道德經 *Dao De Jing* would be *A Classic about the Physics of Psychology* (Schade, Stunning Revelations about Lao Zi's Dao De Jing, 2017).

Lao Zi's style

Dao De Jing is written in a beautiful poetic style that provides profound quotes suitable for almost every occasion. The manuscript certainly stimulates the mind. However, Lao Zi warns us—*My words are very easy to understand and very easy to*

---

[i] Appendix—The Ways of *Dao*

apply. Yet, people cannot understand them and they cannot apply them [70.01-02]. Although *Dao De Jing* is easy reading, it is not so easy to understand its deeper meaning.

Reading *Dao De Jing* without understanding is like interpreting inkblots during a Rorschach test. Such inkblots do not mean anything in itself, but they are a mirror for what is at the forefront of one's mind. Hence, people see their own thoughts in the inkblots. Similarly, people who do not understand *Dao De Jing* may see in it whatever occupies their minds most. As a result, Lao Zi's manuscript means different things to many people. For spiritual people *Dao De Jing* could be a sacred scripture and a guideline to secure their afterlife. Mystics might consider it to be an ancient oracle and put its sayings in their fortune cookies. On the other hand, sceptics consider it to be a dusty collection of simple peasant wisdom and folk tales.

Although Lao Zi's *Dao De Jing* contains only about five thousand pictographs, the more I studied that small manuscript, the more I became convinced that I missed somehow his crucial message. Analysing *Dao De Jing* is like peeling an onion in the hope of finding the truth hidden beneath many layers of ambiguity. Intended or unintended, Lao Zi fosters that ambiguity by his liberal use of poetic metaphors for the *Way of Nature—Father of the Multitude, Great Image, Great Road, Immortal Valley Spirit, Master Carpenter,*

Mother, Mysterious Female, Named, Nameless Simplicity, Nameless, Nothingness, One, River, Simplicity, Valley, and Water.

Our modern literature is written in a rational format in which the details are organized in a logical sequence from cause to conclusion. Paragraphs string together like beads on a string, each additional one building up to the conclusion of the chapter. Each subsequent chapter is a step closer to the conclusion of the manuscript. In contrast, the format of *Dao De Jing* is holistic and has no strong introduction, mid-section or conclusion. Each part seems to embody the entire topic, highlighting that entirety from a different angle. Studying *Dao De Jing* is like looking into a kaleidoscope where no pattern is either the first or last. Consequently, Lao Zi's holistic and ambiguous style hinders a rational understanding of *Dao De Jing*. This problem is addressed in (Schade, Lao Zi's Dao De Jing Demystified, 2017) and (Schade, Stunning Revelations about Lao Zi's Dao De Jing, 2017).

Chinese ambiguity

Each known version of Lao Zi's manuscript was written hundreds of years after the creation of the original. Therefore, even ancient versions, such as the Mawangdui and Guodian versions, might differ from the original text. In addition, translating ancient Chinese pictographs into modern ones adds to the complexity of Lao Zi's manuscript. Every language is alive and changes over time. Therefore, the meaning of some ancient pictographs might have changed, while others might have lost their meaning entirely.

The presented Chinese versions of *Dao De Jing* suggest that each ancient pictograph might have several modern equivalents. For example, in the opinion of experts in ancient Chinese; 呴, 噤, 歍, 灵, and 热 [29.05] represent the same ancient pictograph. Together, those five modern equivalents produce a total of 52 English meanings—*agile, alert, ardent, bellow, bier, blow, breathe, bright, clever, close, coffin, craze, deity, departed soul, eager, easy, effective, efficacious, elf, envious, exhale from nose, fad, fairy, fervent, fever, hearse, heat, heave a sigh, hot, hot weather, howl, intelligence, keep silent, nimble, of the deceased, quick, restless, roar, sensitive, shiver, silent, snort, soul, spirit, spiritual world, sprite, temperature, thermal, unable to speak, warm, warm-hearted, yawn, and zeal* (Schade, Dictionary Lao Zi's Dao De Jing, 2018). That high number of potential meanings suggests that the ambiguity of the ancient pictographs hinders the understanding and translation of *Dao De Jing* even for Chinese speaking scholars.

English ambiguity

Similar to the written symbols used in any other language, the modern Chinese pictographs are versatile and therefore ambiguous. Most pictographs have many different meanings. For example, each pictograph in the phrase—身与货孰多

[44.02]—provides several English meanings. 身 *body, character, clothes, conduct, hull, in person, life, main part of a structure or body, morality, oneself, person, personally, pregnant, status, suit, themselves, torso, trunk, twinset, yourself*; 与 *against, and, associate, careful, final interrogative particle expressing doubt or surprise, for, get along, give, grant, have a hand in, have dealings, help, make contact, offer, on good terms, participate, send, support, take part, to, together, wait, with*; 货, *commodities, goods, money, products*; 孰 *what, which, who*; and 多 *for the most part, lot of, many, more, more than, most, much, multi-, numerous, over* (Schade, Dictionary Lao Zi's Dao De Jing, 2018). Consequently, those five pictographs have the potential to provide more than 13,000 English phrases.[1] This shows that the ambiguity of modern Chinese pictographs hinders also the understanding and translation of *Dao De Jing* into modern English.

Context, consistency, and simplicity

The multiple English meanings of modern Chinese pictographs supports the notion that the meaning of a pictograph can only be determined by the context in which it appears. For example, the pictograph 天 could mean either *Sky* or *Heaven* (Schade, Dictionary Lao Zi's Dao De Jing, 2018). Hence, Lao Zi's phrase 天地之间其犹橐籥与 [05.03] could mean—*What is between the **Sky** and the Earth is like a pair of bellows [05.03]*. Alternatively, it could mean—

What is between **Heaven** *and Earth is like a pair of bellows [05.03].* Both sentences make sense. Hence, we need more information to make the decision whether Lao Zi refers to *Sky* or *Heaven*. However, he did not explain his meaning of 天 in his manuscript. Therefore, we have to take into account the context in which that ambiguous pictograph appears elsewhere in the text and use that meaning as consistently as possible for the entire translation.

The need to understand the context before the specific meaning of a pictograph can be determined creates a linguistic conundrum. Translators need to know the context before they are able to determine the meaning of a pictograph, while they need to know the meaning of the pictograph before they are able to understand the context. Therefore, the translation presented in this book was the result of many cycles in which improving the translation and context were alternated. Each new translation improved the context, while each new context improved the translation. Hence, this meta-translation is based on the principles of context, consistency, and simplicity.

Secular versus sacred

The core of the *Dao* section of Lao Zi's *Dao De Jing* is the transformation from *Nothingness* or the *One* into *All-things*—*The One generated the Two. The Two generated the Three. The Three generated All-things [42.02-04]*. In Lao Zi's theory, the *Two* means *Existence and Non-existence*, which might refer to the modern concepts of *Matter and Antimatter—The world's things originate from Existence. Existence originates from Non-existence [40.03-04]*.[2]

The previous paragraphs support the notion that the *Dao* section is a secular manuscript about physics, rather than a sacred manuscript about spiritual and divine phenomena (Schade, Stunning Revelations about Lao Zi's Dao De Jing, 2017).

The core of the *De* section of Lao Zi's *Dao De Jing* is to maximize the success of 圣人 *sages—obtain what you seek and escape what you suffer [62.09b]. Succeed without boasting. Succeed without attacking. Succeed without arrogance. Succeed without excess. That is called succeeding without force [30.07-11]*.[3] In accord, Lao Zi counsels sages throughout *Dao De Jing* to foster secular virtues such as: *compassion, frugality, humbleness, retreat, simplicity, timing, and tranquillity*. He also urges them to inhibit: *action, arrogance, effort, desire, display, force, hoarding, resistance, strive, and wealth*. In contrast, he does not mention any sacred virtues such as ritual, devotion, worship, sacrifice, or prayer.

The previous paragraphs support the notion that the *De* section is a secular manuscript about psychology, rather than a sacred manuscript about spiritual and divine phenomena. More details about this topic are presented in: Appendix—Secular versus Sacred.

Meta-translation

Each translation is inevitably confounded by linguistic ambiguities and the subjectivity of the translator. As a result, each translator produces a slightly different version of *Dao De Jing*. It is like looking at the facets of a diamond. While each facet is different, they are all part of the same diamond and each facet adds to a clearer perception of the entire gem. In the same way, each translation adds to the holistic understanding of Lao Zi's *Dao De Jing*.

The availability of many high-quality translations justifies a meta-translation, which is a translation that is based on an analysis of more than one previous translations of the same manuscript. The aim of a meta-translation is to produce a translation that takes optimal advantage of the expertise accumulated in the previous translations. The meta-translation for the present study includes an English meta-analysis and a Chinese meta- analysis.

The aim of the English meta-analysis was to provide an initial context for the translation of the Chinese pictographs. This analysis includes the following English translations of

Lao Zi's *Dao De Jing*— (Chan Wing-Tsit, 1988); (Cheng Gia-Fu and English, J, 1972); (Henricks, 1993); (Land, 1990); (Lau, 1985); (Lin, J. P., 1977); (Man-ho Kwok; Palmer, M.; & Ramsay, J., 1997); (Waley, 1968); and (Wing, 1986). Line by line comparisons, across all translations, provided the most likely keywords that were then used to create new draft lines. In turn, those draft lines were used as the initial context for the translation of the Chinese pictographs.

The aim of the Chinese meta-analysis was to create an optimal version of Lao Zi's *Dao De Jing* in modern Chinese pictographs. This analysis includes the following Chinese versions of Lao Zi's *Dao De Jing*— (Wang Bi, 226-249 AD); (He-Shang Gong, 179-157 BC); (Fu Yi, 555-639 AD); (Mawangdui-A, ~200 BC); (Mawangdui-B, ~200 BC); and (Guodian, ~300 BC).[ii] In addition, those modern pictographs were translated with a Chinese-English dictionary that was compiled especially for Lao Zi's *Dao De Jing* (Schade, Dictionary Lao Zi's Dao De Jing, 2018).

The English meaning of each Chinese pictograph was evaluated within the context of the English meta-analysis. In the case of synonym pictographs, each one was evaluated separately. A computer-assisted procedure maximized the consistency of the English meaning of each pictograph across

---

[ii] Appendix—Chinese versions *Dao De Jing*

the entire translation. The cycle of improving alternately the context and translation was repeated until an optimal consistency of the text was obtained.

DAO—WAY OF NATURE[4]

Legend

---	blank space aligning pictographs vertically.
( )	pictographs or words in the same textual position.
a[b]	read pictograph (a) for [b].
>	separates keywords in the same textual position.
□	indicates missing pictograph in the Chinese texts.

■, •, ∠, and ○ indicate breaks in the original Chinese texts.

FE	Final English sentence.
SK	Selected Keywords (synonyms removed).
SC	Selected Chinese pictographs (synonyms removed).
TK	Total Keywords.
TC	Total Chinese pictographs.
WB	Wang Bi version.[5]
HG	He-shang Gong version.[6]
FY	Fu Yi version.[7]
MA	Mawangdui-A version.[8]
MB	Mawangdui-B version.[9]
G_	dummy line indicating missing Guodian text.[10]
GA	Guodian version part-A.[11]
GB	Guodian version part-B.[12]
GC	Guodian version part-C.[13]

Chapter 01

01.010FE	The *Way* that can be discussed is not the eternal *Way*.
01.010SK	*Way* can discuss — not eternal *Way* —
01.010SC	道可道也非恒道也
01.010TK	*Way* can discuss（一 ＞ 一）not（constant ＞ eternal）*Way* —
01.010TC	道可道(也■)非(常恒)道也
01.010WB	道可道(___ ___)非(常 ___)道 ___
01.010HG	道可道(___ ___)非(常 ___)道 ___
01.010FY	道可道(___ ___)非(常 ___)道 ___
45.010MA	道可道(也■)非(___ 恒)道也
45.010MB	道可道(也 ___)□(___ □)□□
00.000G-	___ ___ ___ (___ ___) ___ (___ ___) ___ ___
00.000G-	___ ___ ___ (___ ___) ___ (___ ___) ___ ___

01.020FE	The name that can be named is not the eternal name.
01.020SK	name can named — not eternal name —
01.020SC	名可名也非恒名也
01.020TK	name can named — not（constant ＞ eternal）name —
01.020TC	名可名也非(常恒)名也
01.020WB	名可名 ___ 非(常 ___)名 ___
01.020HG	名可名 ___ 非(常 ___)名 ___
01.020FY	名可名 ___ 非(常 ___)名 ___
45.020MA	名可名也非(___ 恒)名也
45.020MB	□□□□□(___ 恒)名也
00.000G-	___ ___ ___ ___ (___ ___) ___ ___
00.000G-	___ ___ ___ ___ (___ ___) ___ ___

01.030FE   *Nameless:* it is the origin of *All-things.* [14]

01.030SK   (*Nameless*) (*All-things*) ('s) origin 一

01.030SC   （无名）（万物）之始也

01.030TK   (*Nameless*) ((*Sky; Earth*) > (*All-things*)) ('s) origin (一 > 一)

01.030TC   （无名）（（天地）（万物））之始（也■）

01.030WB   （无名）（（天地）（＿＿＿））之始（＿＿＿）

01.030HG   （无名）（（天地）（＿＿＿））之始（＿＿＿）

01.030FY   （无名）（（天地）（＿＿＿））之始（＿＿＿）

45.030MA   （无名）（（＿＿＿）（万物））之始（也■）

45.030MB   （无名）（（＿＿＿）（万物））之始（也＿＿）

00.000G-   （＿＿＿）（（＿＿＿）（＿＿＿））＿＿＿（＿＿＿）

00.000G-   （＿＿＿）（（＿＿＿）（＿＿＿））＿＿＿（＿＿＿）

01.040FE   Being *Named:* it is the *Mother of All-things.* [15]

01.040SK   being named (*All-things*) ('s) *Mother* 一

01.040SC   有名（万物）之母也

01.040TK   being named (*All-things*) ('s) *Mother* 一

01.040TC   有名（万物）之母也

01.040WB   有名（万物）之母＿

01.040HG   有名（万物）之母＿

01.040FY   有名（万物）之母＿

45.040MA   有名（万物）之母也

45.040MB   有名（万物）之母也

00.000G-   ＿＿＿（＿＿＿）＿＿＿

00.000G-   ＿＿＿（＿＿＿）＿＿＿

01.05aFE   Therefore, be always without desire[16]
01.05aSK   therefore always without desire —
01.05aSC   故恒无欲也
01.05aTK   therefore (always > always) without desire —
01.05aTC   故(常恒)无欲也
01.05aWB   故(常＿＿)无欲＿＿
01.05aHG   故(常＿＿)无欲＿＿
01.05aFY   故(常＿＿)无欲＿＿
45.05aMA   □(＿＿恒)无欲也
45.05aMB   故(＿＿恒)无欲也
00.000G-   ＿＿＿ ＿＿＿ ＿＿＿ ＿＿＿ ＿＿＿
00.000G-   ＿＿＿ ＿＿＿ ＿＿＿ ＿＿＿ ＿＿＿

01.05bFE   and see its details.[17]
01.05bSK   accordingly see its detail
01.05bSC   以观其眇
01.05bTK   accordingly see its (fine > detail)
01.05bTC   以观其(妙眇)
01.05bWB   以观其(妙眇)
01.05bHG   以观其(妙眇)
01.05bFY   以观其(妙眇)
45.05bMA   以观其(＿＿眇)
45.05bMB   □□□(＿＿□)
00.000G-   ＿＿＿ ＿＿＿ ＿＿＿ (＿＿＿ ＿＿＿)
00.000G-   ＿＿＿ ＿＿＿ ＿＿＿ (＿＿＿ ＿＿＿)

01.06aFE   Have always desires[18]
01.06aSK   always have desire —
01.06aSC   恒有欲也
01.06aTK   (always > always) (have > and) desire —
01.06aTC   (常恒)(有又)欲也
01.06aWB   (常＿＿)(有＿＿)欲＿＿
01.06aHG   (常＿＿)(有＿＿)欲＿＿
01.06aFY   (常＿＿)(有＿＿)欲＿＿
45.06aMA   (＿＿恒)(有＿＿)欲＿＿
45.06aMB   (＿＿恒)(＿＿又)欲也
00.000G–   (＿＿＿＿)(＿＿＿＿)＿＿＿＿
00.000G–   (＿＿＿＿)(＿＿＿＿)＿＿＿＿

01.06bFE   and see its limits.
01.06bSK   accordingly see their limit
01.06bSC   以观其噭
01.06bTK   accordingly see their — (limit > limit)
01.06bTC   以观其所(徼噭)
01.06bWB   以观其＿＿(徼＿＿)
01.06bHG   以观其＿＿(徼＿＿)
01.06bFY   以观其＿＿(徼＿＿)
45.06bMA   以观其所(＿＿噭)
45.06bMB   以观其所(＿＿噭)
00.000G–   ＿＿＿＿＿＿＿＿(＿＿＿＿)
00.000G–   ＿＿＿＿＿＿＿＿(＿＿＿＿)

01. 07aFE	These two things occur together.
01. 07aSK	these two thing together occur
01. 07aSC	此两者同出
01. 07aTK	these two thing together occur
01. 07aTC	此两者同出
01. 07aWB	此两者同出
01. 07aHG	此两者同出
01. 07aFY	此两者同出
45. 07aMA	＿＿两者同出
45. 07aMB	＿＿两者同出
00. 000G-	＿＿ ＿＿ ＿＿ ＿＿ ＿＿
00. 000G-	＿＿ ＿＿ ＿＿ ＿＿ ＿＿

01. 07bFE	Different names with the same meaning.[19]
01. 07bSK	different name same meaning
01. 07bSC	异名同谓
01. 07bTK	(shows contrast > different) name same (meaning) ('s) mystery
01. 07bTC	（而异）名同（谓［＿＿］）之玄
01. 07bWB	（而异）名同（谓［＿＿］）之玄
01. 07bIIG	（而异）名同（谓［＿＿］）之玄
01. 07bFY	（而异）名同（谓［＿＿］）之玄
45. 07bMA	（＿＿异）名同（谓［胃］）＿＿＿＿
45. 07bMB	（＿＿异）名同（谓［胃］）＿＿＿＿
00. 000G-	（＿＿ ＿＿）＿＿ ＿＿（＿＿［＿＿］）＿＿ ＿＿
00. 000G-	（＿＿ ＿＿）＿＿ ＿＿（＿＿［＿＿］）＿＿ ＿＿

01. 080FE	Profoundly mysterious, they are the gateway to many details.[20]	
01. 080SK	(mystery of mysteries) numerous detail ('s) gateway	
01. 080SC	（玄之又玄）众眇之门	
01. 080TK	((mystery of mysteries) > (mystery of mysteries)) numerous (fine > detail) ('s) gateway	
01. 080TC	((玄之又玄)(玄之有玄))众(妙眇)之门	
01. 080WB	((玄之又玄)(＿＿＿＿＿＿＿))众(妙＿)之门	
01. 080HG	((玄之又玄)(＿＿＿＿＿＿＿))众(妙＿)之门	
01. 080FY	((玄之又玄)(＿＿＿＿＿＿＿))众(妙＿)之门	
45. 080MA	((＿＿＿＿＿＿＿)(玄之有玄))众(＿眇)之□	
45. 080MB	((玄之又玄)(＿＿＿＿＿＿＿))众(＿眇)之门	
00. 000G–	((＿＿＿＿＿＿)(＿＿＿＿＿＿)) ＿ (＿＿＿) ＿＿	
00. 000G–	((＿＿＿＿＿＿)(＿＿＿＿＿＿)) ＿ (＿＿＿) ＿＿	

Chapter 02

02.01aFE	If everyone in the world recognises beauty as beautiful,[21]
02.01aSK	(world) everyone recognise beauty ('s) as beauty —
02.01aSC	（天下）皆知美之为美也
02.01aTK	(world) everyone recognise beauty ('s) as beauty —
02.01aTC	（天下）皆知美之为美也
02.01aWB	（天下）皆知美之为美…
02.01aHG	（天下）皆知美之为美…
02.01aFY	（天下）皆知美之为美…
46.01aMA	（天下）皆知美…为美…
46.01aMB	（天下）皆知美之为美…
09.01aGA	（天下）皆知美之为美也
00.000G-	（……）… … … … … …

02.01bFE	then there is already ugliness.
02.01bSK	then ugly already
02.01bSC	斯恶已
02.01bTK	then (ugly > ugly) already —
02.01bTC	斯（恶亚）已■
02.01bWB	斯（恶…）已…
02.01bHG	斯（恶…）已…
02.01bFY	斯（恶…）已…
46.01bMA	…（恶…）已■
46.01bMB	…（…亚）已…
09.01bGA	…（…亚）已…
00.000G-	…（……）……

02. 02aFE	If everyone recognizes good as goodness,
02. 02aSK	everyone recognise good ('s) as good
02. 02aSC	皆知善之为善
02. 02aTK	everyone recognise good ('s) as good
02. 02aTC	皆知善之为善
02. 02aWB	皆知善之为善
02. 02aHG	皆知善之为善
02. 02aFY	皆知善之为善
46. 02aMA	皆知善___ ___ ___
46. 02aMB	皆知善___ ___ ___
09. 02aGA	皆知善___ ___ ___
00. 000G-	___ ___ ___ ___ ___ ___

02. 02bFE	then there is already badness.
02. 02bSK	then (bad) already —
02. 02bSC	斯(不善)已矣
02. 02bTK	(then > these > is) (bad) already (— > —)
02. 02bTC	(斯此其)(不善)已(矣■)
02. 02bWB	(斯___ ___)(不善)已(___ ___)
02. 02bHG	(斯___ ___)(不善)已(___ ___)
02. 02bFY	(斯___ ___)(不善)已(___ ___)
46. 02bMA	(斯___ ___)(不善)___(矣■)
46. 02bMB	(斯___ ___)(不善)___(矣■)
09. 02bGA	(___此其)(不善)已(___ ___)
00. 000G-	(___ ___ ___)(___ ___)___(___ ___)

02.030FE   Therefore, *Existence* and *Non-existence*
            generate each other.[22]
02.030SK   therefore *Existence* *Non-existence* ('s) (each
            other) generate 一
02.030SC   故有无之相生也
02.030TK   therefore *Existence* (*Non-existence* > missing)
            ('s) (each other) generate 一
02.030TC   故有(无亡)之相生也
02.030WB   故有(无...)...相生...
02.030HG   故有(无...)之相生...
02.030FY   故有(无...)之相生...
46.030MA   ...有(无...)之相生也
46.030MB   ...□(...□)□□生也
09.030GA   ...有(...亡)之相生也
00.000G-   ...... (......) ... ...

02.040FE   Difficult and easy turn into each other.
02.040SK   difficult easy ('s) (each other) (turn into)
            一
02.040SC   难易之相成也
02.040TK   difficult easy ('s) (each other) (turn into)
            一
02.040TC   难易之相成也
02.040WB   难易...相成...
02.040HG   难易之相成...
02.040FY   难易之相成...
46.040MA   难易之相成也
46.040MB   难易之相成也
09.040GA   难易之相成也
00.000G-   ... ...

02. 050FE   Long and short shape each other.
02. 050SK   long short ('s) (each other) shape 一
02. 050SC   长短之相刑也
02. 050TK   long short ('s) (each other) (shape > shape > contrast) 一
02. 050TC   长短之相(形刑较)也
02. 050WB   长短＿相(＿＿较)＿
02. 050HG   长短之相(形＿＿)＿
02. 050FY   长短之相(形＿＿)＿
46. 050MA   长短之相(＿刑＿)也
46. 050MB   长短之相(＿刑＿)也
09. 050GA   长短之相(＿刑＿)也
00. 000G-   ＿＿＿(＿＿)＿

02. 060FE   High and low fill each other.[23]
02. 060SK   high low ('s) (each other) fill 一
02. 060SC   高下之相盈也
02. 060TK   high low ('s) (each other) ((overturn) > fill) (一 > 一)
02. 060TC   高下之相((倾[＿])盈))(也■)
02. 060WB   高下＿相((倾[＿])＿))(＿＿)
02. 060HG   高下之相((倾[倾])＿))(＿＿)
02. 060FY   高下之相((倾[倾])＿))(＿＿)
46. 060MA   高下之相((＿[＿])盈))(也■)
46. 060MB   高下之相((＿[＿])盈))(也＿)
09. 060GA   高下之相((＿[＿])盈))(也＿)
00. 000GC   ＿＿＿((＿[＿]0盈))(＿＿)

02.070FE	Tone and voice harmonise each other.
02.070SK	tone voice ('s) harmony (each other) —
02.070SC	音声之相和也
02.070TK	(tone > intention) voice ('s) harmony (each other) —
02.070TC	(音意)声之相和也
02.070WB	(音__)声__相和__
02.070HG	(音__)声之相和__
02.070FY	(音__)声之相和__
46.070MA	(__意)声之相和也
46.070MB	(音__)声之相和也
09.070GA	(音__)声之相和也
00.000G-	(_____) ___ ___ ___ ___ ___

02.080FE	Before and after follow each other forever.
02.080SK	before after ('s) (each other) follow forever —
02.080SC	先后之相随恒也
02.080TK	(before > before) after ('s) (each other) (follow) forever —
02.080TC	(前先)后之相(随[__])恒也
02.080WB	(前__)后__相(随[__])_____
02.080HG	(前__)后__相(随[随])_____
02.080FY	(前__)后之相(随[随])_____
46.080MA	(__先)后之相(随[__])恒也
46.080MB	(__先)后之相(随[__])恒也
09.080GA	(__先)后之相(随[__])___也
00.000G-	(_____) _______ (__[__])_____

02. 09aFE	Therefore, sages[24]
02. 09aSK	(therefore) (sage)
02. 09aSC	(是以)(圣人)
02. 09aTK	(therefore)((sage) > (reputable person))
02. 09aTC	(是以)((圣人)(声人))
02. 09aWB	(是以)((圣人)(＿＿))
02. 09aHG	(是以)((圣人)(＿＿))
02. 09aFY	(是以)((圣人)(＿＿))
46. 09aMA	(是以)((＿＿)(声人))
46. 09aMB	(是以)((圣人)(＿＿))
09. 09aGA	(是以)((圣人)(＿＿))
00. 000G–	(＿＿)((＿＿)(＿＿))

02. 09bFE	manage their affairs with *Non-action*.[25]
02. 09bSK	manage (*Non-action*) ('s) affair
02. 09bSC	处(无为)之事
02. 09bTK	(manage > claim)((*Non-action*) > (*Non-action*)) ('s) affair
02. 09bTC	(处居)((无为)(亡为))之事
02. 09bWB	(处＿)((无为)(＿＿))之事
02. 09bHG	(处＿)((无为)(＿＿))之事
02. 09bFY	(处＿)((无为)(＿＿))之事
46. 09bMA	(＿居)((无为)(＿＿))之事
46. 09bMB	(＿居)((无为)(＿＿))之事
09. 09bGA	(＿居)((＿＿)(亡为))之事
00. 000G–	(＿＿)((＿＿)(＿＿))＿＿

02.09cFE	They carry out their teachings without speaking.
02.09cSK	(carry out) without speak their teach
02.09cSC	行不言之教
02.09cTK	(carry out) without speak their teach
02.09cTC	行不言之教
02.09cWB	行不言之教
02.09cHG	行不言之教
02.09cFY	行不言之教
46.09cMA	行□□□□
46.09cMB	行不言之教
09.09cGA	行不言之教
00.000G-	--- --- --- --- ---

02.100FE	All-things rise, but do not initiate.
02.100SK	(All-things) rise but not initiate 一
02.100SC	(万物)作而不始也
02.100TK	(All-things) (rise > begin) then but (not > not) do (dismiss > initiate) 一
02.100TC	(万物)(作昔)焉而(不弗)为(辞始)也
02.100WB	(万物)(作___)焉而(不___)___(辞___)___
02.100HG	(万物)(作___)焉而(不___)___(辞___)___
02.100FY	(万物)(作___)___而(不___)为(___始)___
46.100MA	(□□)(_____)□□(___□)___(___□)也
46.100MB	(万物)(___昔)___而(___弗)___(___始)___
09.100GA	(万物)(作___)___而(___弗)___(___始)也
00.000G-	(_____)(_____)___ ___(_____)___(_____)___

02. 110FE   Generate, but do not possess.[26]
02. 110SK   generate but not possess
02. 110SC   生而不有
02. 110TK   generate but not possess
02. 110TC   生而不有
02. 110WB   生而不有
02. 110HG   生而不有
02. 110FY   生而不有
00. 000MA   --- --- --- ---
00. 000MB   --- --- --- ---
00. 000G–   --- --- --- ---
00. 000G–   --- --- --- ---

02. 120FE   Act, but do not rely on it.[27]
02. 120SK   act but not rely 一
02. 120SC   为而弗恃也
02. 120TK   act but (not > not) (rely > desire) 一
02. 120TC   为而(不弗)(恃志)也
02. 120WB   为而(不___)(恃___)___
02. 120HG   为而(不___)(恃___)___
02. 120FY   为而(不___)(恃___)___
46. 110MA   为而(___弗)(___志)也 (not desire)
46. 110MB   为而(___弗)(恃___)也 (not rely)
09. 110GA   为而(___弗)(恃___)也
00. 000G–   --- ---(--- ---)(--- ---)---

02. 130FE　Succeed, but do not claim.

02. 130SK　(succeed) but not claim —

02. 130SC　(成功)而弗居也

02. 130TK　((succeed) > (succeed) > succeed) but (not > not) (claim > (deal with)) (— > —)

02. 130TC　((功成)(成功)(成))而(弗不)(居处)(也■)

02. 130WB　((功成)(＿＿)(＿＿))而(弗＿)(居＿)(＿＿＿)

02. 130HG　((功成)(＿＿)(＿＿))＿(弗＿)(居＿)(＿＿＿)

02. 130FY　((功成)(＿＿)(＿＿))＿(＿不)(＿处)(＿＿＿)

46. 120MA　((＿＿＿)(成功)(＿＿))而(弗＿)(居＿)(也■)

46. 120MB　((＿＿＿)(成功)(＿＿))而(弗＿)(居＿)(也■)

09. 120GA　((＿＿＿)(＿＿＿)(成))而(弗＿)(居＿)(＿＿＿)

00. 000GC　((＿＿＿)(＿＿＿)(成))而(弗＿)(居＿)(＿＿＿)

02. 14aFE　Only that what is not claimed

02. 14aSK　that only not claim —

02. 14aSC　夫唯弗居也

02. 14aTK　that (only > only) (not > not) ((claim > (deal with)) —

02. 14aTC　夫(惟唯)(不弗)(居处)也

02. 14aWD　大(＿唯)(＿弗)(居＿)＿

02. 14aHG　夫(惟＿)(不＿)(居＿)＿

02. 14aFY　夫(惟＿)(不＿)(＿处)＿

46. 13aMA　夫(＿唯)(＿＿＿)(居＿)＿

46. 13aMB　夫(＿唯)(＿弗)(居＿)＿

09. 13aGA　夫(＿唯)(＿弗)(居＿)也

00. 000G-　＿(＿＿＿)(＿＿＿)(＿＿＿)＿

02. 14bFE   can therefore not be taken away.
02. 14bSK   (therefore) not reject 一
02. 14bSC   (是以) 弗去也
02. 14bTK   (therefore) (not > not) reject (一 > 一)
02. 14bTC   (是以) (不弗) 去 (也■)
02. 14bWB   (是以) (不...) 去 (... ...)
02. 14bHG   (是以) (不...) 去 (... ...)
02. 14bFY   (是以) (不...) 去 (... ...)
46. 13bMA   (是以) (... 弗) 去 (... ...)
46. 13bMB   (是以) (... 弗) 去 (... ...)
09. 13bGA   (是以) (... 弗) 去 (也■)
00. 000G-   (... ...) (... ...) ... (... ...)

Chapter 03

03.01aFE	Do not value knowledge
03.01aSK	not promote knowledge
03.01aSC	不上贤
03.01aTK	not (value > promote) knowledge
03.01aTC	不(尚上)贤
03.01aWB	不(尚__)贤
03.01aHG	不(尚__)贤
03.01aFY	不(尚__)贤
47.01aMA	不(__上)贤
47.01aMB	不(__上)贤
00.000G-	__(__ __)__
00.000G-	__(__ __)__

03.01bFE	and the people will not strive.
03.01bSK	let people not strive
03.01bSC	使民不争
03.01bTK	let people not strive
03.01bTC	使民不争
03.01bWB	使民不争
03.01bHG	使民不争
03.01bFY	使民不争
47.01bMA	□□□□
47.01bMB	使民不争
00.000G-	__ __ __ __
00.000G-	__ __ __ __

03. 02aFE	Do not admire goods that are difficult to obtain[28]
03. 02aSK	not admire difficult obtain their goods
03. 02aSC	不贵难得之货
03. 02aTK	not admire difficult obtain their goods
03. 02aTC	不贵难得之货
03. 02aWB	不贵难得之货
03. 02aHG	不贵难得之货
03. 02aFY	不贵难得之货
47. 02aMA	□□□□□□
47. 02aMB	不贵难得之货
00. 000G-	--- --- --- --- ---
00. 000G-	--- --- --- --- ---

03. 02bFE	and the people will not steal.
03. 02bSK	let people not become thief
03. 02bSC	使民不为盗
03. 02bTK	let people not become thief
03. 02bTC	使民不为盗
03. 02bWB	使民不为盗
03. 02bHG	使民不为盗
03. 02bFY	使民不为盗
47. 02bMA	□民不为□
47. 02bMB	使民不为盗
00. 000G-	--- --- --- --- ---
00. 000G-	--- --- --- --- ---

03. 03aFE   Do not display what is desirable
03. 03aSK   not display can desire
03. 03aSC   不见可欲
03. 03aTK   not display can desire
03. 03aTC   不见可欲
03. 03aWB   不见可欲
03. 03aHG   不见可欲
03. 03aFY   不见可欲
47. 03aMA   不□□□
47. 03aMB   不见可欲
00. 000G-   --- --- --- ---
00. 000G-   --- --- --- ---

03. 03bFE   and the people will not revolt.
03. 03bSK   let people mind not revolt
03. 03bSC   使民心不乱
03. 03bTK   let people mind not revolt
03. 03bTC   使民心不乱
03. 03bWB   使民心不乱
03. 03bHG   使___心不乱
03. 03bFY   使民心不乱
47. 03bMA   □民___不乱
47. 03bMB   使民___不乱
00. 000G-   --- --- --- --- ---
00. 000G-   --- --- --- --- ---

03. 04aFE   Therefore, sages rule by[29]
03. 04aSK   (therefore) (sage) ('s) rule —
03. 04aSC   (是以)(圣人)之治也
03. 04aTK   (therefore) ((sage) > (reputable person)) ('s) rule —
03. 04aTC   (是以)((圣人)(声人))之治也
47. 04aWB   (是以)((圣人)(＿＿))之治＿
03. 04aHG   (是以)((圣人)(＿＿))之治＿
03. 04aFY   (是以)((圣人)(＿＿))之治也
47. 04aMA   (是以)((＿＿)(声人))之□□
03. 04aMB   (是以)((圣人)(＿＿))之治也
00. 000G–   (＿＿)((＿＿)(＿＿))＿＿
00. 000G–   (＿＿)((＿＿)(＿＿))＿＿

03. 04bFE   emptying the minds of people,
03. 04bSK   empty their mind
03. 04bSC   虚其心
03. 04bTK   empty their mind
03. 04bTC   虚其心
03. 04bWB   虚其心
03. 04bHG   虚其心
03. 04bFY   虚其心
47. 04bMA   □□□
47. 04bMB   虚其心
00. 000G–   ＿＿＿
00. 000G–   ＿＿＿

03. 04cFE   filling their stomachs,
03. 04cSK   fill their stomach
03. 04cSC   实其腹
03. 04cTK   fill their stomach
03. 04cTC   实其腹
03. 04cWB   实其腹
03. 04cHG   实其腹
03. 04cFY   实其腹
47. 04cMA   □□□
47. 04cMB   实其腹
00. 000G-   --- --- ---
00. 000G-   --- --- ---

03. 04dFE   weakening their ambitions,
03. 04dSK   weak their ambition
03. 04dSC   弱其志
03. 04dTK   weak their ambition
03. 04dTC   弱其志
03. 04dWB   弱其志
03. 04dHG   弱其志
03. 04dFY   弱其志
47. 04dMA   □□□
47. 04dMB   弱其志
00. 000G-   --- --- ---
00. 000G-   --- --- ---

03. 04eFE   and strengthening their bones.
03. 04eSK   strong their bone
03. 04eSC   强其骨
03. 04eTK   (strong > strong) their bone
03. 04eTC   (强彊)其骨
03. 04eWB   (强___)其骨
03. 04eHG   (强___)其骨
03. 04eFY   (___彊)其骨
47. 04eMA   (强___)其骨
47. 04eMB   (强___)其骨
00. 000G–   (___ ___) ___ ___
00. 000G–   (___ ___) ___ ___

03. 050FE   Let the people always be without knowledge and without desire.[30]
03. 050SK   always let people without knowledge without desire —
03. 050SC   恒使民无知无欲也
03. 050TK   (always > always) let people without knowledge without desire —
03. 050TC   (常恒)使民无知无欲也
03. 050WB   (常___)使民无知无欲___
03. 050HG   (常___)使民无知无欲___
03. 050FY   (常___)使民无知无欲___
47. 050MA   (___恒)使民无知无欲也
47. 050MB   (___恒)使民无知无欲也
00. 000G–   (___ ___) ___ ___ ___ ___ ___ ___
00. 000G–   (___ ___) ___ ___ ___ ___ ___ ___

03.060FE   Let those who know, not dare to act but stop.

03.060SK   let that those know those not dare act and
            stop 一

03.060SC   使夫之知者不敢为而已也

03.060TK   let that those know ((those > (sage)) not dare
            not act and stop 一

03.060TC   使夫之知((者)(智者))不敢弗为而已也
03.060WB   使夫＿＿＿((＿))(智者))不敢＿为＿＿＿也
03.060HG   使夫之＿((者)(＿＿＿))不敢＿为＿＿＿也
03.060FY   使夫＿知((者)(＿＿＿))不敢＿为＿＿＿＿
47.060MA   使□＿□((＿))(＿＿＿))□□□□□□＿
47.060MB   使夫＿知((＿))(＿＿＿))不敢弗为而已＿
00.000G-   ＿＿＿＿＿((＿))(＿＿＿))＿＿＿＿＿
00.000G-   ＿＿＿＿＿((＿))(＿＿＿))＿＿＿＿＿＿

03.070FE   Act with *Non-action*, then there will be no
            anarchy.[31]

03.070SK   act (*Non-action*) then no (anarchy) 一

03.070SC   为(无为)则无(不治)矣

03.070TK   act (*Non-action*) then no ((anarchy) > (not;
            act)) 一

03.070TC   为(无为)则无((不治)(不为))矣
03.070WB   为(无为)则无((不治)(＿＿＿))＿
03.070HG   为(无为)则无((不治)(＿＿＿))＿
03.070FY   为(无为)则无((＿＿＿)(不为))矣
47.070MA   ＿(＿＿＿)□□((□□)(＿＿＿))□
47.070MB   ＿(＿＿＿)则无((不治)(＿＿＿))矣
00.000G-   ＿(＿＿＿)＿＿＿((＿＿＿)(＿＿＿))＿
00.000G-   ＿(＿＿＿)＿＿＿((＿＿＿)(＿＿＿))＿

Chapter 04

04. 01aFE   The *Way* is empty,
04. 01aSK   *Way* empty
04. 01aSC   道冲
04. 01aTK   *Way* ((empty) > empty))
04. 01aTC   道((冲[___])盅))
04. 01aWB   道((冲[___])___))
04. 01aHG   道((冲[冲])___))
04. 01aFY   道((___[___])盅))
48. 01aMA   □((□[___])___))
48. 01aMB   道((冲[___])___))
00. 000G-   ___((___[___])___))
00. 000G-   ___((___[___])___))

04. 01bFE   but use it and it has not to be refilled.
04. 01bSK   yet use its have not fill —
04. 01bSC   而用之有弗盈也
04. 01bTK   yet use its ((may be) > and > have)) (not >
              not) (fill > fill) —
04. 01bTC   而用之((或又有))(不弗)(盈满)也
04. 01bWB   而用之((或___ ___))(不___)(盈___)___
04. 01bHG   而用之((或___ ___))(不___)(盈___)___
04. 01bFY   而用之((___又___))(不___)(___满)___
48. 01bMA   □□□((___ ___□))(___□)(盈___)也
48. 01bMB   而用之((___ ___有))(___弗)(盈___)也
00. 000G-   ___ ___ ___((___ ___ ___))(___ ___)(___ ___)___
00. 000G-   ___ ___ ___((___ ___ ___))(___ ___)(___ ___)___

04. 02aFE   It is so deep!
04. 02aSK   deep 一
04. 02aSC   渊呵
04. 02aTK   deep （一 > 一）
04. 02aTC   渊（兮呵）
04. 02aWB   渊（兮___）
04. 02aHG   渊（兮___）
04. 02aFY   渊（兮___）
48. 02aMA   渊（___呵）
48. 02aMB   渊（___呵）
00. 000G-   ___（___ ___）
00. 000G-   ___（___ ___）

04. 02bFE   Like the *Ancestor of All-things*:
04. 02bSK   like （*All-things*） （'s） ancestor
04. 02bSC   似（万物）之宗
04. 02bTK   （（like） > begin） （*All-things*） （'s） ancestor 一
04. 02bTC   （（似［___]）始））（万物）之宗■
04. 02bWB   （（似［___]）___））（万物）之宗___
04. 02bHG   （（似［___]）___））（万物）之宗___
04. 02bFY   （（似［___]）___））（万物）之宗___
48. 02bMA   （（___［___]）始））（万物）之宗■
48. 02bMB   （（似［佁]）___））（万物）之宗___
00. 000G-   （（___［___]）___））（___ ___）___ ___ ___
00. 000G-   （（___［___]）___））（___ ___）___ ___ ___

04. 02cFE	it smoothens their blending;
04. 02cSK	smooth their blend
04. 02cSC	锉其兑
04. 02cTK	(file > smooth) their (sharp > blend)
04. 02cTC	(挫锉)其(锐兑)
04. 02cWB	(挫___)其(锐___)
04. 02cHG	(挫___)其(锐___)
04. 02cFY	(挫___)其(锐___)
48. 02cMA	(___锉)其(___ ___)
48. 02cMB	(___锉)其(___兑)
00. 000G-	(___ ___) ___ (___ ___)
00. 000G-	(___ ___) ___ (___ ___)

04. 02dFE	untangles their disorder;[32]
04. 02dSK	untangle their disorder
04. 02dSC	解其纷
04. 02dTK	untangle their ((disorder) > fragrance)) —
04. 02dTC	解其((纷[___])芬))■
04. 02dWB	解其((纷[___])___))___
04. 02dHG	解其((纷[紛])___))___
04. 02dFY	解其((纷[紛])___))___
48. 02dMA	解其((纷[___])___))■
48. 02dMB	解其((___[___])芬))___
00. 000G-	___ ___ ((___[___])___))___
00. 000G-	___ ___ ((___[___])___))___

04.02eFE softens their glare;[33]
04.02eSK soft their glare
04.02eSC 和其光
04.02eTK soft their glare
04.02eTC 和其光
04.02eWB 和其光
04.02eHG 和其光
04.02eFY 和其光
48.02eMA 和其光
48.02eMB 和其光
00.000G- --- --- ---
00.000G- --- --- ---

04.02fFE and merges their dust.[34]
04.02fSK merge their dust
04.02fSC 同其尘
04.02fTK merge their dust
04.02fTC 同其(尘[塵])
04.02fWB 同其(尘[___])
04.02fHG 同其(尘[___])
04.02fFY 同其(尘[___])
48.02fMA 同□(□[___])
48.02fMB 同其(尘[塵])
00.000G- --- --- (___[___])
00.000G- --- --- (___[___])

04. 030FE	Invisible. Nevertheless, it seems to exist.
04. 030SK	invisible — apparently seem exist
04. 030SC	湛呵似若存
04. 030TK	invisible (— > —) (apparently) (seem > (may be)) exist —
04. 030TC	湛(兮呵)(似[___])(若或)存■
04. 030WB	湛(兮___)(似[___])(___或)存___
04. 030HG	湛(兮___)(似[___])(若___)存___
04. 030FY	湛(兮___)(似[___])(___或)存___
48. 030MA	□(___□)(□[___])(___或)存■
48. 030MB	湛(___呵)(似[佁])(___或)存___
00. 000G-	___(______)(___[___])(______)______
00. 000G-	___(______)(___[___])(______)______

04. 04aFE	I do not know whose child it is,[35]
04. 04aSK	I not know its who ('s) child —
04. 04aSC	吾不知其谁之子也
04. 04aTK	I not know its who ('s) child (— > —)
04. 04aTC	吾不知其谁之子(也■)
04. 04aWB	吾不知___谁之子(______)
04. 04aHG	吾不知其谁之子(______)
04. 04aFY	吾不知___谁之子(______)
48. 04aMA	吾不知□______子(也■)
48. 04aMB	吾不知其谁之子(也___)
00. 000G-	________________________(______)
00. 000G-	________________________(______)

04. 04bFE	but it seems to predate the Emperor.[36]
04. 04bSK	seem Emperor ('s) predate
04. 04bSC	象帝之先
04. 04bTK	seem Emperor ('s) predate —
04. 04bTC	象帝之先■
04. 04bWB	象帝之先...
04. 04bHG	象帝之先...
04. 04bFY	象帝之先...
48. 04bMA	象帝之先■
48. 04bMB	象帝之先...
00. 000G-	--- --- --- --- ---
00. 000G-	--- --- --- --- ---

Chapter 05

05.01aFE	The *Sky* and the *Earth* do not have to be benevolent[37]
05.01aSK	*Sky Earth* not benevolence
05.01aSC	天地不仁
05.01aTK	*Sky Earth* not benevolence
05.01aTC	天地不仁
05.01aWB	天地不仁
05.01aHG	天地不仁
05.01aFY	天地不仁
49.01aMA	天地不仁
49.01aMB	天地不仁
00.000G-	--- --- --- ---
00.000G-	--- --- --- ---

05.01bFE	if *All-things* would act as straw dogs.[38]
05.01bSK	because (*All-things*) act straw dog
05.01bSC	以(万物)为刍狗
05.01bTK	because (*All-things*) act straw dog —
05.01bTC	以(万物)为刍狗■
05.01bWB	以(万物)为刍狗 ...
05.01bHG	以(万物)为刍狗 ...
05.01bFY	以(万物)为刍狗 ...
49.01bMA	以(万物)为刍狗■
49.01bMB	以(万物)为刍狗 ...
00.000G-	--- (--- ---) --- --- --- ---
00.000G-	--- (--- ---) --- --- --- ---

05.02aFE   Sages do not have to be benevolent[39]
05.02aSK   (sage) not benevolence
05.02aSC   (圣人)不仁
05.02aTK   ((sage) > (reputable person)) not benevolence
            —
05.02aTC   ((圣人)(声人))不仁■
05.02aWB   ((圣人)(_____))不仁___
05.02aHG   ((圣人)(_____))不仁___
05.02aFY   ((圣人)(_____))不仁___
49.02aMA   ((_____)(声人))不仁■
49.02aMB   ((圣人)(_____))不仁___
00.000G-   ((_____)(_____))_______
00.000G-   ((_____)(_____))_______

05.02bFE   if common people would act as straw dogs.[40]
05.02bSK   because (common people) act straw dog
05.02bSC   以(百姓)为刍狗
05.02bTK   because (common people) act straw dog
05.02bTC   以(百姓)为刍狗
05.02bWB   以(百姓)为刍狗
05.02bHG   以(百姓)为刍狗
05.02bFY   以(百姓)为刍狗
49.02bMA   以(百姓)□□狗
49.02bMB   □(百姓)为刍狗
00.000G-   ___(_____)_______
00.000G-   ___(_____)_______

05.030FE	What is between the *Sky* and the *Earth* is like a pair of bellows.[41]
05.030SK	*Sky Earth* ('s) separate is like (pair of bellows) —
05.030SC	天地之间其犹(橐籥)与
05.030TK	*Sky Earth* ('s) separate is (like > planned) (pair of bellows) (— > —)
05.030TC	天地之间其(犹猷)(橐籥)(乎与)
05.030WB	天地之间其(犹＿)(橐籥)(乎＿)
05.030HG	天地之间其(犹＿)(橐籥)(乎＿)
05.030FY	天地之间其(犹＿)(橐籥)(乎＿)
49.030MA	天地口间口(犹＿)(橐籥)(＿与)
49.030MB	天地之间其(＿猷)(橐籥)(＿与)
12.010GA	天地之间其(犹＿)(橐籥)(＿与)
00.000GC	＿＿＿＿＿＿(＿＿)(＿＿)(＿与)

05.040FE	It is empty, but not exhausted.
05.040SK	empty but not exhaust
05.040SC	虚而不渴
05.040TK	empty but not (subdue > lack > exhaust)
05.040TC	虚而不(屈诎渴)
05.040WB	虚而不(屈＿＿)
05.040HG	虚而不(屈＿＿)
05.040FY	虚而不(＿诎＿)
49.040MA	虚而不(＿＿渴)
49.040MB	虚而不(＿＿渴)
12.020GA	虚而不(屈＿＿)
00.000G-	＿＿＿(＿＿＿)

05. 050FE	Use it and more will be produced.
05. 050SK	use and more produce
05. 050SC	动而俞出
05. 050TK	(use > move) and (more > more) produce 一
05. 050TC	(动蹱)而(愈俞)出 ■
05. 050WB	(动___)而(愈___)出___
05. 050HG	(动___)而(愈___)出___
05. 050FY	(动___)而(___俞)出___
49. 050MA	(___蹱)而(___俞)出___
49. 050MB	(动___)而(___俞)出___
12. 030GA	(动___)而(愈___)出 ■
00. 000G-	(___ ___) ___ (___ ___) ___ ___

05. 06aFE	Listening to many details is exhausting
05. 06aSK	many listen detail exhaust
05. 06aSC	多闻数穷
05. 06aTK	many (declare > listen) detail exhaust
05. 06aTC	多(言闻)数穷
05. 06aWB	多(言___)数穷
05. 06aHG	多(言___)数穷
05. 06aFY	多(言___)数穷
49. 06aMA	多(___闻)数穷
49. 06aMB	多(___闻)数穷
00. 000G-	___ (___ ___) ___ ___
00. 000G-	___ (___ ___) ___ ___

05. 06bFE   and not as good as following your heart.[42]
05. 06bSK   (not as good as) follow at inside
05. 06bSC   (不若)守于中
05. 06bTK   ((not as good as) > (not as good as)) follow
              at inside
05. 06bTC   ((不如)(不若))守于中
05. 06bWB   ((不如)(______))守___中
05. 06bHG   ((不如)(______))守___中
05. 06bFY   ((不如)(______))守___中
49. 06bMA   ((______)(不若))守于中
49. 06bMB   ((______)(不若))守于中
00. 000G-   ((______)(______))___ ___ ___
00. 000G-   ((______)(______))___ ___ ___

Chapter 06

06.010FE	The *Immortal Valley Spirit* is called the *Mysterious Female*. [43]
06.010SK	*Valley Spirit* (immortal) is call mystery female
06.010SC	谷神(不死)是谓玄牝
06.010TK	(valley > valley) spirit (immortal) is (call) mystery female
06.010TC	(谷浴)神(不死)是(谓[___])玄牝
06.010WB	(谷___)神(不死)是(谓[___])玄牝
06.010HG	(谷___)神(不死)是(谓[___])玄牝
06.010FY	(谷___)神(不死)是(谓[___])玄牝
50.010MA	(___浴)神(口死)是(谓[胃])玄牝
50.010MB	(___浴)神(不死)是(谓[胃])玄牝
00.000G-	(___ ___) ___ (___ ___) ___ (___ [___]) ___ ___
00.000G-	(___ ___) ___ (___ ___) ___ (___ [___]) ___ ___

06.020FE	The home of this *Mysterious Female* is called the origin of the *Sky* and the *Earth*. [44]
06.020SK	mystery female ('s) home is call *Sky Earth* ('s) origin
06.020SC	玄牝之门是谓天地之根
06.020TK	mystery female ('s) home is (call) *Sky Earth* ('s) origin
06.020TC	玄牝之门是(谓[___])天地之根
06.020WB	玄牝之门是(谓[___])天地___根
06.020HG	玄牝之门是(谓[___])天地之根
06.020FY	玄牝之门是(谓[___])天地之根
50.020MA	玄牝之门是(谓[胃])口地之根
50.020MB	玄牝之门是(谓[___])天地之根
00.000G-	___ ___ ___ ___ (___ [___]) ___ ___ ___
00.000G-	___ ___ ___ ___ (___ [___]) ___ ___ ___

06. 030FE It seems to exist forever and using it is no hard work.

06. 030SK (forever) it seem exist use ('s) not (hard-working)

06. 030SC (绵绵)其若存用之不勤

06. 030TK (forever) 一 it seem exist use ('s) not (hard-working)

06. 030TC (绵绵)呵其若存用之不(勤[＿])

06. 030WB (绵绵)＿＿若存用之不(勤[＿])

06. 030HG (绵绵)＿＿若存用之不(勤[＿])

06. 030FY (绵绵)＿＿若存用之不(勤[＿])

50. 030MA (绵绵)呵＿若存用之不(勤[堇])

50. 030MB (绵绵)呵其若存用之不(勤[堇])

00. 000G- (＿＿)＿＿＿＿＿＿＿(＿[＿])

00. 000G- (＿＿)＿＿＿＿＿＿＿(＿[＿])

Chapter 07

07.010FE	The *Sky* endures and the *Earth* last long.[45]
07.010SK	*Sky* endure *Earth* (last long)
07.010SC	天长地久
07.010TK	*Sky* endure *Earth* (last long)
07.010TC	天长地久
07.010WB	天长地久
07.010HG	天长地久
07.010FY	天长地久
51.010MA	天长地久
51.010MB	天长地久
00.000G-	--- --- --- ---
00.000G-	--- --- --- ---

07.020FE	Why do the *Sky* and the *Earth* last long and endure?[46]
07.020SK	*Sky* *Earth* ('s) (why) can endure and (last long) those
07.020SC	天地之(所以)能长且久者
07.020TK	*Sky* *Earth* ('s) (why) can endure and (last long) those
07.020TC	天地之(所以)能长且久者
07.020WB	天地＿＿(所以)能长且久者
07.020HG	天地＿＿(所以)能长且久者
07.020FY	天地＿＿(所以)能长且久者
51.020MA	天地之(所以)能□且久者
51.020MB	天地之(所以)能长且久者
00.000G-	--- --- --- (--- ---) --- --- --- ---
00.000G-	--- --- --- (--- ---) --- --- --- ---

07. 030FE   That is, because they do not foster themselves. [47]

07. 030SK   because they not themselves foster —

07. 030SC   以其不自生也

07. 030TK   because they not themselves foster —

07. 030TC   以其不自生也

07. 030WB   以其不自生...

07. 030HG   以其不自生...

07. 030FY   以其不自生...

51. 030MA   以其不自生也

51. 030MB   以其不自生也

00. 000G-   --- --- --- --- --- ---

00. 000G-   --- --- --- --- --- ---

07. 040FE   Therefore, they can live long.

07. 040SK   therefore can long life

07. 040SC   故能长生

07. 040TK   therefore can long life —

07. 040TC   故能长生■

07. 040WB   故能长生...

07. 040HG   故能长生...

07. 040FY   故能长生...

51. 040MA   故能长生■

51. 040MB   故能长生...

00. 000G-   --- --- --- --- --- ---

00. 000G-   --- --- --- --- --- ---

07.05aFE   Accordingly, sages withdraw themselves.[48]
07.05aSK   (therefore) (sage) withdraw (themselves)
07.05aSC   (是以)(圣人)退(其身)
07.05aTK   (therefore) ((sage > (reputable person))
            (behind > withdraw > (thongs of a
            shield))(themselves)
07.05aTC   (是以)((圣人)(声人))(后退芮)(其身)
07.05aWB   (是以)((圣人)(＿＿))(后＿＿)(其身)
07.05aHG   (是以)((圣人)(＿＿))(后＿＿)(其身)
07.05aFY   (是以)((圣人)(＿＿))(后＿＿)(其身)
51.05aMA   (是以)((＿＿)(声人))(＿＿芮)(其身)
51.05aMB   (是以)((圣人)(＿＿))(＿退＿)(其身)
00.000G-   (＿＿)((＿＿)(＿＿))(＿＿＿)(＿＿)
00.000G-   (＿＿)((＿＿)(＿＿))(＿＿＿)(＿＿)

07.05bFE   Yet they are first.[49]
07.05bSK   yet oneself first
07.05bSC   而身先
07.05bTK   yet oneself first 一
07.05bTC   而身先■
07.05bWB   而身先＿
07.05bHG   而身先＿
07.05bFY   而身先＿
51.05bMA   而身先■
51.05bMB   而身先＿
00.000G-   ＿＿＿＿＿
00.000G-   ＿＿＿＿＿

```
07.06aFE    They put themselves outside.
07.06aSK    outside (themselves)
07.06aSC    外(其身)
07.06aTK    outside (themselves)
07.06aTC    外(其身)
07.06aWB    外(其身)
07.06aHG    外(其身)
07.06aFY    外(其身)
51.06aMA    外(其身)
51.06aMB    外(其身)
00.000G-    ___(_____)
00.000G-    ___(_____)
```

```
07.06bFE    Yet they are inside.
07.06bSK    yet oneself inside
07.06bSC    而身存
07.06bTK    yet oneself inside
07.06bTC    而身存
07.06bWB    而身存
07.06bHG    而身存
07.06bFY    而身存
51.06bMA    而身存
51.06bMB    而身存
00.000G-    ________
00.000G-    ________
```

07.07aFE   Because they are selfless,
07.07aSK   not because they (selfless) 一
07.07aSC   不以其(无私)欤
07.07aTK   (not ＞ not) because they (selfless) irregular
            (一 ＞ 一)
07.07aTC   (不非)以其(无私)邪(欤■)
07.07aWB   (__非)以其(无私)邪(__ __)
07.07aHG   (__ __)以其(无私)__(__ __)
07.07aFY   (不__)以其(无私)邪(__ __)
51.07aMA   (不__)以其(无□)__(欤■)
51.07aMB   (不__)以其(无私)__(欤__)
00.000G-   (__ __)__ __(__ __)__(__ __)
00.000G-   (__ __)__ __(__ __)__(__ __)

07.07bFE   therefore, their self-interest is fulfilled.
07.07bSK   therefore can accomplish their selfish
07.07bSC   故能成其私
07.07bTK   therefore can accomplish their selfish
07.07bTC   故能成其私
07.07bWB   故能成其私
07.07bHG   故能成其私
07.07bFY   故能成其私
51.07bMA   故能成其私
51.07bMB   故能成其私
00.000G-   __ __ __ __ __
00.000G-   __ __ __ __ __

Chapter 08

08.010FE	Superior goodness is like water.[50]
08.010SK	superior good like water
08.010SC	上善如水
08.010TK	superior good (like > like > manage) water
08.010TC	上善(若如治)水
08.010WB	上善(若＿＿)水
08.010HG	上善(若＿＿)水
08.010FY	上善(若＿＿)水
52.010MA	上善(＿＿治)水
52.010MB	上善(＿如＿)水
00.000G-	＿＿(＿＿＿)＿
00.000G-	＿＿(＿＿＿)＿

08.020FE	The goodness of water benefits *All-things* and it does not strive.[51]
08.020SK	water good benefit (*All-things*) and not strive
08.020SC	水善利(万物)而不争
08.020TK	water good benefit (*All-things*) and ((not; strive) > (is; tranquil) > (is; strive))
08.020TC	水善利(万物)而((不争)(有静)(有争))
08.020WB	水善利(万物)而((不争)(＿＿)(＿＿))
08.020HG	水善利(万物)而((不争)(＿＿)(＿＿))
08.020FY	水善利(万物)而((不争)(＿＿)(＿＿))
52.020MA	水善利(万物)而((＿＿)(有静)(＿＿))
52.020MB	水善利(万物)而((＿＿)(＿＿)(有争))
00.000G-	＿＿＿(＿＿)＿((＿＿)(＿＿)(＿＿))
00.000G-	＿＿＿(＿＿)＿((＿＿)(＿＿)(＿＿))

08.030FE	It occupies places everybody dislikes.
08.030SK	occupy (everybody) ('s) place dislike
08.030SC	处(众人)之所恶
08.030TK	(claim > occupy) ((everybody) > (many people)) ('s) place (dislike > ugly)
08.030TC	(居处)((众人)众))之所(恶亚)
08.030WB	(＿＿处)((众人)＿＿))之所(恶＿＿)
08.030HG	(＿＿处)((众人)＿＿))之所(恶＿＿)
08.030FY	(居处)((众人)＿＿))之所(恶＿＿)
52.030MA	(居处)((＿＿＿＿)众))之所(恶＿＿)
52.030MB	(居处)((众人)＿＿))之所(＿＿亚)
00.000G-	(＿＿＿＿)((＿＿＿＿)＿＿)) ＿＿＿＿ (＿＿＿＿)
00.000G-	(＿＿＿＿)((＿＿＿＿)＿＿)) ＿＿＿＿ (＿＿＿＿)

08.040FE	Therefore, it is close to the *Way*.
08.040SK	therefore near to *Way* —
08.040SC	故几于道矣
08.040TK	therefore near to *Way* (— > —)
08.040TC	故几于道(矣■)
08.040WB	故几于道(＿＿＿＿)
08.040HG	故几于道(＿＿＿＿)
08.040FY	故几于道(矣＿＿)
52.040MA	故几于道(矣■)
52.040MB	故几于道(矣＿＿)
00.000G-	＿＿＿＿＿＿＿＿ (＿＿＿＿)
00.000G-	＿＿＿＿＿＿＿＿ (＿＿＿＿)

08. 050FE   In dwelling, the goodness is location.
08. 050SK   dwell good location
08. 050SC   居善地
08. 050TK   dwell good location
08. 050TC   居善地
08. 050WB   居善地
08. 050HG   居善地
08. 050FY   居善地
52. 050MA   居善地
52. 050MB   居善地
00. 000G–   --- --- ---
00. 000G–   --- --- ---

08. 060FE   In thinking, the goodness is depth.
08. 060SK   mind good deep
08. 060SC   心善渊
08. 060TK   mind good (deep > deep) 一
08. 060TC   心善(渊瀟) ■
08. 060WB   心善(渊 ___) ___
08. 060HG   心善(渊 ___) ___
08. 060FY   心善(渊 ___) ___
52. 060MA   心善(___ 瀟) ■
52. 060MB   心善(渊 ___) ___
00. 000G–   --- --- (--- ---) ---
00. 000G–   --- --- (--- ---) ---

08.070FE	In giving, the goodness is benevolence.
08.070SK	give good benevolence[52]
08.070SC	予善仁
08.070TK	(give > give) good (people > benevolence > sincere > natural)
08.070TC	(与予)善(人仁信天)
08.070WB	(与__)善(__仁____)
08.070HG	(与__)善(人______)
08.070FY	(与__)善(人______)
52.070MA	(__予)善(____信__)
52.070MB	(__予)善(______天)
00.000G-	(______)__(________)
00.000G-	(______)__(________)

08.080FE	In speaking, the goodness is truth.
08.080SK	speak good truth
08.080SC	言善信
08.080TK	speak good truth
08.080TC	言善信
08.080WB	言善信
08.080HG	言善信
08.080FY	言善信
00.000MA	______
52.080MB	言善信
00.000G-	______
00.000G-	______

08.090FE	In ruling, the goodness is order.
08.090SK	rule good control
08.090SC	正善治
08.090TK	(rule > rule) good control —
08.090TC	(政正)善治■
08.090WB	(＿正)善治＿
08.090HG	(政＿)善治＿
08.090FY	(政＿)善治＿
52.080MA	(＿正)善治■
52.090MB	(＿正)善治＿
00.000G-	(＿＿)＿＿＿
00.000G-	(＿＿)＿＿＿

08.100FE	In working, the goodness is skill.
08.100SK	work good skill
08.100SC	事善能
08.100TK	work good skill
08.100TC	事善能
08.100WB	事善能
08.100HG	事善能
08.100FY	事善能
52.090MA	事善能
52.100MB	事善能
00.000G-	＿＿＿
00.000G-	＿＿＿

08.110FE   In action, the goodness is timing.
08.110SK   act good time
08.110SC   动善时
08.110TK   (act > move) good time —
08.110TC   (动躃)善时 ∎
08.110WB   (动＿)善时＿
08.110HG   (动＿)善时＿
08.110FY   (动＿)善时＿
52.100MA   (＿躃)善时 ∎
52.110MB   (动＿)善时＿
00.000G-   (＿＿)＿＿＿
00.000G-   (＿＿)＿＿＿

08.12aFE   Only those who do not strive
08.12aSK   those only not strive
08.12aSC   夫唯不争
08.12aTK   those (only > only) not (strive > tranquil)
08.12aTC   夫(唯惟)不(争静)
08.12aWB   夫(唯＿)不(争＿)
08.12aHG   夫(唯＿)不(争＿)
08.12aFY   夫(＿惟)不(争＿)
52.11aMA   夫(唯＿)不(＿静)
52.12aMB   夫(唯＿)不(争＿)
00.000G-   ＿(＿＿)＿(＿＿)
00.000G-   ＿(＿＿)＿(＿＿)

08.12bFE	will therefore not fail.
08.12bSK	therefore not fail —
08.12bSC	故无尤矣
08.12bTK	therefore not fail —
08.12bTC	故无尤矣
08.12bWB	故无尤...
08.12bHG	故无尤...
08.12bFY	故无尤矣
52.11bMA	故无尤...
52.12bMB	故无尤...
00.000G-	--- --- --- ---
00.000G-	--- --- --- ---

Chapter 09

09.01aFE	Accumulating and filling up
09.01aSK	accumulate and fill ('s)
09.01aSC	持而盈之
09.01aTK	(accumulate > accumulate) and fill ('s)
09.01aTC	(持殖)而盈之
09.01aWB	(持＿＿)而盈之
09.01aHG	(持＿＿)而盈之
09.01aFY	(持＿＿)而盈之
53.01aMA	(持＿＿)而盈之
53.01aMB	(持＿＿)而盈之
20.01aGA	(＿＿殖)而盈之
00.000G-	(＿＿ ＿＿) ＿＿ ＿＿ ＿＿

09.01bFE	are not as good as stopping in time.
09.01bSK	(not as good as) is stop
09.01bSC	(不若)其已
09.01bTK	((not) > (not as good as) > (not as good as)) is stop
09.01bTC	((不)(不如)(不若))其已
09.01bWB	((＿＿)(不如)(＿＿ ＿＿))其已
09.01bHG	((＿＿)(不如)(＿＿ ＿＿))其已
09.01bFY	((＿＿)(不如)(＿＿ ＿＿))其已
53.01bMA	((＿＿)(＿＿ ＿＿)(不□))□□
53.01bMB	((＿＿)(＿＿ ＿＿)(不若))其已
20.01bGA	((不)(＿＿ ＿＿)(不若))＿＿已
00.000G-	((＿＿)(＿＿ ＿＿)(＿＿ ＿＿)) ＿＿ ＿＿

09.02aFE	Hammer it too sharp
09.02aSK	Hammer to sharp its
09.02aSC	揣而锐之
09.02aTK	(Hammer > forge > clean) to (sharp > extreme > clean) its
09.02aTC	(揣锻湍)而(锐至湍)之
09.02aWB	(揣﹍﹍)而(锐﹍﹍)之
09.02aHG	(揣﹍﹍)而(锐﹍﹍)之
09.02aFY	(揣﹍﹍)而(锐﹍﹍)之
53.02aMA	(﹍□﹍)□(﹍□﹍)之
53.02aMB	(﹍锻﹍)而(﹍至﹍)之
20.02aGA	(﹍﹍湍)而(﹍﹍湍)之
00.000G-	(﹍﹍﹍)﹍(﹍﹍﹍)﹍

09.02bFE	and it cannot last long.
09.02bSK	(cannot) long last ('s) 一
09.02bSC	(不可)长保之也
09.02bTK	□ ('s) (cannot) long last ('s) (一 > 一)
09.02bTC	□之(不可)长保之(也■)
09.02bWB	﹍﹍(不可)长保﹍(﹍﹍)
09.02bHG	﹍﹍(不可)长保﹍(﹍﹍)
09.02bFY	﹍﹍(不可)长保﹍(﹍﹍)
53.02bMA	□之(□可)长保之(﹍■)
53.02bMB	﹍﹍(不可)长保﹍(也﹍)
20.02bGA	﹍﹍(不可)长保﹍(也﹍)
00.000G-	﹍﹍(﹍﹍)﹍﹍(﹍﹍)

09.03aFE	A room filled with gold and jade
09.03aSK	gold jade full room
09.03aSC	金玉盈室
09.03aTK	gold jade (full > full) (room > room)
09.03aTC	金玉(满盈)(堂室)
09.03aWB	金玉(满＿)(堂＿)
09.03aHG	金玉(满盈)(堂室)
09.03aFY	金玉(满＿)(＿室)
53.03aMA	金玉(＿盈)(＿室)
53.03aMB	金玉(＿盈)(＿室)
20.03aGA	金玉(＿盈)(＿室)
00.000G-	＿＿(＿＿)(＿＿)

09.03bFE	cannot be defended competently.
09.03bSK	cannot its competent defend —
09.03bSC	莫之能守也
09.03bTK	cannot its competent defend —
09.03bTC	莫之能守也
09.03bWB	莫之能守＿
09.03bHG	莫之能守＿
09.03bFY	莫之能守＿
53.03bMA	莫之＿守也
53.03bMB	莫之能守也
20.03bGA	莫＿能守也
00.000G-	＿＿＿＿＿

09.04aFE	Admiring wealth and arrogance
09.04aSK	admire wealth and arrogance
09.04aSC	贵富而骄
09.04aTK	((wealth; admire) > (admire; wealth) > (admire; fortune)) and (arrogance > arrogance)
09.04aTC	((富贵)(贵富)(贵福))而(骄乔)
09.04aWB	((富贵)(___)(___))而(骄__)
09.04aHG	((富贵)(___)(___))而(骄__)
09.04aFY	((富贵)(___)(___))而(骄__)
53.04aMA	((___)(贵富)(___))而(骄__)
53.04aMB	((___)(贵富)(___))而(骄__)
20.04aGA	((___)(___)(贵福))__(__乔)
00.000G-	((___)(___)(___))__(___)

09.04bFE	brings personal loss and misfortune.
09.04bSK	personal loss misfortune —
09.04bSC	自遗咎也
09.04bTK	personal loss them misfortune (— > —)
09.04bTC	自遗其咎(也■)
09.04bWB	自遗其咎(___)
09.04bHG	自遗其咎(___)
09.04bFY	自遗其咎(___)
53.04bMA	自遗__咎(也■)
53.04bMB	自遗__咎(也__)
20.04bGA	自遗__咎(也__)
00.000G-	___ ___ ___(___)

09.05aFE	When merit is achieved,
09.05aSK	merit achieve
09.05aSC	功遂
09.05aTK	((merit; achieve) > (fame; merit) > (merit; achieve))
09.05aTC	((功成)(名成)(名功)(功遂))
09.05aWB	((＿＿)(＿＿)(＿＿)(功遂))
09.05aHG	((功成)(名＿)(＿＿)(＿遂))
09.05aFY	((＿＿)(＿成)(名功)(＿遂))
53.05aMA	((＿＿)(＿＿)(＿＿)(功遂))
53.05aMB	((＿＿)(＿＿)(＿＿)(功遂))
20.05aGA	((＿＿)(＿＿)(＿＿)(功遂))
00.000G-	((＿＿)(＿＿)(＿＿)(＿＿))

09.05bFE	withdrawing yourself is the *Way of Nature*.[53]
09.05bSK	yourself withdraw nature ('s) *Way* —
09.05bSC	身退天之道也
09.05bTK	yourself ((withdraw > (thongs of a shield)) nature ('s) *Way* (— > —)
09.05bTC	身((退芮))天之道(也■)
09.05bWB	身((退＿))天之道(＿＿)
09.05bHG	身((退＿))天之道(＿＿)
09.05bFY	身((退＿))天之道(＿＿)
53.05bMA	身((＿芮))天□□(□＿)
53.05bMB	身((退＿))天之道(也＿)
20.05bGA	身((退＿))天之道(也■)
00.000G-	＿((＿＿))＿＿＿＿(＿＿)

Chapter 10

10. 01aFE	Carry the team spirit[54]
10. 01aSK	carry (team spirit)
10. 01aSC	载(营魄)
10. 01aTK	carry (team spirit)
10. 01aTC	载(营魄)
10. 01aWB	载(营魄)
10. 01aHG	载(营魄)
10. 01aFY	载(营魄)
54. 01aMA	□(□□)
54. 01aMB	载(营魄)
00. 000G-	___(___ ___)
00. 000G-	___(___ ___)

10. 01bFE	and unite it inseparable with the *One*.
10. 01bSK	unite *One* (inseparable) 一
10. 01bSC	抱一(能毋离)乎
10. 01bTK	(unite > hold) *One* ((inseparable) > (inseparable)) 一
10. 01bTC	(抱裹)一(能无离)(能毋离)乎
10. 01bWB	(抱___)一(能无离)(___ ___ ___)乎
10. 01bHG	(抱___)一(能无离)(___ ___ ___)乎
10. 01bFY	(___裹)一(能无离)(___ ___ ___)乎
54. 01bMA	(□□)___(___ ___ ___)(□□□)□
54. 01bMB	(抱___)一(___ ___ ___)(能毋离)乎
00. 000G-	(___ ___)___(___ ___ ___)(___ ___ ___)___
00. 000G-	(___ ___)___(___ ___ ___)(___ ___ ___)___

10.020FE   Concentrate vital energy and be as flexible as an infant.

10.020SK   concentrate (vital energy) softest can as (infant) 一

10.020SC   专气(至柔)能如(婴儿)乎

10.020TK   (concentrate > knead) (vital energy) ((softest) > (softest)) can as (infant) (一 > 一)

10.020TC   (专抟)(气)((致柔)(至柔))能如(婴儿)(乎■)

10.020WB   (专＿)(气)((致柔)(＿＿))能＿(婴儿)(乎＿)

10.020HG   (专＿)(气)((致柔)(＿＿))能如(婴儿)(乎＿)

10.020FY   (专＿)(气)((致柔)(＿＿))能如(婴儿)(乎＿)

54.020MA   (＿□)(□)((□□)(＿＿))能＿(婴儿)(乎■)

54.020MB   (＿抟)(气)((＿＿)(至柔))能＿(婴儿)(乎＿)

00.000G-   (＿＿)(＿)((＿＿)(＿＿))＿＿(＿＿)(＿＿)

00.000G-   (＿＿)(＿)((＿＿)(＿＿))＿＿(＿＿)(＿＿)

10.030FE   Study and eliminate problems. Inspect them competently without flaws.

10.030SK   study eliminate mystery inspect competent without have flaw 一

10.030SC   修除玄监能毋有疵乎

10.030TK   (purify > study > study) eliminate mystery (inspect > inspect > inspect) competent (not > not) have flaw 一

10.030TC   (涤修脩)除玄(览鉴监)能(无毋)有疵乎

10.030WB   (涤＿＿)除玄(览＿＿)能(无＿)＿疵乎

10.030HG   (涤＿＿)除玄(览＿＿)能(无＿)＿疵乎

10.030FY   (涤＿＿)除玄(览＿＿)能(无＿)＿疵乎

54.030MA   (＿＿脩)除玄(＿鉴＿)能(＿毋)＿疵乎

54.030MB   (＿修＿)除玄(＿＿监)能(＿毋)有疵乎

00.000G-   (＿＿＿)＿＿(＿＿＿)＿(＿＿)＿＿＿

00.000G-   (＿＿＿)＿＿(＿＿＿)＿(＿＿)＿＿＿

10. 04aFE	Love the people and rule the country[55]
10. 04aSK	love people rule country can
10. 04aSC	爱民治国能
10. 04aTK	love people ((rule > (work)) country can
10. 04aTC	爱民((治(活[＿＿]))国能
10. 04aWB	爱民((治(＿＿[＿＿]))国能
10. 04aHG	爱民((治(＿＿[＿＿]))国能
10. 04aFY	爱民((治(＿＿[＿＿]))国能
54. 04aMA	爱□((＿＿(□[＿＿]))□□
54. 04aMB	爱民((＿＿(活[栝]))国能
00. 000G-	＿＿＿＿((＿＿(＿＿[＿＿])) ＿＿＿＿
00. 000G-	＿＿＿＿((＿＿(＿＿[＿＿])) ＿＿＿＿

10. 04bFE	without using knowledge.
10. 04bSK	without use knowledge —
10. 04bSC	毋以知乎
10. 04bTK	*Non-action*) > ((without; use; knowledge) > (without; knowledge) > (without; use; knowledge)) —
10. 04bTC	(无为)(无以知)(无知)(毋以知))乎
10. 04bWB	((＿＿＿＿)(＿＿＿＿＿＿)(无知)(＿＿＿＿＿＿))乎
10. 04bHG	((无为)(＿＿＿＿＿＿)(＿＿＿＿)(＿＿＿＿＿＿))乎
10. 04bFY	((＿＿＿＿)(无以知)(＿＿＿＿)(＿＿＿＿＿＿))乎
54. 04bMA	((＿＿＿＿)(＿＿＿＿＿＿)(＿＿＿＿)(□□□□))□
54. 04bMB	((＿＿＿＿)(＿＿＿＿＿＿)(＿＿＿＿)(毋以知))乎
00. 000G-	((＿＿＿＿)(＿＿＿＿＿＿)(＿＿＿＿)(＿＿＿＿＿＿)) ＿＿
00. 000G-	((＿＿＿＿)(＿＿＿＿＿＿)(＿＿＿＿)(＿＿＿＿＿＿)) ＿＿

10. 050FE   Open and close the gates of nature as a
             female.[56]
10. 050SK   nature gate open close can (serve as) female
             —
10. 050SC   天门开阖能为雌乎
10. 050TK   nature gate (open > open) close can ((not;
             female) > (serve as; female)) —
10. 050TC   天门(开启)阖能((无雌)(为雌))乎
10. 050WB   天门(开＿＿)阖能((无雌)(＿＿＿＿))乎
10. 050HG   天门(开＿＿)阖能((无雌)(＿＿＿＿))乎
10. 050FY   天门(开＿＿)阖能((＿＿＿＿)(为雌))乎
54. 050MA   □□(＿＿□)□□((＿＿＿＿)(□□))□
54. 050MB   天门(＿＿启)阖能((＿＿＿＿)(为雌))乎
00. 000G-   ＿＿＿＿(＿＿＿＿)＿＿＿＿((＿＿＿＿)(＿＿＿＿))＿＿
00. 000G-   ＿＿＿＿(＿＿＿＿)＿＿＿＿((＿＿＿＿)(＿＿＿＿))＿＿

10. 06aFE   Understand the surroundings
10. 06aSK   (understand) (surrounding) can
10. 06aSC   (明白)(四达)能
10. 06aTK   (understand) (surrounding) can
10. 06aTC   (明白)(四达)能
10. 06aWB   (明白)(四达)能
10. 06aHG   (明白)(四达)能
10. 06aFY   (明白)(四达)能
54. 06aMA   (□□)(□□)□
54. 06aMB   (明白)(四达)能
00. 000G-   (＿＿＿＿)(＿＿＿＿)＿＿
00. 000G-   (＿＿＿＿)(＿＿＿＿)＿＿

10. 06bFE   without using knowledge.
10. 06bSK   without use knowledge —
10. 06bSC   毋以知乎
10. 06bTK   ((without; knowledge) > (without; using; act)
             > (without; act) > (without; use; knowledge))
             —

10. 06bTC   ((无知)(无以为)(无为)(毋以知))乎
10. 06bWB   ((___ ___)(___ ___)(无为)(___ ___))乎
10. 06bHG   ((无知)(___ ___)(___ ___)(___ ___))乎
10. 06bFY   ((___ ___)(无以为)(___ ___)(___ ___))乎
54. 06bMA   ((___ ___)(___ ___)(___ ___)(□□□))□
54. 06bMB   ((___ ___)(___ ___)(___ ___)(毋以知))乎
00. 000G-   ((___ ___)(___ ___)(___ ___)(___ ___)) ___
00. 000G-   ((___ ___)(___ ___)(___ ___)(___ ___)) ___

10. 070FE   Generate them and raise them.
10. 070SK   generate them raise them
10. 070SC   生之畜之
10. 070TK   generate them raise them
10. 070TC   生之畜之
10. 070WB   生之畜之
10. 070HG   生之畜之
10. 070FY   生之畜之
54. 070MA   生之畜之
54. 070MB   生之畜之
00. 000G-   --- --- --- ---
00. 000G-   --- --- --- ---

10. 080FE   Generate, but do not possess. [57]
10. 080SK   generate but not possess
10. 080SC   生而弗有
10. 080TK   generate but (not > not) possess
10. 080TC   生而(不弗)有
10. 080WB   生而(不＿)有
10. 080HG   生而(不＿)有
10. 080FY   生而(不＿)有
54. 080MA   生而(＿弗)□
54. 080MB   生而(＿弗)有
00. 000G-   ＿＿(＿＿)＿
00. 000G-   ＿＿(＿＿)＿

10. 090FE   Act, but do not rely on it. [58]
10. 090SK   act but not rely
10. 090SC   为而不恃
10. 090TK   act but not rely
10. 090TC   为而不恃
10. 090WB   为而不恃
10. 090HG   为而不恃
10. 090FY   为而不恃
00. 000MA   ＿＿＿＿
00. 000MB   ＿＿＿＿
00. 000G-   ＿＿＿＿
00. 000G-   ＿＿＿＿

10. 100FE	Develop but do not exploit.[59]	
10. 100SK	develop but not exploit 一	
10. 100SC	长而弗宰也	
10. 100TK	develop but (not > not) exploit 一	
10. 100TC	长而(不弗)宰也	
10. 100WB	长而(不___)宰___	
10. 100HG	长而(不___)宰___	
10. 100FY	长而(不___)宰___	
54. 090MA	□□(___□)□___	
54. 090MB	长而(___弗)宰也	
00. 000G-	___ ___ (___ ___) ___ ___	
00. 000G-	___ ___ (___ ___) ___ ___	

10. 110FE	This is called profound virtue.[60]	
10. 110SK	this call profound virtue	
10. 110SC	是谓玄德	
10. 110TK	this (call) is profound virtue	
10. 110TC	是(谓[___])为玄德	
10. 110WB	是(谓[___])___玄德	
10. 110HG	是(谓[___])___玄))德	
10. 110FY	是(___[___])为玄德	
54. 100MA	□(□[___])___□德	
54. 100MB	是(谓[胃])___玄德	
00. 000G-	___ (___[___]) ___ ___ ___	
00. 000G-	___ (___[___]) ___ ___ ___	

Chapter 11

11.01aFE	Thirty spokes merge into one hub,
11.01aSK	(thirty) spoke merge one hub
11.01aSC	(三十)辐同一毂
11.01aTK	((thirty) > thirty) spoke (merge > merge) one hub
11.01aTC	((三十)卅))辐(共同)一毂
11.01aWB	((三十)＿))辐(共＿)一毂
11.01aHG	((三十)＿))辐(共＿)一毂
11.01aFY	((三十)＿))辐(共＿)一毂
55.01aMA	((＿＿)卅))□(＿□)□□
55.01aMB	((＿＿)卅))辐(＿同)一毂
00.000G-	((＿＿)＿))＿(＿＿)＿＿
00.000G-	((＿＿)＿))＿(＿＿)＿＿

11.01bFE	but its *Non-existence* is useful for a carriage.[61]
11.01bSK	is its (*Non-existence*) carriage ('s) use —
11.01bSC	当其(无有)车之用也
11.01bTK	is its (*Non-existence*) carriage ('s) use —
11.01bTC	当其(无有)车之用也
11.01bWB	当其(无有)车之用＿
11.01bHG	当其(无有)车之用＿
11.01bFY	当其(无有)车之用＿
55.01bMA	□其(无□)□之用□
55.01bMB	当其(无有)车之用也
00.000G-	＿＿(＿＿)＿＿＿＿
00.000G-	＿＿(＿＿)＿＿＿＿

11.02aFE	Moulded clay makes a cup,
11.02aSK	mould clay to make cup
11.02aSC	捻埴以为器
11.02aTK	((clay > fire > (mould)) clay (to > and) (make) cup
11.02aTC	((埏然(捻[___]))埴(以而)为器
11.02aWB	((埏___(___[___]))埴(以___)为器
11.02aHG	((埏___(___[___]))埴(以___)为器
11.02aFY	((埏___(___[___]))埴(以___)为器
55.02aMA	((___然(___[___]))埴(___ ___)为器
55.02aMB	((___ ___(捻[撚]))埴(___而)为器
00.000G-	((___ ___(___[___]))___(___ ___)___ ___
00.000G-	((___ ___(___[___]))___(___ ___)___ ___

11.02bFE	but the *Non-existence* of clay is useful for a cup.[62]
11.02bSK	is its (*Non-existence*) clay cup ('s) use —
11.02bSC	当其(无有)埴器之用也
11.02bTK	is its (*Non-existence*) clay cup ('s) use —
11.02bTC	当其(无有)埴器之用也
11.02bWB	当其(无有)___器之用___
11.02bHG	当其(无有)___器之用___
11.02bFY	当其(无有)___器之用___
55.02bMA	当其(无有)埴器□□□
55.02bMB	当其(无有)埴器之用也
00.000G-	___ ___(___ ___)___ ___ ___ ___
00.000G-	___ ___(___ ___)___ ___ ___ ___

11.03aFE	Chiselled doors and windows make a room,
11.03aSK	chisel door window (in order) for room
11.03aSC	凿户牖以为室
11.03aTK	chisel door window (in order) for room
11.03aTC	凿户牖(以)为室
11.03aWB	凿户牖(以)为室
11.03aHG	凿户牖(以)为室
11.03aFY	凿户牖(以)为室
55.03aMA	□□□(___) ___ ___
55.03aMB	凿户牖(___) ___ ___
00.000G-	___ ___ ___ (___) ___ ___
00.000G-	___ ___ ___ (___) ___ ___

11.03bFE	but their *Non-existence* is useful for a room.[63]
11.03bSK	is its (*Non-existence*) room ('s) use —
11.03bSC	当其(无有)室之用也
11.03bTK	is its (*Non-existence*) room ('s) use —
11.03bTC	当其(无有)室之用也
11.03bWB	当其(无有)室之用___
11.03bHG	当其(无有)室之用___
11.03bFY	当其(无有)室之用___
55.03bMA	当其(无有)□之用也
55.03bMB	当其(无有)室之用也
00.000G-	___ ___ (___ ___) ___ ___ ___
00.000G-	___ ___ (___ ___) ___ ___ ___

11.04aFE	Therefore, using *Existence* is beneficial,
11.04aSK	therefore *Existence* ('s) use is benefit
11.04aSC	故有之以为利
11.04aTK	therefore *Existence* ('s) use is benefit
11.04aTC	故有之以为利
11.04aWB	故有之以为利
11.04aHG	故有之以为利
11.04aFY	故有之以为利
55.04aMA	故有之以为利
55.04aMB	故有之以为利
00.000G-	--- --- --- --- --- ---
00.000G-	--- --- --- --- --- ---

11.04bFE	while using *Non-existence* is useful. [64]
11.04bSK	*Non-existence* ('s) use is useful
11.04bSC	无之以为用
11.04bTK	*Non-existence* ('s) use is useful
11.04bTC	无之以为用
11.04bWB	无之以为用
11.04bHG	无之以为用
11.04bFY	无之以为用
55.04bMA	无之以为用
55.04bMB	无之以为用
00.000G-	--- --- --- --- ---
00.000G-	--- --- --- --- ---

Chapter 12

12.010FE	The five colours will blind people's eyes.[65]
12.010SK	five colour make people eye blind
12.010SC	五色使人目盲
12.010TK	five colour (make > make) people eye (blind > bright) 一
12.010TC	五色(令使)人目(盲明)■
12.010WB	五色(令…)人目(盲…)…
12.010HG	五色(令…)人目(盲…)…
12.010FY	五色(令…)人目(盲…)…
56.010MA	五色(…使)人目(…明)■
56.010MB	五色(…使)人目(盲…)…
00.000G-	… …(… …)… …(… …)…
00.000G-	… …(… …)… …(… …)…

12.020FE	The five tones will deafen people's ears.
12.020SK	five tones make people ('s) ear deaf
12.020SC	五音使人之耳聾
12.020TK	five tones (make > make) people ('s) ear deaf 一
12.020TC	五音(令使)人之耳聾■
12.020WB	五音(令…)人…耳聾…
12.020HG	五音(令…)人…耳聾…
12.020FY	五音(令…)人…耳聾…
56.050MA	五音(…使)人之耳聾■
56.050MB	五音(…使)人之耳口…
00.000G-	… …(… …)… … … … …
00.000G-	… …(… …)… … … … …

12. 030FE	The five flavours will refresh people's mouth.
12. 030SK	five flavour make people ('s) mouth refresh
12. 030SC	五味使人之口爽
12. 030TK	five flavour (make > make) people ('s) mouth refresh
12. 030TC	五味（令使）人之口爽
12. 030WB	五味（令＿＿）人＿＿口爽
12. 030HG	五味（令＿＿）人＿＿口爽
12. 030FY	五味（令＿＿）人＿＿口爽
56. 040MA	五味（＿＿使）人之口爽
56. 040MB	五味（＿＿使）人之口爽
00. 000G-	＿＿＿＿（＿＿＿＿）＿＿＿＿＿＿
00. 000G-	＿＿＿＿（＿＿＿＿）＿＿＿＿＿＿

12. 040FE	Galloping and hunting in the field will madden people's minds.
12. 040SK	(gallop) field hunt make people mind (madden)
12. 040SC	（驰骋）田猎使人心（发狂）
12. 040TK	(gallop) (field > field) ((hunt > (meat)) (make > make) people mind (madden)
12. 040TC	（驰骋）（田畋）（（猎（腊［＿＿］））（令使）人心（发狂）
12. 040WB	（驰骋）（＿＿畋）（（猎（＿＿［＿＿］））（令＿＿）人心（发狂）
12. 040HG	（驰骋）（田＿＿）（（猎（＿＿［＿＿］））（令＿＿）人心（发狂）
12. 040FY	（驰骋）（田＿＿）（（猎（＿＿［＿＿］））（令＿＿）人心（发狂）
56. 020MA	（驰骋）（田＿＿）（（＿＿（腊［臘］））（＿＿使）人口（口口）
56. 020MB	（驰骋）（田＿＿）（（＿＿（腊［＿＿］））（＿＿使）人心（发狂）
00. 000G-	（＿＿＿＿）（＿＿＿＿）（（＿＿（＿＿［＿＿］））（＿＿＿＿）＿＿＿＿（＿＿＿＿）
00. 000G-	（＿＿＿＿）（＿＿＿＿）（（＿＿（＿＿［＿＿］））（＿＿＿＿）＿＿＿＿（＿＿＿＿）

12.050FE Goods that are difficult to obtain will harm people.

12.050SK difficult obtain ('s) goods make people ('s) do harm

12.050SC 难得之货使人之行妨

12.050TK difficult obtain ('s) goods — (make > make) people ('s) do ((harm) > hesitate))

12.050TC 难得之货■(令使)人之行((妨[___])仿))

12.050WB 难得之货___(令___)人___行((妨[___])仿))

12.050HG 难得之货___(令___)人___行((妨[___])仿))

12.050FY 难得之货___(令___)人___行((妨[___])仿))

56.030MA 难得之货___(___使)人之行((妨[___])仿))

56.030MB 难得之货■(___使)人之行((___[方])仿))

00.000G- ___ ___ ___ ___ (___ ___) ___ ___ ___ ((___[___])___))

00.000G- ___ ___ ___ ___ (___ ___) ___ ___ ___ ((___[___])___))

12.06aFE Therefore, sages will rule for the stomach[66]

12.06aSK (therefore) (sage) ('s) rule for stomach

12.06aSC (是以)(圣人)之治为腹

12.06aTK (therefore) ((sage)(reputable person)) ('s) rule — for stomach

12.06aTC (是以)((圣人)(声人))之治也为腹

12.06aWB (是以)((圣人)(___ ___))___ ___ ___为腹

12.06aHG (是以)((圣人)(___ ___))___ ___ ___为腹

12.06aFY (是以)((圣人)(___ ___))___ ___ ___为腹

56.06aMA (是以)((___ ___)(声人))之治也为腹

56.06aMB (是以)((圣人)(___ ___))之治也为腹

00.000G- (___ ___)((___ ___)(___ ___))___ ___ ___ ___

00.000G- (___ ___)((___ ___)(___ ___))___ ___ ___ ___

12. 06bFE   and not for the eyes.
12. 06bSK   and not for eye
12. 06bSC   而不为目
12. 06bTK   and not for eye
12. 06bTC   而不为目
12. 06bWB   ___不为目
12. 06bHG   ___不为目
12. 06bFY   ___不为目
56. 06bMA   ___不□□
56. 06bMB   而不为目
00. 000G-   --- --- --- ---
00. 000G-   --- --- --- ---

12. 070FE   Therefore, reject that and accept this.[67]
12. 070SK   therefore reject that accept this
12. 070SC   故去罢耳此
12. 070TK   therefore reject ((that; abandon) > (that; accept) > (abandon; both sides) > (and accept)) this
12. 070TC   故去((彼取)(罢耳)(而取))此
12. 070WB   故去((彼取)(___ ___)(___ ___))此
12. 070HG   故去((彼取)(___ ___)(___ ___))此
12. 070FY   故去((彼取)(___ ___)(___ ___))此
56. 070MA   故去((___ ___)(罢耳)(___ ___))此
56. 070MB   故去((___ ___)(___ ___)(而取))此
00. 000G-   --- --- ((___ ___)(___ ___)(___ ___)) ---
00. 000G-   --- --- ((___ ___)(___ ___)(___ ___)) ---

Chapter 13

13.01aFE	Favour and disgrace are just like distress.
13.01aSK	favour disgrace (just like) distress
13.01aSC	宠辱若惊
13.01aTK	(favour > imperial > get) disgrace (just like) ((distress > (suffer)))
13.01aTC	(宠龙弄)辱若((惊(缨[___])))
13.01aWB	(宠___)辱若((惊(___[___])))
13.01aHG	(宠___)辱若((惊(___[___])))
13.01aFY	(宠___)辱若((惊(___[___])))
57.01aMA	(___龙___)辱若((惊(___[___])))
57.01aMB	(______弄)辱若((惊(___[___])))
24.01aGB	(宠___)辱若((___(缨[纓])))
00.000G-	(______) ______ ((___(___[___])))

13.01bFE	They cause great suffering just like the body.
13.01bSK	cost great suffer (just like) body
13.01bSC	贵大患若身
13.01bTK	cost great (suffer > sacrifice) (just like) body
13.01bTC	贵大(患梡)若身■
13.01bWB	贵大(患___)若身___
13.01bHG	贵大(患___)若身___
13.01bFY	贵大(患___)若身___
57.01bMA	贵大(___梡)若身■
57.01bMB	贵大(患___)若身___
24.01bGB	贵大(患___)若身___
00.000G-	______ (______) ______

13. 020FE   Why saying that favour and disgrace are just like distress?

13. 020SK   why say favour disgrace (just like) distress

13. 020SC   何谓宠辱若惊

13. 020TK   (why > harsh) (say) (favour > imperial > get) disgrace (just like) distress

13. 020TC   (何苛) (谓[＿＿]) (宠龙弄) 辱若惊

13. 020WB   (何＿＿) (谓[＿＿]) (宠＿＿＿＿) 辱若惊

13. 020HG   (何＿＿) (谓[＿＿]) (宠＿＿＿＿) 辱＿＿＿＿

13. 020FY   (何＿＿) (谓[＿＿]) (宠＿＿＿＿) 辱＿＿＿＿

57. 020MA   (＿＿苛) (谓[胃]) (＿＿龙＿＿) 辱若惊

57. 020MB   (何＿＿) (谓[胃]) (＿＿＿＿弄) 辱若惊

24. 020GB   (何＿＿) (谓[＿＿]) (宠＿＿＿＿) 辱＿＿＿＿

00. 000G-   (＿＿＿＿) (＿＿[＿＿]) (＿＿＿＿＿) ＿＿＿＿

13. 030FE   Favour is inferior.

13. 030SK   favour ('s) is inferior —

13. 030SC   宠之为下也

13. 030TK   ((disgrace) > (just like; distress; favour) > (favour) > (imperial) > (get)) ('s) is inferior —

13. 030TC   ((辱) (若惊宠) (宠) (龙) (弄)) 之为下也

13. 030WB   ((＿＿) (＿＿＿＿＿＿) (宠) (＿＿) (＿＿)) ＿＿为下＿＿

13. 030HG   ((辱) (＿＿＿＿＿＿) (＿＿) (龙) (＿＿)) ＿＿为下＿＿

13. 030FY   ((＿＿) (若惊宠) (＿＿) (＿＿) (＿＿)) ＿＿为下＿＿

57. 030MA   ((＿＿) (＿＿＿＿＿＿) (＿＿) (龙) (＿＿)) 之为下＿＿

57. 030MB   ((＿＿) (＿＿＿＿＿＿) (＿＿) (＿＿) (弄)) 之为下也

24. 030GB   ((＿＿) (＿＿＿＿＿＿) (宠) (＿＿) (＿＿)) ＿＿为下也

00. 000G-   ((＿＿) (＿＿＿＿＿＿) (＿＿) (＿＿) (＿＿)) ＿＿＿＿＿＿

13.040FE Receiving it is like distress and losing it is like distress.

13.040SK receive its (just like) distress lose its (just like) distress

13.040SC 得之若惊失之若惊

13.040TK receive its (just like) ((distress > (suffer))) lose its (just like)((distress > (suffer))) —

13.040TC 得之若((惊(缨[___])))失之若((惊(缨[___])))■

13.040WB 得之若((惊(___[___])))失之若((惊(___[___])))___

13.040HG 得之若((惊(___[___])))失之若((惊(___[___])))___

13.040FY 得之若((惊(___[___])))失之若((惊(___[___])))___

57.040MA 得之若((惊(___[___])))失□若((惊(___[___])))■

57.040MB 得之若((惊(___[___])))失之若((惊(___[___])))___

24.040GB 得之若((___(缨[纓])))失之若(((___(缨[纓])))___

00.000G- ___ ___ ___(((___(___[___]))) ___ ___ ___(((___(___[___])))___

13.050FE Whether it is called favour or disgrace, it is like distress.

13.050SK is call favour disgrace (just like) distress

13.050SC 是谓宠辱若惊

13.050TK is (call) (favour > imperial > get) disgrace (just like)(distress > suffer)

13.050TC 是谓[___](宠龙弄)辱若(惊缨)[纓]

13.050WB 是谓[___](宠___ ___)辱若(惊___)[___]

13.050HG 是谓[___](宠___ ___)辱若(惊___)[___]

13.050FY 是谓[___](宠___ ___)辱若(惊___)[___]

57.050MA 是谓[胃](___龙___)辱若(惊___)[___]

57.050MB 是谓[胃](___ ___弄)辱若(惊___)[___]

24.050GB 是谓[___](宠___ ___)辱___(___缨)[纓]

00.000G- ___ ___[___](___ ___ ___)___ ___(___ ___)[___]

13. 060FE	Why saying that it cost great suffering just like the body?
13. 060SK	why say cost great suffer (just like) body
13. 060SC	何谓贵大患若身
13. 060TK	why (say) get cost great (suffer > sacrifice)(just like) body
13. 060TC	何(谓[___])弄贵大(患桅)若身
13. 060WB	何(谓[___])___贵大(患___)若身
13. 060HG	何(谓[___])弄贵大(患___)若身
13. 060FY	何(谓[___])___贵大(患___)若身
57. 060MA	何(谓[胃])___贵大(___桅)若身
57. 060MB	何(谓[胃])___贵大(患___)若身
24. 060GB	□(□[___])___□□(□___)若身
00. 000G-	___(___[___])___ ___(___ ___)___ ___

13. 070FE	Why do I have great suffering?[68]
13. 070SK	I (why) have great suffer
13. 070SC	吾(所以)有大患
13. 070TK	I (why) have great (suffer > sacrifice)
13. 070TC	吾(所以)有大(患桅)
13. 070WB	吾(所以)有大(患___)
13. 070HG	吾(所以)有大(患___)
13. 070FY	吾(所以)有大(患___)
57. 070MA	吾(所以)有大(___桅)
57. 070MB	吾(所以)有大(患___)
24. 070GB	吾(所以)有大(患___)
00. 000G-	___(___ ___)___ ___(___ ___)

13. 080FE	That is, because I have a body.
13. 080SK	that because I have body —
13. 080SC	者为吾有身也
13. 080TK	that because I have body —
13. 080TC	者为吾有身也
13. 080WB	者为吾有身…
13. 080HG	者为吾有身…
13. 080FY	者为吾有身…
57. 080MA	者为吾有身也
57. 080MB	者为吾有身也
24. 080GB	者为吾有身…
00. 000G-	--- --- --- --- --- ---

13. 090FE	If I had no body, how could I suffer?
13. 090SK	if I no body I have how suffer —
13. 090SC	及吾无身吾有何患乎
13. 090TK	(if > if) I (no > missing) body I have how suffer —
13. 090TC	(及苟)吾(无亡)身吾有何患乎
13. 090WB	(及…)吾(无…)身吾有何患…
13. 090HG	(及…)吾(无…)身吾有何患…
13. 090FY	(…苟)吾(无…)身吾有何患乎
57. 090MA	(及…)吾(无…)身…有何患…
57. 090MB	(及…)吾(无…)身…有何患…
24. 090GB	(及…)吾(…亡)身…有何□…
00. 000G-	(… …)…(… …)--- --- --- ---

13. 10aFE   Therefore, those who purposely value their
             body for serving the world[69]
13. 10aSK   therefore value purpose body for serve (world)
13. 10aSC   故贵以身于为（天下）
13. 10aTK   therefore value purpose body for serve (world)
             —
13. 10aTC   故贵以身于为（天下）■
13. 10aWB   故贵以身＿＿为（天下）＿＿
13. 10aHG   故贵以身＿＿为（天下）＿＿
13. 10aFY   故贵以身＿＿为（天下）＿＿
57. 10aMA   故贵为身于为（天下）■
57. 10aMB   故贵为身于为（天下）＿＿
24. 10aGB   □□□□□为（天下）＿＿
00. 000G-   ＿＿ ＿＿ ＿＿ ＿＿ ＿＿（＿＿ ＿＿）＿＿

13. 10bFE   can be entrusted with the purpose of the
             world.[70]
13. 10bSK   according can purpose entrust for (world) —
13. 10bSC   若可以寄于（天下）矣
13. 10bTK   ((those; then) > (according)) can purpose
             (entrust > entrust > bag > administer) for
             (world) (— > —)
13. 10bTC   （（者则）若））可以（寄托橐庀）于（天下）矣■
13. 10bWB   （（＿＿）若））可＿（寄＿＿＿）＿（天下）＿＿
13. 10bHG   （（者则）＿）可以（寄＿＿＿）于（天下）＿＿
13. 10bFY   （（者则）＿））可以（＿托＿＿）＿（天下）矣＿
57. 10bMA   （（＿＿）若））可以（＿托＿＿）＿（天下）矣■
57. 10bMB   （（＿＿）若））可以（＿＿橐＿）＿（天下）□＿
24. 10bGB   （（＿＿）若））可以（＿＿＿庀）＿（天下）矣■
00. 000G-   （（＿＿）＿））＿＿（＿＿＿＿）＿（＿＿）＿＿

13. 11aFE	Those who purposely love their body for the world[71]
13. 11aSK	love purpose body for (world) those
13. 11aSC	爱以身为(天下)者
13. 11aTK	love purpose body for (world) those
13. 11aTC	爱以身为(天下)者
13. 11aWB	爱以身为(天下)...
13. 11aHG	爱以身为(天下)者
13. 11aFY	爱以身为(天下)者
57. 11aMA	爱以身为(天下)...
57. 11aMB	爱以身为(天下)...
24. 11aGB	爱以身为(天下)...
00. 000G-	... ... (... ...) ...

13. 11bFE	can be
13. 11bSK	can according
13. 11bSC	可以
13. 11bTK	((thus > then > (according) > according > (can; according))
13. 11bTC	((乃则(如[...])若(可以))
13. 11bWB	((... ...(... [...])若(可...))
13. 11bHG	((乃...(... [...]) ...(可以))
13. 11bFY	((...则(... [...]) ...(可以))
57. 11bMA	((... ...(如[女]) ...(可以))
57. 11bMB	((... ...(如[女]) ...(可以))
24. 11bGB	((... ...(... [...])若(可以))
00. 000G-	((... ...(... [...]) ...(... ...))

13. 11cFE	entrusted with the world.[72]
13. 11cSK	entrust (world) 一
13. 11cSC	寄(天下)矣
13. 11cTK	(entrust > for > entrust > repeatedly) (world) (一 > 一)
13. 11cTC	(托于寄迭)(天下)(矣■)
13. 11cWB	(托＿＿＿＿)(天下)(＿＿)
13. 11cHG	(托于＿＿)(天下)(＿＿)
13. 11cFY	(＿＿寄＿)(天下)(矣＿)
57. 11cMA	(＿＿寄＿)(天下)(＿＿)
57. 11cMB	(＿＿寄＿)(天下)(矣＿)
24. 11cGB	(＿＿＿迭)(天下)(矣■)
00. 000G−	(＿＿＿＿＿)(＿＿)(＿＿)

Chapter 14

14. 01aFE	Look at it, yet it cannot be seen.
14. 01aSK	look its yet not see
14. 01aSC	視之而弗见
14. 01aTK	look its yet (not > not) see
14. 01aTC	視之而(不弗)见
14. 01aWB	視之___(不___)见
14. 01aHG	視之___(不___)见
14. 01aFY	視之___(不___)见
58. 01aMA	視之而(___弗)见
58. 01aMB	視之而(___弗)见
00. 000G-	___ ___ ___ (___ ___) ___
00. 000G-	___ ___ ___ (___ ___) ___

14. 01bFE	Its name is called invisible.
14. 01bSK	name its call tiny
14. 01bSC	名之曰微
14. 01bTK	name its call (smooth > tiny)
14. 01bTC	名之曰(夷微)
14. 01bWB	名___曰(夷___)
14. 01bHG	名___曰(夷___)
14. 01bFY	名___曰(夷___)
58. 01bMA	名之曰(___微)
58. 01bMB	口之曰(___微)
00. 000G-	___ ___ ___ (___ ___)
00. 000G-	___ ___ ___ (___ ___)

14. 02aFE   Listen to it, yet it cannot be heard.
14. 02aSK   listen its yet not hear
14. 02aSC   听之而弗闻
14. 02aTK   listen its yet (not > not) hear
14. 02aTC   听之而(不弗)闻■
14. 02aWB   听之＿(不＿)闻＿
14. 02aHG   听之＿(不＿)闻＿
14. 02aFY   听之＿(不＿)闻＿
58. 02aMA   听之而(＿弗)闻■
58. 02aMB   听之而(＿弗)闻＿
00. 000G-   ＿＿＿(＿＿)＿＿
00. 000G-   ＿＿＿(＿＿)＿＿

14. 02bFE   Its name is called inaudible.
14. 02bSK   name its call uncommon
14. 02bSC   名之曰希
14. 02bTK   (name > name) its call uncommon —
14. 02bTC   (名命)之曰希■
14. 02bWB   (名＿)＿曰希＿
14. 02bHG   (名＿)＿曰希＿
14. 02bFY   (名＿)＿曰希＿
58. 02bMA   (名＿)之曰希＿
58. 02bMB   (＿命)之曰希■
00. 000G-   (＿＿)＿＿＿
00. 000G-   (＿＿)＿＿＿

14.03aFE   Seize it, yet it cannot be caught.
14.03aSK   seize its yet not caught
14.03aSC   搏之而弗得
14.03aTK   (seize > 揝) its yet (not > not) caught
14.03aTC   (搏揝)之而(不弗)得
14.03aWB   (搏＿)之＿(不＿)得
14.03aHG   (搏＿)之＿(不＿)得
14.03aFY   (搏＿)之＿(不＿)得
58.03aMA   (＿揝)之而(不＿)得
58.03aMB   (＿揝)之而(＿弗)得
00.000G－   (＿＿)＿＿(＿＿)＿
00.000G－   (＿＿)＿＿(＿＿)＿

14.03bFE   Its name is called insubstantial.
14.03bSK   name its call insubstantial
14.03bSC   名之曰微
14.03bTK   (name > name) its call (insubstantial > root
            out) 一
14.03bTC   (名命)之曰(微夷)■
14.03bWB   (名＿)＿曰(微＿)＿
14.03bHG   (名＿)＿曰(微＿)＿
14.03bFY   (名＿)＿曰(微＿)＿
58.03bMA   (名＿)之曰(＿夷)■
58.03bMB   (＿命)之曰(＿夷)■
00.000G－   (＿＿)＿＿(＿＿)＿
00.000G－   (＿＿)＿＿(＿＿)＿

14. 040FE	These three phenomena cannot be extensively evaluated,
14. 040SK	these three thing (cannot) extensive measured
14. 040SC	此三者(不可)致计
14. 040TK	these three thing (cannot)(extensive > optimal)(examined > measured)
14. 040TC	此三者(不可)(致至)(诘计)
14. 040WB	此三者(不可)(致___)(诘___)
14. 040HG	此三者(不可)(致___)(诘___)
14. 040FY	此三者(不可)(致___)(诘___)
58. 040MA	___三者(不可)(___至)(___计)
58. 040MB	___三者(不可)(___至)(___计)
00. 000G–	___ ___ ___ (___ ___) (___ ___) (___ ___)
00. 000G–	___ ___ ___ (___ ___) (___ ___) (___ ___)

14. 050FE	because they merge into the *One*.[73]
14. 050SK	therefore merge into as one
14. 050SC	故混而为一
14. 050TK	therefore merge into as one
14. 050TC	故混而为一
14. 050WB	故混而为一
14. 050HG	故混而为一
14. 050FY	故混而为一
58. 050MA	故混□□□
58. 050MB	故混而为一
00. 000G–	___ ___ ___ ___ ___
00. 000G–	___ ___ ___ ___ ___

14. 06aFE   Above the *One* there is no void.
14. 06aSK   one thing it above not void
14. 06aSC   一者其上不谬
14. 06aTK   one thing it above ('s) not (light > distant
             > void)
14. 06aTC   一者其上之不(皦攸谬)
14. 06aWB   ＿＿其上＿不(皦＿＿)
14. 06aHG   ＿＿其上＿＿(皦＿＿)
14. 06aFY   一者其上之不(皦＿＿)
58. 06aMA   一者其上＿不(＿攸＿)
58. 06aMB   一者其上＿不(＿＿谬)
00. 000G-   ＿＿＿＿＿＿(＿＿)
00. 000G-   ＿＿＿＿＿＿(＿＿)

14. 06bFE   Below it there is no substance.
14. 06bSK   it below ('s) no substance
14. 06bSC   其下之不忽
14. 06bTK   it below ('s) no (dark > (substance))
14. 06bTC   其下之不(昧忽)
14. 06bWB   其下＿不(昧＿)
14. 06bHG   其下＿不(昧＿)
14. 06bFY   其下之不(昧＿)
58. 06bMA   其下＿不(＿忽)
58. 06bMB   其下＿不(＿忽)
00. 000G-   ＿＿＿＿＿(＿＿)
00. 000G-   ＿＿＿＿＿(＿＿)

14. 070FE It is infinite.
14. 070SK (infinite) 一
14. 070SC (寻寻) 呵
14. 070TK ((infinite) > (infinite)) (一 > 一)
14. 070TC ((绳绳) (寻寻)) (兮呵)
14. 070WB ((绳绳) (＿＿)) (＿＿)
14. 070HG ((绳绳) (＿＿)) (兮＿)
14. 070FY ((绳绳) (＿＿)) (兮＿)
58. 070MA ((＿＿) (寻寻)) (＿呵)
58. 070MB ((＿＿) (寻寻)) (＿呵)
00. 000G- ((＿＿) (＿＿)) (＿＿)
00. 000G- ((＿＿) (＿＿)) (＿＿)

14. 08aFE It cannot be named.
14. 08aSK (cannot) named 一
14. 08aSC (不可) 名也
14. 08aTK ((cannot) > (not; be)) (named > name) 一
14. 08aTC ((不可) (不为)) (名命) 也
14. 08aWB ((不可) (＿＿)) (名＿) ＿
14. 08aHG ((不可) (＿＿)) (名＿) ＿
14. 08aFY ((不可) (＿＿)) (名＿) ＿
58. 08aMA ((不可) (＿＿)) (名＿) 也
58. 08aMB ((＿＿) (不为)) (＿命) 也
00. 000G- ((＿＿) (＿＿)) (＿＿) ＿
00. 000G- ((＿＿) (＿＿)) (＿＿) ＿

14. 08bFE　Every time it returns to *Nothingness*.
14. 08bSK　(every time) return to (nothing)
14. 08bSC　复归于(无物)
14. 08bTK　(every time) return to (nothing)
14. 08bTC　复归于(无物)
14. 08bWB　复归于(无物)
14. 08bHG　复归于(无物)
14. 08bFY　复归于(无物)
58. 08bMA　复归于(无物)
58. 08bMB　复归于(无物)
00. 000G-　--- --- --- (--- ---)
00. 000G-　--- --- --- (--- ---)

14. 09aFE　It is called shapeless.
14. 09aSK　is call (shapeless)
14. 09aSC　是谓(无状)
14. 09aTK　is (call) (shapeless)
14. 09aTC　是(谓[___])(无状)
14. 09aWB　是(谓[___])(无状)
14. 09aHG　是(谓[___])(无状)
14. 09aFY　是(谓[___])(无状)
58. 09aMA　是(谓[胃])(无状)
58. 09aMB　是(谓[胃])(无状)
00. 000G-　--- (--- [___]) (--- ---)
00. 000G-　--- (--- [___]) (--- ---)

14. 09bFE	Like the shape of *Nothingness*.
14. 09bSK	its shape (nothing) its like
14. 09bSC	之状(无物)之象
14. 09bTK	its shape (nothing) its like
14. 09bTC	之状(无物)之象
14. 09bWB	之状(无物)之象
14. 09bHG	之状(无物)之象
14. 09bFY	之状(无物)之象
58. 09bMA	之状(无物)之□
58. 09bMB	之状(无物)之象
00. 000G-	‒‒ ‒‒ (‒‒ ‒‒) ‒‒ ‒‒
00. 000G-	‒‒ ‒‒ (‒‒ ‒‒) ‒‒ ‒‒

14. 100FE	It is called dim and elusive.[74]
14. 100SK	is call dim elusive
14. 100SC	是谓惚恍
14. 100TK	is (call) (dim > dim) (indistinct > indistinct > elusive > gaze)
14. 100TC	是(谓[___])(惚芴)(怳芒恍望)
14. 100WB	是(谓[___])(惚___)(___ ___恍___)
14. 100HG	是(谓[___])(惚___)(怳___ ___)
14. 100FY	是(谓[___])(___芴)(___芒___ ___)
58. 100MA	□(□[___])(□___)(___ ___□)
58. 100MB	是(谓[胃])(惚___)(___ ___望)
00. 000G-	___(___[___])(___ ___)(___ ___ ___)
00. 000G-	___(___[___])(___ ___)(___ ___ ___)

14.110FE	Face it, yet you do not see its head.
14.110SK	face its yet not see its head
14.110SC	迎之而不见其首
14.110TK	face its yet not see its head
14.110TC	迎之而不见其首
14.110WB	迎之___不见其首
14.110HG	迎之___不见其首
14.110FY	迎之___不见其首
58.120MA	□___而不见其首
58.120MB	迎___而不见其首
00.000G-	--- --- --- --- --- ---
00.000G-	--- --- --- --- --- ---

14.120FE	Follow it, yet you do not see its back.
14.120SK	follow its yet not see its back
14.120SC	随之而不见其后
14.120TK	(follow) its yet not see its back
14.120TC	(随[___])之而不见其后
14.120WB	(随[___])之___不见其后
14.120HG	(随[随])之___不见其后
14.120FY	(随[随])之___不见其后
58.110MA	(□[___])___□□□□□
58.110MB	(随[___])___而不见其后
00.000G-	(___[___])___ --- --- --- ---
00.000G-	(___[___])___ --- --- --- ---

14. 130FE   Adhere to the present *Way* in order to manage
             the present *Existence*.[75]
14. 130SK   adhere present ('s) *Way* (in order to) manage
             present ('s) *Existence*
14. 130SC   执今之道以御今之有
14. 130TK   adhere (ancient > present)('s) *Way* can (in
             order to) manage present ('s) *Existence* —
14. 130TC   执(古今)之道可以御今之有■
14. 130WB   执(古＿)之道＿以御今之有＿
14. 130HG   执(古＿)之道＿以御今之有＿
14. 130FY   执(古＿)之道可以御今之有＿
58. 130MA   执(＿今)之道＿以御今之有■
58. 130MB   执(＿今)之道＿以御今之有＿
00. 000G-   ＿(＿＿)＿＿＿＿＿＿＿＿＿＿＿
00. 000G-   ＿(＿＿)＿＿＿＿＿＿＿＿＿＿＿

14. 140FE   Use it to understand its ancient origin.
14. 140SK   use understand ancient origin
14. 140SC   以知古始
14. 140TK   (use > able) understand ancient origin
14. 140TC   (以能)知古始
14. 140WB   (＿能)知古始
14. 140HG   (以＿)知古始
14. 140FY   (＿能)知古始
58. 140MA   (以＿)知古始
58. 140MB   (以＿)知古始
00. 000G-   (＿＿)＿＿＿＿
00. 000G-   (＿＿)＿＿＿＿

14. 150FE	That is called the principle of the *Way*.
14. 150SK	is call *Way* principle
14. 150SC	是谓道纪
14. 150TK	is (call) *Way* principle
14. 150TC	是(谓[___])道纪
14. 150WB	是(谓[___])道纪
14. 150HG	是(谓[___])道纪
14. 150FY	是(谓[___])道纪
58. 150MA	是(谓[胃])□□
58. 150MB	是(谓[胃])道纪
00. 000G-	___(___[___])___ ___
00. 000G-	___(___[___])___ ___

Chapter 15

15.01aFE	Those Ancients who practised the *Way* competently,
15.01aSK	ancient ('s) competent practise *Way* those
15.01aSC	古之善为道者
15.01aTK	ancient ('s) (competent > fly) practise ((commendable) > *Way*) those
15.01aTC	古之(善仚)为(士道)者
15.01aWB	古之(善__)为(士__)者
15.01aHG	古之(善__)为(士__)者
15.01aFY	古之(善__)为(__道)者
59.01aMA	□□(__□)□(__□)□
59.01aMB	古之(__仚)为(__道)者
05.01aGA	古之(善__)为(士__)者
00.000G–	__ __ (__ __) __ (__ __) __

15.01bFE	understood profoundly the smallest details. [76]
15.01bSK	small detail profound understand
15.01bSC	微眇玄达
15.01bTK	certainly ((subtle) > (small detail)) profound (understand > understand)
15.01bTC	必((微妙)(微眇))玄(通达)
15.01bWB	__((微妙)(__ __))玄(通__)
15.01bHG	__((微妙)(__ __))玄(通__)
15.01bFY	__((微妙)(__ __))玄(通__)
59.01bMA	__((__ __)(□□))□(__□)
59.01bMB	__((__ __)(微眇))玄(__达)
05.01bGA	必((微妙)(__ __))玄(__达)
00.000G–	__((__ __)(__ __))__(__ __)

15.020FE	Their depth cannot be known.
15.020SK	deep (cannot) known
15.020SC	深（不可）识
15.020TK	deep (cannot) (known > measure) 一
15.020TC	深（不可）（识志）■
15.020WB	深（不可）（识＿）＿
15.020HG	深（不可）（识＿）＿
15.020FY	深（不可）（识＿）＿
59.020MA	深（不可）（＿志）＿
59.020MB	深（不可）（＿志）＿
05.020GA	深（不可）（＿志）■
00.000G-	＿（＿＿）（＿＿）＿

15.030FE	They cannot be understood.
15.030SK	they only (cannot) understand
15.030SC	夫唯（不可）识
15.030TK	they (only > only) (cannot) (understand > measure)
15.030TC	夫（唯惟）（不可）（识志）
15.030WB	夫（唯＿）（不可）（识＿）
15.030HG	夫（唯＿）（不可）（识＿）
15.030FY	夫（＿惟）（不可）（识＿）
59.030MA	夫（唯＿）（不可）（＿志）
59.030MB	夫（唯＿）（不可）（＿志）
00.000G-	＿（＿＿）（＿＿）（＿＿）
00.000G-	＿（＿＿）（＿＿）（＿＿）

15.040FE　Therefore, they are difficult to describe and called:

15.040SK　therefore difficult are their describe call

15.040SC　故强为之容曰

15.040TK　(therefore ﹥ (therefore))(difficult ﹥ difficult) are their (describe ﹥ praise) — call

15.040TC　((故(是以))(强彊)为之(容颂)■曰

15.040WB　((故(＿＿＿))(强＿＿)为之(容＿＿)＿＿＿

15.040HG　((故(＿＿＿))(强＿＿)＿＿之(容＿＿)＿＿＿

15.040FY　((故(＿＿＿))(＿＿彊)为之(容＿＿)＿＿曰

59.040MA　((故(＿＿＿))(强＿＿)为之(容＿＿)■曰

59.040MB　((故(＿＿＿))(强＿＿)为之(容＿＿)＿＿曰

05.030GA　((＿＿(是以))(＿＿＿＿)为之(＿＿颂)＿＿＿

00.000G-　((＿＿(＿＿＿＿))(＿＿＿＿)＿＿＿＿＿(＿＿＿＿)＿＿＿

15.050FE　"Careful, like they were wading through a river in the winter.

15.050SK　careful — they like winter wade river

15.050SC　与呵其若冬涉川

15.050TK　(carefree ﹥ careful)(— ﹥ — ﹥ —)(then ﹥ they)(like ﹥ like) winter (wade ﹥ wade)(river ﹥ water) —

15.050TC　(豫与)(兮乎呵)(焉其)(若如)冬(涉涉)(川水)■

15.050WB　(豫＿＿)(＿＿＿＿＿＿)(焉＿＿)(若＿＿)冬(涉＿＿)(川＿＿)＿＿

15.050HG　(豫＿＿)(兮＿＿＿)(＿＿＿＿)(若＿＿)冬(＿＿涉)(川＿＿)＿＿

15.050FY　(豫＿＿)(兮＿＿＿)(＿＿＿＿)(若＿＿)冬(＿＿涉)(川＿＿)＿＿

59.050MA　(＿＿与)(＿＿＿呵)(＿＿其)(若＿＿)冬(□＿＿)(＿＿□)＿＿

59.050MB　(＿＿与)(＿＿＿呵)(＿＿其)(若＿＿)冬(涉＿＿)(＿＿水)＿＿

05.040GA　(豫＿＿)(＿＿乎＿＿)(＿＿＿＿)(＿＿如)冬(涉＿＿)(川＿＿)■

00.000G-　(＿＿＿＿)(＿＿＿＿)(＿＿＿＿)(＿＿＿＿)＿＿(＿＿＿＿)(＿＿＿＿)＿＿

15. 060FE   Hesitant, like they were afraid of their
             surrounding neighbours.
15. 060SK   hesitant — they like afraid four neighbour
15. 060SC   犹呵其如畏四邻
15. 060TK   (hesitant > plan) (— > — > —) they (like >
             like)(afraid > consider) four (neighbour) —
15. 060TC   (犹猷)(兮呵乎)其(若如)(畏思)四(邻[＿＿])■
15. 060WB   (犹＿＿)(兮＿＿＿＿)＿＿＿(若＿＿)(畏＿＿)四(邻[＿＿])＿＿＿
15. 060HG   (犹＿＿)(兮＿＿＿＿)＿＿＿(若＿＿)(畏＿＿)四(邻[＿＿])＿＿＿
15. 060FY   (犹＿＿)(兮＿＿＿＿)＿＿＿(若＿＿)(畏＿＿)四(邻[＿＿])＿＿＿
59. 060MA   (＿＿□)(＿＿□＿＿)□(□＿＿)(畏＿＿)四(□[＿＿])＿＿＿
59. 060MB   (＿＿猷)(＿＿呵＿＿)其(若＿＿)(畏＿＿)四(邻[翼])＿＿＿
05. 050GA   (＿＿猷)(＿＿＿＿乎)其(＿＿如)(＿＿思)四(邻[＿＿])■
00. 000G-   (＿＿＿＿)(＿＿＿＿＿)＿＿＿(＿＿＿)(＿＿＿＿)＿＿＿(＿＿[＿＿])＿＿＿

15. 070FE   Solemn, like they were guests.
15. 070SK   solemn — they like guest
15. 070SC   俨呵其若客
15. 070TK   solemn (— > — > —) they (like > like)(hold
             > guest) —
15. 070TC   俨(兮呵乎)其(若如)(容客)■
15. 070WB   俨(兮＿＿＿＿)其(若＿＿)(＿＿客)＿＿＿
15. 070HG   俨(兮＿＿＿＿)其(若＿＿)(容＿＿)＿＿＿
15. 070FY   俨(＿＿＿＿＿＿)＿＿＿(若＿＿)(＿＿客)＿＿＿
59. 070MA   □(＿＿呵＿＿)其(若＿＿)(＿＿客)■
59. 070MB   俨(＿＿呵＿＿)其(若＿＿)(＿＿客)＿＿＿
05. 060GA   俨(＿＿＿＿乎)其(＿＿如)(＿＿客)■
00. 000G-   ＿＿＿(＿＿＿＿＿)＿＿＿(＿＿＿＿)(＿＿＿＿)＿＿＿

15.080FE   Dissipating, like they were melting snow.
15.080SK   dissipate — they like snow damp
15.080SC   涣呵其若凌泽
15.080TK   dissipate (— > — > —) they (like > like) (snow > snow)('s) ((were; cheerful) > > damp > damp) —
15.080TC   涣(兮呵乎)其(若如)(冰凌)之((将释)泽泽))■
15.080WB   涣(兮＿＿)＿(若＿)(冰＿)之((将释)＿＿))＿
15.080HG   涣(兮＿＿)＿(若＿)(冰＿)之((将释)＿＿))＿
15.080FY   涣(＿＿＿)＿(若＿)(冰＿)＿((将释)＿＿))＿
59.080MA   涣(＿呵＿)其(若＿)(＿凌)＿((＿＿)泽＿))＿
59.080MB   涣(＿呵＿)其(若＿)(＿凌)＿((＿＿)泽＿))＿
05.070GA   涣(＿＿乎)其(＿如)(冰＿)＿((＿＿)＿泽))■
00.000G-   ＿(＿＿＿)＿(＿＿)(＿＿)＿((＿＿)＿＿))＿

15.090FE   Vague, like they were simple.
15.090SK   vague — they like simple
15.090SC   沌呵其若朴
15.090TK   (candid > vague > difficult) (— > —) — they (like > like)(simple > master) —
15.090TC   (敦沌屯)(兮呵乎)其(若如)(朴楃)■
15.090WB   (敦＿＿)(兮＿＿)其(若＿)(朴＿)＿
15.090HG   (敦＿＿)(兮＿＿)其(若＿)(朴＿)＿
15.090FY   (敦＿＿)(兮＿＿)其(若＿)(朴＿)＿
59.090MA   (＿□＿)(＿呵＿)其(若＿)(＿楃)＿
59.090MB   (＿沌＿)(＿呵＿)其(若＿)(朴＿)＿
05.080GA   (＿＿屯)(＿＿乎)其(＿如)(朴＿)■
00.000G-   (＿＿＿)(＿＿＿)＿(＿＿)(＿＿)＿

15. 100FE   Empty, like they were a valley.[77]
15. 100SK   empty — they like valley
15. 100SC   旷呵其若浴
15. 100TK   empty (— > —) they like (valley > valley) —
15. 100TC   旷(兮呵)其若(谷浴)■
15. 100WB   旷(兮___)其若(谷___)___
15. 100HG   旷(兮___)其若(谷___)___
15. 100FY   旷(兮___)其若(谷___)___
59. 110MA   □(___□)□若(___浴)■
59. 110MB   旷(___呵)其若(___浴)___
00. 000G-   ___(______)______(______)___
00. 000G-   ___(______)______(______)___

15. 110FE   Merging, like they were mud. ”[78]
15. 110SK   merge — they like muddy
15. 110SC   溷呵其若浊
15. 110TK   (merge > merge > merge > vague) (— > — > —)
              they (like > like) muddy
15. 110TC   (浑混溷沌)(兮呵乎)其(若如)浊
15. 110WB   (浑________)(兮______)其(若___)浊
15. 110HG   (浑________)(兮______)其(若___)浊
15. 110FY   (___混______)(兮______)其(若___)浊
59. 100MA   (______溷___)(___□___)□(□___)□
59. 100MB   (______溷___)(___呵___)其(若___)浊
05. 090GA   (________沌)(______乎)其(___如)浊
00. 000G-   (__________)(________)___(______)___

15. 12aFE   Do not stir mud
15. 12aSK   muddy use unstirred ('s)
15. 12aSC   浊以静之
15. 12aTK   what can muddy (use > change) ((only;
             unstirred) > (clear; tranquil) > unstirred >
             (condition)) ('s)
15. 12aTC   孰能浊(以而)((止静)(澄靖)静情))之
15. 12aWB   孰能浊(以＿)((＿＿)(＿＿)静＿))之
15. 12aHG   孰能浊(以＿)((止静)(＿＿)＿＿))之
15. 12aFY   孰能浊(以＿)((＿＿)(澄靖)＿＿))之
59. 12aMA   ＿＿浊(＿而)((＿＿)(＿＿)＿情))之
59. 12aMB   ＿＿浊(＿而)((＿＿)(＿＿)静＿))之
05. 10aGA   孰能浊(以＿)((＿＿)(＿＿)静＿))＿
00. 000G-   ＿＿＿(＿＿)((＿＿)(＿＿)＿＿))＿

15. 12bFE   and it will slowly clear.
15. 12bSK   it will slow clear
15. 12bSC   者将徐清
15. 12bTK   and it will (slow > leave) clear —
15. 12bTC   而者将(徐余)清■
15. 12bWB   ＿＿＿(徐＿)清＿
15. 12bHG   ＿＿＿(徐＿)清＿
15. 12bFY   而＿＿(徐＿)清＿
59. 12bMA   ＿＿＿(＿余)清＿
59. 12bMB   ＿＿＿(徐＿)清＿
05. 10bGA   ＿者将(徐＿)清■
00. 000G-   ＿＿＿(＿＿)＿＿

15.130FE	If settled, stir it and then it will slowly come alive.
15.130SK	settle use stir ('s) and it will slow alive
15.130SC	安以动之而者将徐生
15.130TK	what can (settle) use ((always; stir) > stir > iterate) ('s) and it will ((slow > leave)) alive
15.130TC	孰能(安[＿＿])以((久动)动重))之而者将(徐余)生
15.130WB	孰能(安[＿＿])以((久动)＿＿))之＿＿＿＿(徐＿)生
15.130HG	孰能(安[＿＿])以((久动)＿＿))之＿＿＿＿(徐＿)生
15.130FY	孰能(安[＿＿])以((久动)＿＿))之而＿＿(徐＿)生
59.130MA	＿＿＿(安[女])以((＿＿＿)＿重))之＿＿＿＿(＿余)生
59.130MB	＿＿＿(安[女])以((＿＿＿)＿重))之＿＿＿＿(徐＿)生
05.110GA	孰能(安[＿＿])以((＿＿＿)动＿))＿＿＿者将(徐＿)生
00.000G-	＿＿＿(＿[＿＿])＿((＿＿＿)＿＿＿))＿＿＿＿＿(＿＿＿)＿

15.140FE	Those who keep the *Way* do not desire fullness.
15.140SK	keep this *Way* those not desire fullness
15.140SC	葆此道者不欲盈
15.140TK	(keep > keep) this *Way* those not desire esteem fullness
15.140TC	(保葆)此道者不欲尚盈
15.140WB	(保＿)此道者不欲＿盈
15.140HG	(保＿)此道者不欲＿盈
15.140FY	(保＿)此道者不欲＿盈
59.140MA	(＿葆)此道＿不欲＿盈
59.140MB	(＿葆)此道□□欲＿盈
05.120GA	(保＿)此道者不欲尚盈
00.000G-	(＿＿＿)＿＿＿＿＿＿＿＿

15. 15aFE	Only those who desire no fullness
15. 15aSK	those only not desire fullness
15. 15aSC	夫唯不欲盈
15. 15aTK	those (only > only) not desire fullness
15. 15aTC	夫(唯惟)不欲盈
15. 15aWB	夫(唯＿＿)不＿＿盈
15. 15aHG	夫(唯＿＿)不＿＿盈
15. 15aFY	夫(＿＿惟)不＿＿盈
59. 15aMA	夫(唯＿＿)不欲□
00. 00aMB	＿＿＿(＿＿＿＿＿) ＿＿＿＿＿＿＿
00. 000G–	＿＿＿(＿＿＿＿＿) ＿＿＿＿＿＿＿
00. 000G–	＿＿＿(＿＿＿＿＿) ＿＿＿＿＿＿＿

15. 15bFE	are therefore able to exhaust themselves without renewal.
15. 15bSK	(therefore) able exhaust without renewed
15. 15bSC	(是以)能敝不成
15. 15bTK	(therefore > (therefore)) able (harm > exhaust > conceal) yet without new renewed
15. 15bTC	故(是以)能(弊敝蔽)而不新成
15. 15bWB	故(＿＿＿＿)能(＿＿＿＿蔽)＿＿不新成
15. 15bHG	故(＿＿＿＿)能(弊＿＿＿＿)＿＿不新成
15. 15bFY	＿＿＿(是以)能(＿＿敝＿＿)而不＿＿成
59. 15bMA	＿＿＿(□以)能(＿＿□＿＿)□□＿＿成
59. 15bMB	＿＿＿(是以)能(＿＿敝＿＿)而不＿＿成
00. 000G–	＿＿＿(＿＿＿＿) ＿＿(＿＿＿＿＿＿) ＿＿＿＿＿＿＿＿
00. 000G–	＿＿＿(＿＿＿＿) ＿＿(＿＿＿＿＿＿) ＿＿＿＿＿＿＿＿

Chapter 16

16.01aFE	Concentrate on removing extremes.
16.01aSK	concentrate empty extreme —
16.01aSC	致虚极也
16.01aTK	(concentrate > reach) empty extreme —
16.01aTC	(致至)虚极也
16.01aWB	(致___)虚极___
16.01aHG	(致___)虚极___
16.01aFY	(致___)虚极___
60.01aMA	(___至)虚极也
60.01aMB	(___至)虚极也
13.01aGA	(___至)虚极也
00.000G-	(______)_______

16.01bFE	Nurture tranquillity diligently.
16.01bSK	nurse tranquil diligently —
16.01bSC	守静笃也
16.01bTK	nurse (tranquil > tranquil > kindness > agreeable) (faithful > administer > supervise)
16.01bTC	守(静靖情中)(笃表督)也
16.01bWB	守(静________)(笃______)___
16.01bHG	守(静________)(笃______)___
16.01bFY	守(___靖_____)(笃______)___
60.01bMA	守(______情___)(___表___)也
60.01bMB	守(静________)(______督)也
13.01bGA	守(________中)(笃______)也
00.000G-	___(__________)(________)___

16. 02aFE	*All-things* around us rise,
16. 02aSK	(*All-things*) around rise
16. 02aSC	(万物) 傍作
16. 02aTK	(*All-things*) (together > around > near) rise
16. 02aTC	(万物) (并傍旁) 作
16. 02aWB	(万物) (并___ ___) 作
16. 02aHG	(万物) (并___ ___) 作
16. 02aFY	(万物) (并___ ___) 作
60. 02aMA	(万物) (___傍___) 作
60. 02aMB	(万物) (___傍___) 作
13. 02aGA	(万物) (___ ___旁) 作
00. 000G-	(___ ___) (___ ___ ___) ___

16. 02bFE	and I watch them return.[79]
16. 02bSK	I according watch them return —
16. 02bSC	吾以观其复也
16. 02bTK	(I > claim) according this (watch > must) them return —
16. 02bTC	(吾居) 以是 (观须) 其复也
16. 02bWB	(吾___) 以___ (观___) ___复___
16. 02bHG	(吾___) 以是 (观___) 其复___
16. 02bFY	(吾___) 以___ (观___) 其复___
60. 02bMA	(吾___) 以___ (观___) 其复也
60. 02bMB	(吾___) 以___ (观___) 其复也
13. 02bGA	(___居) 以___ (___须) ___复也
00. 000G-	(___ ___) ___ ___ (___ ___) ___ ___ ___

16.03aFE   Those things are numerous
16.03aSK   those thing (numerous)
16.03aSC   夫物（耘耘）
16.03aTK   (those > all) (thing > *Way*) ((numerous) >
            (numerous) > (numerous) > (numerous))
16.03aTC   (夫凡)(物道)((芸芸)(耘耘)(云云)(员员))
16.03aWB   (夫＿)(物＿)((芸芸)(＿＿)(＿＿)(＿＿))
16.03aHG   (夫＿)(物＿)((芸芸)(＿＿)(＿＿)(＿＿))
16.03aFY   (＿凡)(物＿)((＿＿)(耘耘)(＿＿)(＿＿))
60.03aMA   (夫＿)(物＿)((＿＿)(＿＿)(云云)(＿＿))
60.03aMB   (夫＿)(物＿)((＿＿)(耘耘)(＿＿)(＿＿))
13.03aGA   (夫＿)(＿道)((＿＿)(＿＿)(＿＿)(员员))
00.000G-   (＿＿)(＿＿)((＿＿)(＿＿)(＿＿)(＿＿))

16.03bFE   and each one returns to its roots.
16.03bSK   each again return to its root
16.03bSC   各复归于其根
16.03bTK   each again (return > return) to its root —
16.03bTC   各复(归复)于其根■
16.03bWB   各复(归＿)＿其根＿
16.03bHG   各复(归＿)＿其根＿
16.03bFY   各＿(归＿)＿其根＿
60.03bMA   各复(归＿)于其□＿
60.03bMB   各复(归＿)于其根＿
13.03bGA   各＿(＿复)＿其根■
00.000G-   ＿＿(＿＿)＿＿＿＿

16. 040FE	Returning to the roots is called tranquillity.
16. 040SK	return root call tranquil
16. 040SC	归根曰静
16. 040TK	return root call (tranquil > tranquil)
16. 040TC	归根曰(静靖)
16. 040WB	归根曰(静＿＿)
16. 040HG	归根曰(静＿＿)
16. 040FY	归根曰(＿＿靖)
60. 040MA	＿＿ ＿＿□(□＿＿)
60. 040MB	＿＿ ＿＿曰(静＿＿)
00. 000G-	＿＿ ＿＿ ＿＿(＿＿ ＿＿)
00. 000G-	＿＿ ＿＿ ＿＿(＿＿ ＿＿)

16. 050FE	Tranquillity is called returning to order.
16. 050SK	tranquil is call return order
16. 050SC	静是谓复命
16. 050TK	(tranquil > tranquil) is ((call > (call)) return order
16. 050TC	(静靖)是((曰(谓[＿＿]))复命
16. 050WB	(＿＿ ＿＿)是((＿＿(谓[＿＿]))复命
16. 050HG	(静＿＿)＿＿((曰(＿＿[＿＿]))复命
16. 050FY	(＿＿靖)＿＿((曰(＿＿[＿＿]))复命
60. 050MA	(静＿＿)是((＿＿(谓[胃]))复命
60. 050MB	(静＿＿)是((＿＿(谓[胃]))复命
00. 000G-	(＿＿ ＿＿)＿＿((＿＿(＿＿[＿＿]))＿＿ ＿＿
00. 000G-	(＿＿ ＿＿)＿＿((＿＿(＿＿[＿＿]))＿＿ ＿＿

16. 060FE	Returning to order is a constant.
16. 060SK	return order constant 一
16. 060SC	复命常也
16. 060TK	return order call constant 一
16. 060TC	复命曰常也
16. 060WB	复命曰常___
16. 060HG	复命曰常___
16. 060FY	复命曰常___
60. 060MA	复命___常也
60. 060MB	复命___常也
00. 000G-	--- --- --- --- ---
00. 000G-	--- --- --- --- ---

16. 070FE	Knowing this constant is brilliant.
16. 070SK	know constant brilliant 一
16. 070SC	知常明也
16. 070TK	know constant call brilliant 一
16. 070TC	知常曰明也
16. 070WB	知常曰明___
16. 070HG	知常曰明___
16. 070FY	知常曰明___
60. 070MA	知常___明也
60. 070MB	知常___明也
00. 000G-	--- --- --- --- ---
00. 000G-	--- --- --- --- ---

16. 080FE   Not acknowledging this constant is arrogant.
16. 080SK   not know constant arrogant
16. 080SC   不知常妄
16. 080TK   not know constant (arrogant > scarf > blurred)
16. 080TC   不知常妄帗芒
16. 080WB   不知常＿＿＿
16. 080HG   不知常＿＿＿
16. 080FY   不知常＿＿＿
60. 080MX   不知常妄＿＿
60. 080MA   不知常＿帗＿
60. 080MB   不知常＿＿芒
00. 000G-   ＿＿＿＿＿
00. 000G-   ＿＿＿＿＿

16. 090FE   Arrogance causes misfortune.
16. 090SK   arrogant cause misfortune
16. 090SC   妄作凶
16. 090TK   (arrogant > scarf > blurred) cause misfortune
16. 090TC   (妄帗芒)作凶
16. 090WB   (妄＿＿)作凶
16. 090HG   (妄＿＿)作凶
16. 090FY   (妄＿＿)作凶
60. 090MA   (＿帗＿)作凶
60. 090MB   (＿＿芒)作凶
00. 000G-   (＿＿＿)＿＿
00. 000G-   (＿＿＿)＿＿

16. 100FE   Knowing this constant is embracing.
16. 100SK   know constant embrace
16. 100SC   知常容
16. 100TK   know constant embrace
16. 100TC   知常容
16. 100WB   知常容
16. 100HG   知常容
16. 100FY   知常容
60. 100MA   知常容
60. 100MB   知常容
00. 000G-   --- --- ---
00. 000G-   --- --- ---

16. 110FE   Embracing is honourable.
16. 110SK   embrace is honourable
16. 110SC   容乃公
16. 110TK   embrace is honourable
16. 110TC   容乃公
16. 110WB   容乃公
16. 110HG   容乃公
16. 110FY   容乃公
60. 110MA   容乃公
60. 110MB   容乃公
00. 000G-   --- --- ---
00. 000G-   --- --- ---

16. 120FE   Honourable is Kingly.
16. 120SK   honourable is King
16. 120SC   公乃王
16. 120TK   honourable is King
16. 120TC   公乃王
16. 120WB   公乃王
16. 120HG   公乃王
16. 120FY   公乃王
60. 120MA   公乃王
60. 120MB   公乃王
00. 000G–   --- --- ---
00. 000G–   --- --- ---

16. 130FE   Kingly is natural.[80]
16. 130SK   King is nature
16. 130SC   王乃天
16. 130TK   King is nature
16. 130TC   王乃天
16. 130WB   王乃天
16. 130HG   王乃天
16. 130FY   王乃天
60. 130MA   王乃天
60. 130MB   □□天
00. 000G–   --- --- ---
00. 000G–   --- --- ---

16. 140FE　　Natural is the *Way*.[81]
16. 140SK　　nature is *Way*
16. 140SC　　天乃道
16. 140TK　　nature is *Way*
16. 140TC　　天乃道
16. 140WB　　天乃道
16. 140HG　　天乃道
16. 140FY　　天乃道
60. 140MA　　天乃道
60. 140MB　　天乃道
00. 000G-　　--- --- ---
00. 000G-　　--- --- ---

16. 15aFE　　The *Way* is forever.
16. 15aSK　　*Way* is forever
16. 15aSC　　道乃久
16. 15aTK　　*Way* is forever
16. 15aTC　　道乃久
16. 15aWB　　道乃久
16. 15aHG　　道乃久
16. 15aFY　　道乃久
60. 15aMA　　□□□
60. 15aMB　　道乃___
00. 000G-　　--- --- ---
00. 000G-　　--- --- ---

16. 15bFE   It produces a life without danger.[82]
16. 15bSK   produce life without danger
16. 15bSC   没身不殆
16. 15bTK   ((produce) > content)) life without (danger >
             neglect)
16. 15bTC   ((没沕))身不(殆怠)
16. 15bWB   ((没＿))身不(殆＿)
16. 15bHG   ((没＿))身不(殆＿)
16. 15bFY   ((没＿))身不(殆＿)
60. 15bMA   ((＿沕))身不(＿怠)
60. 15bMB   ((没＿))身不(殆＿)
00. 000G-   ((＿＿))＿＿(＿＿)
00. 000G-   ((＿＿))＿＿(＿＿)

Chapter 17

17.010FE	Great leaders are those known by their subjects to exist.
17.010SK	great leader subject know exist their
17.010SC	大上下知有之
17.010TK	(great > great) leader subject know (exist > and) their
17.010TC	(太大)上下知(有又)之
17.010WB	(太...)上下知(有...)之
17.010HG	(太...)上下知(有...)之
17.010FY	(太...)上下知(有...)之
61.010MA	(...大)上下知(有...)之
61.010MB	(...大)上下知(...又)□
00.000G-	(......)...............(......)...
29.010GC	(太...)上下知(有...)之

17.020FE	Next are those who are loved and praised.
17.020SK	(Next) love praise those
17.020SC	(其次)亲誉之
17.020TK	((Next) (those immediately)) love (('o) > and) (next) praise those
17.020TC	((其次)(其即))亲之而(其次)誉之
17.020WB	((其次)(......))亲...而(......)誉之
17.020HG	((其次)(......))亲...而(......)誉之
17.020FY	((其次)(......))亲之...(其次)誉之
61.020MA	((其次)(......))亲......(......)誉之
61.020MB	((其□)(......))亲......(......)誉之
00.000G-	((......)(......))...............(......)......
29.020GC	((......)(其即))亲......(......)誉之

17.030FE	Next are those who are feared.
17.030SK	(Next) fear those
17.030SC	(其次)畏之
17.030TK	(Next) those immediately fear those
17.030TC	(其次)其即畏之
17.030WB	(其次)＿＿畏之
17.030HG	(其次)＿＿畏之
17.030FY	(其次)＿＿畏之
61.030MA	(其次)＿＿畏之
61.030MB	(其次)＿＿畏之
00.000G-	(＿＿)＿＿＿＿
29.030GC	(＿＿)其即畏之

17.040FE	Next are those low ones who are insulting.
17.040SK	(Next) those low insult them
17.040SC	(其次)其下侮之
17.040TK	(Next) those low immediately (insult > *Mother*) them
17.040TC	(其次)其下即(侮母)之
17.040WB	(其次)＿＿＿＿(侮＿)之
17.040HG	(其次)＿＿＿＿(侮＿)之
17.040FY	(其次)＿＿＿＿(侮＿)之
61.040MA	(＿＿)其下＿(＿母)之
61.040MB	(＿＿)其下＿(＿母)之
00.000G-	(＿＿)＿＿＿＿(＿＿)＿
29.040GC	(＿＿)其＿即(侮＿)之

17. 050FE   If there is not enough trust,
17. 050SK   trust not enough
17. 050SC   信不足
17. 050TK   (have > therefore) trust not enough
17. 050TC   (有故)信不足
17. 050WB   (＿＿)信不足
17. 050HG   (有＿)＿不足
17. 050FY   (＿故)信不足
61. 050MA   (＿＿)信不足
61. 050MB   (＿＿)信不足
00. 000G−   (＿＿)＿＿＿
29. 050GC   (＿＿)信不足

17. 060FE   then there is distrust.
17. 060SK   then (there is) (distrust)
17. 060SC   焉有(不信)
17. 060TK   (then > propose > settle)(there is) (distrust)
17. 060TC   (焉案安)有(不信)
17. 060WB   (焉＿＿)有(不信)
17. 060HG   (焉＿＿)有(不信)
17. 060FY   (焉＿＿)有(不信)
61. 060MA   (＿案＿)有(不信)
61. 060MB   (＿＿安)有(不信)
00. 000G−   (＿＿＿)＿(＿＿)
29. 060GC   (焉＿＿)有(不信)

17. 070FE   Those of value speak about their plans

17. 070SK   plan — those value speak —

17. 070SC   猷呵其贵言也

17. 070TK   then ((hesitant) > leisure > plan))
(— > — > —) those value speak (— > —)

17. 070TC   焉((犹[＿＿])悠猷))(兮呵乎)其贵言也哉

17. 070WB   焉((＿＿[＿＿])悠＿＿))(兮＿＿＿)其贵言＿＿＿

17. 070HG   焉((犹[＿＿])＿＿＿))(兮＿＿＿)其贵言＿＿＿

17. 070FY   ＿＿((犹[猶])＿＿＿))(兮＿＿＿)其贵言＿＿哉

61. 070MA   ＿＿((＿＿[＿＿])＿＿□))(＿＿□＿＿)其贵言也＿＿

61. 070MB   ＿＿((＿＿[＿＿])＿＿猷))(＿＿呵＿＿)其贵言也＿＿

00. 000G–   ＿＿((＿＿[＿＿])＿＿＿＿))(＿＿＿＿＿) ＿＿＿＿＿＿＿＿＿

29. 070GC   ＿＿((＿＿[＿＿])＿＿猷))(＿＿＿＿乎)其贵言也＿＿

17. 080FE   and succeed in completing their affairs.

17. 080SK   (succeed) (satisfy affair)

17. 080SC   (成功)(遂事)

17. 080TK   ((succeed) > (succeed)) > achieve > ((affair;
satisfy) > (satisfy; affair)) > merit

17. 080TC   ((功成)(成功))成((事遂)(遂事))功

17. 080WB   ((功成)(＿＿＿＿))＿＿((事遂)(＿＿＿＿))＿＿

17. 080HG   ((功成)(＿＿＿＿))＿＿((事遂)(＿＿＿＿))＿＿

17. 080FY   ((功成)(＿＿＿＿))＿＿((事遂)(＿＿＿＿))＿＿

61. 080MA   ((＿＿＿＿)(成功))＿＿((＿＿＿＿)(遂事))＿＿

61. 080MB   ((＿＿＿＿)(成功))＿＿((＿＿＿＿)(遂事))＿＿

00. 000G–   ((＿＿＿＿)(＿＿＿＿))＿＿((＿＿＿＿)(＿＿＿＿))＿＿

29. 080GC   ((＿＿＿＿)(＿＿＿＿))成((事遂)(＿＿＿＿))功

17.090FE	Yet, the common people will say;
17.090SK	yet (common people) say
17.090SC	而(百姓)谓
17.090TK	yet ((common people) > (common people) > all)) ((say > (say)) daily
17.090TC	而((百姓)(百省)皆))((曰(谓[___]))日
17.090WB	___((百姓)(______)皆))((___(谓[___]))___
17.090HG	___((百姓)(______)皆))((___(谓[___]))___
17.090FY	___((百姓)(______)皆))((曰(___[___]))___
61.090MA	而((______)(百省)___))((___(谓[胃]))___
61.090MB	而((百姓)(______)___))((___(谓[胃]))___
00.000G-	___((______)(______)___))((___(___[___]))___
29.090GC	而((百姓)(______)___))((___(___[___]))日

17.100FE	it happened naturally.
17.100SK	us (natural) 一
17.100SC	我(自然)也
17.100TK	us (natural) (一 > 一)
17.100TC	我(自然)也■
17.100WB	我(自然)______
17.100HG	我(自然)______
17.100FY	我(自然)______
61.100MA	我(自然)___■
61.100MB	我(自然)______
00.000G-	___(______)______
29.100GC	我(自然)也___

Chapter 18

18.01aFE	Therefore, if the great *Way* is rejected,[83]
18.01aSK	therefore great *Way* reject
18.01aSC	故大道废
18.01aTK	therefore great *Way* reject 一
18.01aTC	故大道废■
18.01aWB	...大道废...
18.01aHG	...大道废...
18.01aFY	..大道废...
62.01aMA	故大道废■
62.01aMB	故大道废...
00.000G-	... ...
30.01aGC	故大道废...

18.01bFE	then there will be benevolence and justice.
18.01bSK	then (there is) benevolence justice
18.01bSC	焉有仁义
18.01bTK	(then > propose > install) (there is) benevolence justice
18.01bTC	(焉案安)有仁义
18.01bWB	(...........)有仁义
18.01bHG	(...........)有仁义
18.01bFY	(焉......)有仁义
62.01bMA	(...案...)有仁义
62.01bMB	(......安)有仁义
00.000G-	(.........) ... ...
30.01bGC	(焉......)有仁义

18. 02aFE   Knowledge and cleverness will appear
18. 02aSK   know clever appear
18. 02aSC   知快出
18. 02aTK   ((know; intelligent) > (intelligent; know) >
             (know; clever) > (know; intelligent)) appear
             —
18. 02aTC   ((智慧)(慧智)(知快)(知慧))出■
18. 02aWB   ((＿＿)(慧智)(＿＿)(＿＿))出＿
18. 02aHG   ((智慧)(＿＿)(＿＿)(＿＿))出＿
18. 02aFY   ((智慧)(＿＿)(＿＿)(＿＿))出＿
62. 02aMA   ((＿＿)(＿＿)(知快)(＿＿))出■
62. 02aMB   ((＿＿)(＿＿)(＿＿)(知慧))出＿
00. 000G-   ((＿＿)(＿＿)(＿＿)(＿＿))＿＿
00. 000G-   ((＿＿)(＿＿)(＿＿)(＿＿))＿＿

18. 02bFE   and then there is great hypocrisy.
18. 02bSK   then (there is) great hypocrisy
18. 02bSC   焉有大伪
18. 02bTK   (then > propose > install)(there is) great
             hypocrisy
18. 02bTC   (焉案安)有大伪
18. 02bWB   (＿＿＿)有大伪
18. 02bHG   (＿＿＿)有大伪
18. 02bFY   (焉＿＿)有大伪
62. 02bMA   (＿案＿)有大伪
62. 02bMB   (＿＿安)有□□
00. 000G-   (＿＿＿)＿＿＿
00. 000G-   (＿＿＿)＿＿＿

18.03aFE	Family relationships will be disharmonious
18.03aSK	(family relationship) (disharmony)
18.03aSC	(六亲) (不和)
18.03aTK	(family relationship) (disharmony)
18.03aTC	(六亲) (不和)
18.03aWB	(六亲) (不和)
18.03aHG	(六亲) (不和)
18.03aFY	(六亲) (不和)
62.03aMA	(六亲) (不和)
62.03aMB	(六亲) (不和)
00.000G-	(＿＿) (＿＿)
30.02aGC	(六亲) (不和)

18.03bFE	and then there is animal dirt everywhere.
18.03bSK	then (there is) animals dirt
18.03bSC	焉有畜兹
18.03bTK	(then > propose > install) ((there is) > and)) ((filial piety) > animals)) (compassion > dirt)
18.03bTC	(焉案安) ((有) 又)) ((孝) 畜)) (慈兹)
18.03bWB	(＿＿＿) ((有) ＿)) ((孝) ＿)) (慈 ＿)
18.03bHG	(＿＿＿) ((有) ＿)) ((孝) ＿)) (慈 ＿)
18.03bFY	(＿＿＿) ((有) ＿)) ((孝) ＿)) (慈 ＿)
62.03bMA	(＿案＿) ((有) ＿)) ((＿) 畜)) (＿兹)
62.03bMB	(＿＿安) ((＿) 又)) ((孝) ＿)) (＿兹)
00.000G-	(＿＿＿) ((＿) ＿)) ((＿) ＿)) (＿＿)
30.02bGC	(焉＿＿) ((有) ＿)) ((孝) ＿)) (慈 ＿)

18. 04aFE	The State's household will be a confused disorder[84]
18. 04aSK	state household confuse disorder
18. 04aSC	国家昏乱
18. 04aTK	shepherd support (state > state) household (confuse > depressed) disorder
18. 04aTC	牧养(国邦)家(昏闷)乱
18. 04aWB	＿＿＿(国＿)家(昏＿)乱
18. 04aHG	牧养(国＿)家(昏＿)乱
18. 04aFY	＿＿＿(国＿)家(昏＿)乱
62. 04aMA	＿＿＿(＿邦)家(＿闷)乱
62. 04aMB	＿＿＿(国＿)家(＿闷)乱
00. 000G-	＿＿＿(＿＿＿) ＿(＿＿＿) ＿
30. 03aGC	＿＿＿(国＿)家(昏＿)乱

18. 04bFE	and then there is bureaucracy.
18. 04bSK	then (there is) (virtuous official)
18. 04bSC	焉有(贞臣)
18. 04bTK	(then > propose > settle) (there is) (loyal > virtuous > right) official —
18. 04bTC	(焉案安)有(忠贞正)臣■
18. 04bWB	(＿＿＿＿)有(忠＿＿)臣＿
18. 04bHG	(＿＿＿＿)有(忠＿＿)臣＿
18. 04bFY	(＿＿＿＿)有(＿贞＿)臣＿
62. 04bMA	(＿案＿)有(＿贞＿)臣＿
62. 04bMB	(＿＿安)有(＿贞＿)臣＿
00. 000G-	(＿＿＿＿) ＿(＿＿＿＿) ＿＿
30. 03bGC	(焉＿＿)有(＿＿正)臣■

Chapter 19

19. 01aFE	Discard adoration and reject knowledge
19. 01aSK	discard adoration reject knowledge
19. 01aSC	绝圣弃知
19. 01aTK	discard (adoration > voice > knowledge) reject (knowledge > knowledge > recognition)
19. 01aTC	绝(圣声智)弃(智知辨)
19. 01aWB	绝(圣＿＿＿)弃(智＿＿＿)
19. 01aHG	绝(圣＿＿＿)弃(智＿＿＿)
19. 01aFY	绝(圣＿＿＿)弃(＿＿知＿0
63. 01aMA	绝(＿＿声＿)弃(＿＿知＿)
63. 01aMB	绝(圣＿＿＿)弃(＿＿知＿)
01. 01aGA	绝(＿＿＿智)弃(＿＿＿辨)
00. 000G-	＿＿(＿＿＿＿＿) ＿＿(＿＿＿＿＿)

19. 01bFE	and the people will benefit a hundred times.
19. 01bSK	and people benefit hundred times
19. 01bSC	而民利百倍
19. 01bTK	and people benefit hundred times (一)
19. 01bTC	而民利百倍■
19. 01bWB	＿＿民利百倍＿＿
19. 01bHG	＿＿民利百倍＿＿
19. 01bFY	＿＿民利百倍＿＿
63. 01bMA	＿＿民利百倍■
63. 01bMB	而民利百倍＿＿
01. 01bGA	＿＿民利百倍■
00. 000G-	＿＿ ＿＿ ＿＿ ＿＿ ＿＿

19.02aFE	Discard benevolence and reject righteousness
19.02aSK	discard benevolence reject righteousness
19.02aSC	绝仁弃义
19.02aTK	discard (benevolence > hypocrisy) reject righteousness.
19.02aTC	绝(仁伪)弃义
19.02aWB	绝(仁___)弃义
19.02aHG	绝(仁___)弃义
19.02aFY	绝(仁___)弃义
63.02aMA	绝(仁___)弃义
63.02aMB	绝(仁___)弃义
01.03aGA	绝(___伪)弃___
00.000G-	___(______)______

19.02bFE	and the people will return to filial piety and compassion.
19.02bSK	and people return (filial piety) compassion
19.02bSC	而民复孝慈
19.02bTK	(and > concern) people (return) ((filial piety) > raise) (compassion > year > season) —
19.02bTC	(而虑)民(复[___])(孝畜)(慈兹季)子■
19.02bWB	(______)民(复[___])(孝___)(慈______)______
19.02bHG	(______)民(复[復])(孝___)(慈______)______
19.02bFY	(______)民(复[___])(孝___)(慈______)______
63.02bMA	(______)民(复[___])(___畜)(___兹___)___■
63.02bMB	(而___)民(复[___])(孝___)(___兹___)______
01.03bGA	(___虑)民(复[___])(______)(______季)子■
00.000G-	(______)___(___[___])(______)(______)______

19. 03aFE	Discard cleverness and reject profit
19. 03aSK	discard clever reject profit
19. 03aSC	绝巧弃利
19. 03aTK	discard clever reject profit
19. 03aTC	绝巧弃利
19. 03aWB	绝巧弃利
19. 03aHG	绝巧弃利
19. 03aFY	绝巧弃利
63. 03aMA	绝巧弃利
63. 03aMB	绝巧弃利
01. 02aGA	绝巧弃利
00. 000G-	--- --- --- ---

19. 03bFE	and there will be no burglars and thieves.
19. 03bSK	thief burglar no (there are)
19. 03bSC	盗贼无有
19. 03bTK	((thief) > burglar)) (no > missing) (there are) —
19. 03bTC	((盗[___])贼))无亡有■
19. 03bWB	((盗[___])贼))无___有___
19. 03bHG	((盗[盗])贼))无___有___
19. 03bFY	((盗[盗])贼))无___有___
63. 03bMA	((盗[___])贼))无___有___
63. 03bMB	((盗[___])贼))无___有___
01. 02bGA	((盗[___])贼))___亡有■
00. 000G-	((___[___])___))--- --- ---

19. 04aFE   These three declarations
19. 04aSK   these three declaration 一
19. 04aSC   此三言也
19. 04aTK   these three (thing > declaration) 一
19. 04aTC   此三(者言)也
19. 04aWB   此三(者＿＿)＿＿
19. 04aHG   此三(者＿＿)＿＿
19. 04aFY   此三(者＿＿)＿＿
63. 04aMA   此三(＿＿言)也
63. 04aMB   此三(＿＿言)也
01. 04aGA   ＿＿三(＿＿言)＿＿
00. 000G−   ＿＿＿＿(＿＿＿＿)＿＿

19. 04bFE   could be regarded to be inadequate slogans.
19. 04bSK   use as slogan and not enough 一
19. 04bSC   以为文而未足也
19. 04bTK   use as (slogan > dispatch) and (not > not)
             enough (一 > 一)
19. 04bTC   以为(文使)而(不未)足也■
19. 04bWB   以为(文＿＿)＿＿(不＿＿)足＿＿＿＿
19. 04bHG   以为(文＿＿)＿＿(不＿＿)足＿＿＿＿
19. 04bFY   以为(文＿＿)而(＿＿未)足也＿＿
63. 04bMA   以为(文＿＿)＿＿(＿＿未)足＿＿■
63. 04bMB   以为(文＿＿)＿＿(＿＿未)足＿＿＿＿
01. 04bGA   以为(＿＿使)＿＿(不＿＿)足＿＿＿＿
00. 000G−   ＿＿＿＿(＿＿＿＿)＿＿(＿＿＿＿)＿＿＿＿

19. 050FE	Therefore, let the people have institutions.
19. 050SK	therefore let them have (institution)
19. 050SC	故令之有(所属)
19. 050TK	therefore let them (have > (may be)) (institution) —
19. 050TC	故令之(有或)(所属) ■
19. 050WB	故令＿＿(有＿＿)(所属)＿＿
19. 050HG	故令＿＿(有＿＿)(所属)＿＿
19. 050FY	故令＿＿(有＿＿)(所属)＿＿
63. 050MA	故令之(有＿＿)(所属)＿＿
63. 050MB	故令之(有＿＿)(所属)＿＿
01. 050GA	故令之(＿＿或)(所属) ■
00. 000G–	＿＿＿＿＿＿ (＿＿＿＿) (＿＿＿＿) ＿＿

19. 060FE	Show modesty and embrace simplicity.[85]
19. 060SK	show modest embrace simple
19. 060SC	见素抱朴
19. 060TK	(show > look) modest (embrace > embrace > keep) simple
19. 060TC	(见视)素(抱裹保)朴
19. 060WB	(见＿＿)素(抱＿＿＿＿)朴
19. 060HG	(见＿＿)素(抱＿＿＿＿)朴
19. 060FY	(见＿＿)素(＿＿裹＿＿)朴
63. 060MA	(见＿＿)素(抱＿＿＿＿)□
63. 060MB	(见＿＿)素(抱＿＿＿＿)朴
01. 060GA	(＿＿视)素(＿＿＿＿保)朴
00. 000G–	(＿＿＿＿) ＿＿ (＿＿＿＿＿＿) ＿＿

19. 070FE	Lack selfishness and restrain desires.
19. 070SK	lack selfish and lack desire
19. 070SC	少私而寡欲
19. 070TK	lack selfish and lack desire 一
19. 070TC	少私而寡欲■
63. 070WB	少私…寡欲…
19. 070HG	少私…寡欲…
19. 070FY	少私…寡欲…
63. 070MA	□□…□□…
19. 070MB	少□而寡欲…
01. 070GA	少私…寡欲■
00. 000G-	———————

Chapter 20

20. 010FE	Discard knowledge and there are no worries.[86]
20. 010SK	discard knowledge no worry
20. 010SC	绝学无忧
20. 010TK	discard knowledge (no > missing) worry
20. 010TC	绝学（无亡）忧
20. 010WB	绝学（无＿）忧
20. 010HG	绝学（无＿）忧
20. 010FY	绝学（无＿）忧
63. 080MA	□□（□＿）□
63. 080MB	绝学（无＿）忧
23. 010GB	绝学（＿亡）忧
00. 000G–	＿＿（＿＿）＿

20. 02aFE	Flattery and rebuke:
20. 02aSK	flatter ('s) and rebuke
20. 02aSC	唯之与诃
20. 02aTK	flatter ('s) and (flatter > rebuke > rebuke)
20. 02aTC	唯之与（阿呵诃）
20. 02aWB	唯之与（阿＿＿）
20. 02aHG	唯之与（阿＿＿）
20. 02aFY	唯之与（阿＿＿）
64. 01aMA	唯＿与（＿＿诃）
64. 01aMB	唯＿与（＿呵＿）
23. 02aGB	唯＿与（＿＿诃）
00. 000G–	＿＿＿（＿＿＿）

20.02bFE   how much do they differ from each other?[87]
20.02bSK   they (each other) difference (how much)
20.02bSC   其相去（几何）
20.02bTK   they (each other) difference (how much)
20.02bTC   其相去（几何）
20.02bWB   ⎯相去（几何）
20.02bHG   ⎯相去（几何）
20.02bFY   ⎯相去（几何）
64.01bMA   其相去（几何）
64.01bMB   其相去（几何）
23.02bGB   ⎯相去（几何）
00.000G-   ⎯⎯⎯（⎯⎯）

20.03aFE   Satisfaction and dissatisfaction:
20.03aSK   satisfy) and dissatisfy
20.03aSC   美与恶
20.03aTK   (competent > satisfy) and (dissatisfy >
            inferior)
20.03aTC   （善美）之与（恶亚）
20.03aWB   （善⎯）之与（恶⎯）
20.03aHG   （善⎯）之与（恶⎯）
20.03aFY   （⎯美）之与（恶⎯）
64.02aMA   （⎯美）⎯与（恶⎯）
64.02aMB   （⎯美）⎯与（⎯亚）
23.03aGB   （⎯美）⎯与（⎯亚）
00.000G-   （⎯⎯）⎯⎯（⎯⎯）

20. 03bFE	how much do they differ from each other?[88]
20. 03bSK	they (each other) different how seem
20. 03bSC	其相去何若
20. 03bTK	they (each other) different ((how; seem) > (seem; how)) —
20. 03bTC	其相去((何若)(若何))
20. 03bWB	___相去((______)(若何))
20. 03bHG	___相去((何若)(______))
20. 03bFY	___相去((何若)(______))
64. 02bMA	其相去((何若)(______))
64. 02bMB	其相去((何若)(______))
23. 03bGB	___相去((何若)(______))
00. 000G-	___ ___ ___((______)(______))

20. 040FE	What everybody fears, one has to fear as well.
20. 040SK	everybody ('s) actual fear also not can according not fear everybody
20. 040SC	人之所畏亦不可以不畏人
20. 040TK	everybody ('s) actual fear also not can according not fear everybody
20. 040TC	人之所畏亦不可以不畏人
20. 040WB	人之所畏___不可___不畏___
20. 040HG	人之所畏___不可___不畏___
20. 040FY	人之所畏___不可___不畏___
64. 030MA	人之□□亦不□□□□___
64. 030MB	人之所畏亦不可以不畏___
23. 040GB	人之所畏亦不可以不畏人
00. 000G-	___ ___ ___ ___ ___ ___ ___ ___ ___ ___ ___

20.050FE	Everybody stares at me. They do not stop.
20.050SK	everybody stare — they not stop —
20.050SC	人望呵其未央哉
20.050TK	absurd everybody stare (一 > 一) they not stop —
20.050TC	荒人望(兮呵)其未央哉
20.050WB	荒＿＿＿(兮＿)其未央哉
20.050HG	荒＿＿＿(兮＿)其未央哉
20.050FY	荒＿＿＿(兮＿)其未央＿
64.040MA	＿□＿(＿□)□□□＿
64.040MB	＿人望(＿呵)其未央＿
00.000G-	＿＿＿(＿＿)＿＿＿
00.000G-	＿＿＿(＿＿)＿＿＿

20.060FE	Everybody is very happy.
20.060SK	(everybody) (very happy)
20.060SC	(众人)(熙熙)
20.060TK	only (everybody) (very happy)
20.060TC	才(众人)(熙熙)
20.060WB	＿(众人)(熙熙)
20.060HG	＿(众人)(熙熙)
20.060FY	＿(众人)(熙熙)
64.050MA	□(众人)(熙熙)
64.050MB	才(众人)(熙熙)
00.000G-	＿(＿＿)(＿＿)
00.000G-	＿(＿＿)(＿＿)

20.07aFE Just like a big sacrificial feast in the village
20.07aSK (just like) village in big (sacrificial feast)
20.07aSC 若乡于大牢
20.07aTK ((just like) > (just like)) (enjoy > village) in (big > big)(sacrificial feast) 一
20.07aTC ((如若))(享乡)于(太大)牢■
20.07aWB ((如＿))(享＿)＿(太＿)牢＿
20.07aHG ((如＿))(享＿)＿(太＿)牢＿
20.07aFY ((＿若))(享＿)＿(太＿)牢＿
64.06aMA ((＿若))(＿乡)于(＿大)牢■
64.06aMB ((＿若))(＿乡)于(＿大)牢＿
00.000G- ((＿＿))(＿＿)＿(＿＿)＿＿
00.000G- ((＿＿))(＿＿)＿(＿＿)＿＿

20.07bFE and stepping on stage in the springtime.[89]
20.07bSK and spring (step on) stage
20.07bSC 而春登台
20.07bTK ((just like) > (just like) > and) spring (step on) stage
20.07bTC (如若而)春登台
20.07bWB (如＿＿)春登台
20.07bHG (如＿＿)春登台
20.07bFY (＿若＿)春登台
64.06bMA (＿＿而)春登台
64.06bMB (＿＿而)春登台
00.000G- (＿＿＿)＿＿＿
00.000G- (＿＿＿)＿＿＿

20. 08aFE	I am quiet and not predictable.[90]
20. 08aSK	I quiet — not predictable
20. 08aSC	我泊兮未兆
20. 08aTK	I alone (scared > bold > quiet > learned) — (such > then) ((not; predictable) > (not; sacrifice))
20. 08aTC	我独(怕魄泊博)兮其焉((未兆)(未朓))
20. 08aWB	我独(___ ___泊___)兮其___((未兆)(___ ___))
20. 08aHG	我独(怕___ ___ ___)兮其___((未兆)(___ ___))
20. 08aFY	我独(___魄___ ___)兮其___((未兆)(___ ___))
64. 07aMA	我___(___ ___泊___)___ ___焉((未兆)(___ ___))
64. 07aMB	我___(___ ___ ___博)___ ___焉((___ ___)(未朓))
00. 000G-	___ ___(___ ___ ___)___ ___ ___((___ ___)(___ ___))
00. 000G-	___ ___(___ ___ ___)___ ___ ___((___ ___)(___ ___))

20. 08bFE	Just like a baby that has not coughed yet.
20. 08bSK	just like infant not cough
20. 08bSC	若婴儿未咳
20. 08bTK	((just like) > (just like))(infant)('s) not (child > cough)
20. 08bTC	(如若)(婴儿)之未(孩咳)
20. 08bWB	(如___)(婴儿)之未(孩___)
20. 08bHG	(如___)(婴儿)之未(孩___)
20. 08bFY	(___若)(婴儿)之未(___咳)
64. 07bMA	(___若)(□□)___□(___□)
64. 07bMB	(___若)(婴儿)___未(___咳)
00. 000G-	(___ ___)(___ ___)___ ___(___ ___)
00. 000G-	(___ ___)(___ ___)___ ___(___ ___)

20.09aFE   Tired;
20.09aSK   tired 一
20.09aSC   儳呵
20.09aTK   (much travel) ((very tired) > (very tired) >
             tired)) (一 > 一)
20.09aTC   (乘乘)((儑儑)(累累)儳))(兮呵)
20.09aWB   (___ ___)((___ ___)(累累)___))(兮___)
20.09aHG   (乘乘)((___ ___)(___ ___)___))(兮___)
20.09aFY   (___ ___)((儑儑)(___ ___)___))(兮___)
64.08aMA   (___ ___)((___ ___)(___ ___)儳))(___呵)
64.08aMB   (___ ___)((___ ___)(___ ___)儳))(___呵)
00.000G-   (___ ___)((___ ___)(___ ___)___))(___ ___)
00.000G-   (___ ___)((___ ___)(___ ___)___))(___ ___)

20.09bFE   without a place to return to.
20.09bSK   like without place return
20.09bSC   似无所归
20.09bTK   ((like > its > (like) > like)) not enough
             purpose without place return
20.09bTC   ((若其(似[___])如))不足以无所归
20.09bWB   ((若___(___[___])___))___ ___ ___无所归
20.09bHG   ((若___(___[___])___))___ ___ ___无所归
20.09bFY   ((___其(___[___])___))不足以无所归
64.08bMA   ((___ ___(___[___])如))___ ___ ___□□□
64.08bMB   ((___ ___(似[佁])___))___ ___ ___无所归
00.000G-   ((___ ___(___[___])___))___ ___ ___ ___ ___
00.000G-   ((___ ___(___[___])___))___ ___ ___ ___ ___

20. 10aFE	Everybody has a surplus.
20. 10aSK	(everybody) have surplus
20. 10aSC	(众人)有余
20. 10aTK	(everybody) all (have > and) surplus
20. 10aTC	(众人)皆(有又)余
20. 10aWB	(众人)皆(有＿)余
20. 10aHG	(众人)皆(有＿)余
20. 10aFY	(众人)皆(有＿)余
64. 09aMA	(□□)皆(有＿)余
64. 09aMB	(众人)皆(＿又)余
00. 000G-	(＿＿)＿(＿＿)＿
00. 000G-	(＿＿)＿(＿＿)＿

20. 10bFE	Yet, only I seem to be lacking.[91]
20. 10bSK	yet I only seem loss
20. 10bSC	而我独若遗
20. 10bTK	yet I only seem loss
20. 10bTC	而我独若遗
20. 10bWB	而我独若遗
20. 10bHG	而我独若遗
20. 10bFY	＿我独若遗
64. 09bMA	＿我独＿遗
00. 00bMB	＿＿＿＿＿
00. 000G-	＿＿＿＿＿
00. 000G-	＿＿＿＿＿

20.110FE	I am a very stupid fool in other people's minds.
20.110SK	I fool (other people) ('s) mind — (very stupid) —
20.110SC	我愚人之心也(惷惷)兮
20.110TK	I fool (other people) ('s) mind — why ((very unclear) > (very stupid) > (湷湷)) (— > —)
20.110TC	我愚人之心也哉((沌沌)(惷惷)(湷湷))(兮呵)
20.110WB	我愚人之心也哉((沌沌)(___ ___)(___ ___))(兮___)
20.110HG	我愚人之心也哉((沌沌)(___ ___)(___ ___))(兮___)
20.110FY	我愚人之心也哉((沌沌)(___ ___)(___ ___))(兮___)
64.100MA	我愚人之心也___((___ ___)(惷惷)(___ ___))(___呵)
64.100MB	我愚人之心也___((___ ___)(___ ___)(湷湷))(___呵)
00.000G-	___ ___ ___ ___ ___ ___ ___((___ ___)(___ ___)(___ ___))(___ ___)
00.000G-	___ ___ ___ ___ ___ ___ ___((___ ___)(___ ___)(___ ___))(___ ___)

20.12aFE	Everybody is very clear.
20.12aSK	(everybody (very clear)
20.12aSC	(俗人)(昭昭)
20.12aTK	((everybody) > (everybody) > (sales; people)) all (very clear)
20.12aTC	(众人)(俗人)(鬻人)皆(昭昭)
20.12aWB	(___ ___)(俗人)(___ ___)___(昭昭)
20.12aHG	(众人)(___ ___)(___ ___)___(昭昭)
20.12aFY	(___ ___)(俗人)(___ ___)皆(昭昭)
64.11aMA	(___ ___)(___ ___)(鬻□)___(□□)
64.11aMB	(___ ___)(___ ___)(鬻人)___(昭昭)
00.000G-	(___ ___)(___ ___)(___ ___)___(___ ___)
00.000G-	(___ ___)(___ ___)(___ ___)___(___ ___)

20.12bFE   Only I seem to be confused.[92]
20.12bSK   I only seem confuse —
20.12bSC   我独若昏呵
20.12bTK   I only seem (confuse > (very confused) > (脣))
             —

20.12bTC   我独若((昏)(昏昏)(脣))呵
20.12bWB   我独＿＿((＿＿)(昏昏)(＿＿))＿＿
20.12bHG   我独若((昏)(＿＿＿)(＿＿))＿＿
20.12bFY   我独若((昏)(＿＿＿)(＿＿))＿＿
64.11bMA   □□□((＿＿)(＿＿＿)(脣))呵
64.11bMB   我独若((昏)(＿＿＿)(＿＿))呵
00.000G-   ＿＿＿＿＿((＿＿)(＿＿＿)(＿＿))＿＿
00.000G-   ＿＿＿＿＿((＿＿)(＿＿＿)(＿＿))

20.13aFE   Everybody is very certain.[93]
20.13aSK   (everybody) (very strict)
20.13aSC   (俗人)(察察)
20.13aTK   ((everybody) > (everybody) > (sales; people))
             all ((very strict) > (extreme sacrifice) >
             (turtle; turtle))
20.13aTC   ((众人)(俗人)(鬻人))皆((察察)(祭祭)(蔡蔡))
20.13aWB   ((＿＿＿)(俗人)(＿＿＿))＿＿((察察)(＿＿＿)(＿＿＿))
20.13aHG   ((众人)(＿＿＿)(＿＿＿))＿＿((察察)(＿＿＿)(＿＿＿))
20.13aFY   ((＿＿＿)(俗人)(＿＿＿))皆((＿＿＿)(祭祭)(＿＿＿))
64.12aMA   ((＿＿＿)(＿＿＿)(鬻人))＿＿((＿＿＿)(＿＿＿)(蔡蔡))
64.12aMB   ((＿＿＿)(＿＿＿)(鬻人))＿＿((察察)(＿＿＿)(＿＿＿))
00.000G-   ((＿＿＿)(＿＿＿)(＿＿＿))＿＿((＿＿＿)(＿＿＿)(＿＿＿))
00.000G-   ((＿＿＿)(＿＿＿)(＿＿＿))＿＿((＿＿＿)(＿＿＿)(＿＿＿))

20. 13bFE	Only I seem to be very uncertain.[94]
20. 13bSK	I only (very depressed) —
20. 13bSC	我独(闷闷)呵
20. 13bTK	I only seem ((very depressed) > (very confused) > (闽闽)) —
20. 13bTC	我独若((闷闷)(闵闵)(闽闽))呵
20. 13bWB	我独＿＿((闷闷)(＿＿＿)(＿＿＿))＿＿
20. 13bHG	我独＿＿((闷闷)(＿＿＿)(＿＿＿))＿＿
20. 13bFY	我独若((＿＿＿)(闵闵)(＿＿＿))＿＿
64. 12bMA	我独＿＿((闷闷)(＿＿＿)(＿＿＿))呵
64. 12bMB	我独＿＿((＿＿＿)(＿＿＿)(闽闽))呵
00. 000G-	＿＿＿＿((＿＿＿)(＿＿＿)(＿＿＿))＿＿
00. 000G-	＿＿＿＿((＿＿＿)(＿＿＿)(＿＿＿))＿＿

20. 14aFE	They are indifferent.
20. 14aSK	indifferent —
20. 14aSC	淡呵
20. 14aTK	(inattention > indifferent > calm) (— > —)
20. 14aTC	(忽淡澹)(兮呵)
20. 14aWB	(＿＿＿澹)(兮＿)
20. 14aHG	(忽＿＿＿)(兮＿)
20. 14aFY	(＿淡＿)(兮＿)
64. 13aMA	(忽＿＿＿)(＿呵)
64. 13aMB	(忽＿＿＿)(＿呵)
00. 000G-	(＿＿＿＿)(＿＿＿)
00. 000G-	(＿＿＿＿)(＿＿＿)

20. 14bFE	It is like staring at the sea.	
20. 14bSK	its (just like) sea gaze 一	
20. 14bSC	其若海望呵	
20. 14bTK	its (just like) sea ((drift 〉 drift) 〉 wind 〉 〉 gaze 〉 gaze)) (一 〉 一)	
20. 14bTC	其若海((漂(飘[___])飚望塱))(兮呵)	
20. 14bWB	其若海((___(___[___])飚______))(兮___)	
20. 14bHG	___若海((漂(___[___])______))(兮___)	
20. 14bFY	其若海((___(飘[飘])______))(兮___)	
64. 13bMA	其若□((___(___[___])___望___))(___呵)	
64. 13bMB	其若海((___(___[___])______塱))(___呵)	
00. 000G-	______((___(___[___])______))(______)	
00. 000G-	______((___(___[___])______))(______)	

20. 150FE	It is like having no place to rest.	
20. 150SK	its (just like) no place rest	
20. 150SC	其若无所止	
20. 150TK	its ((just like) 〉 (just like)) no place rest	
20. 150TC	其((若似))无所止	
20. 150WB	___((若___))无___止	
20. 150HG	___((若___))无所止	
20. 150FY	___((___似))无所止	
64. 140MA	其((若___))无所止	
64. 140MB	___((若___))无所止	
00. 000G-	___((______))______	
00. 000G-	___((______))______	

20. 160FE	Everybody has a purpose.	
20. 160SK	(everybody) all have purpose	
20. 160SC	（众人）皆有以	
20. 160TK	(everybody) all have purpose	
20. 160TC	（众人）皆有以	
20. 160WB	（众人）皆有以	
20. 160HG	（众人）皆有以	
20. 160FY	（众人）皆有以	
64. 150MA	（□□）□□□	
64. 150MB	（众人）皆有以	
00. 000G–	（__ __）__ __ __	
00. 000G–	（__ __）__ __ __	

20. 170FE	Only I am stubborn and my purpose seems to be ridiculous.
20. 170SK	I only stubborn purpose ridicule
20. 170SC	我独顽以悝
20. 170TK	yet I only (stubborn > method) (fundamental > like > and > purpose) ((scorn > (pursue) > ridicule))
20. 170TC	而我独（顽门）（元似且以）（（鄙（图[___]）悝））
20. 170WB	而我独（顽__）（__似__ __）（（鄙（__[___]）__））
20. 170HG	而我独（顽__）（__似__ __）（（鄙（__[___]）__））
20. 170FY	__我独（顽__）（__ __且__）（（__（图[圖]）__））
64. 160MA	__□□（__□）（__ __ __以）（（__（__[___]）悝））
64. 160MB	__我独（__门）（元__ __以）（（鄙（__[___]）__））
00. 000G–	__ __ __（__ __）（__ __ __ __）（（__（__[___]）__））
00. 000G–	__ __ __（__ __）（__ __ __ __）（（__（__[___]）__））

20. 18aFE	I desire only to differ from other people
20. 18aSK	I desire only different from (other people)
20. 18aSC	吾欲独异于人
20. 18aTK	(I > I) (only > (only; desire) > (desire; only)) different from (other people)
20. 18aTC	(我吾) ((独 (独欲) (欲独)) 异于人
20. 18aWB	(我＿) ((独 (＿＿) (＿＿)) 异于人
20. 18aHG	(我＿) ((独 (＿＿) (＿＿)) 异于人
20. 18aFY	(＿吾) ((＿ (独欲) (＿＿)) 异于人
64. 17aMA	(＿吾) ((＿ (＿＿) (欲独)) 异于人
64. 17aMB	(＿吾) ((＿ (＿＿) (欲独)) 异于人
00. 000G-	(＿＿) ((＿ (＿＿) (＿＿)) ＿＿＿
00. 000G-	(＿＿) ((＿ (＿＿) (＿＿)) ＿＿＿

20. 18bFE	and value the nourishment from the *Mother*.
20. 18bSK	and value food *Mother*
20. 18bSC	而贵食母
20. 18bTK	and value food *Mother*
20. 18bTC	而贵食母
20. 18bWB	而贵食母
20. 18bHG	而贵食母
20. 18bFY	而贵食母
64. 17bMA	而贵食母
64. 17bMB	而贵食母
00. 000G-	＿＿＿＿
00. 000G-	＿＿＿＿

Chapter 21

21.010FE	The greatest virtue is following only the *Way*.
21.010SK	great virtue its for only *Way* is follow
21.010SC	孔德之容唯道是从
21.010TK	great virtue its for (only > only) *Way* is follow
21.010TC	孔德之容(唯惟)道是从
21.010WB	孔德之容(___惟)道是从
21.010HG	孔德之容(唯___)道是从
21.010FY	孔德之容(___惟)道是从
65.010MA	孔德之容(唯___)道是从
65.010MB	孔德之容(唯___)道是从
00.000G-	--- --- --- (--- ---) --- --- ---
00.000G-	--- --- --- (--- ---) --- --- ---

21.020FE	The contents of the *Way* are only elusive and dim.[95]
21.020SK	*Way* ('s) content only elusive only dim
21.020SC	道之物唯恍唯惚
21.020TK	*Way* ('s) are content (only > only) (blurred > blurred > elusive > gaze) (only > only) (overlook > dim > dim)
21.020TC	道之为物(唯惟)(怳芒恍望)(唯惟)(忽芴惚)
21.020WB	道之为物(___惟)(______恍___)(___惟)(______惚)
21.020HG	道之为物(唯___)(怳__________)(唯___)(忽______)
21.020FY	道之为物(___惟)(___芒______)(___惟)(___芴___)
65.020MA	道之___物(唯___)(__________望)(唯___)(忽______)
65.020MB	道之___物(唯___)(__________望)(唯___)(______惚)
00.000G-	--- --- --- (--- ---) (--- --- ---) (--- ---) (--- ---)
00.000G-	--- --- --- (--- ---) (--- --- ---) (--- ---) (--- ---)

21.030FE	Dim. Elusive.[96]	
21.030SK	dim — elusive —	
21.030SC	惚呵恍呵	
21.030TK	(overlook > dim > dim) (— > —) (blurred > blurred > elusive > gaze) (— > —)	
21.030TC	(忽芴惚)(兮呵)(怳芒恍望)(兮呵)	
21.030WB	(＿＿惚)(兮＿)(＿＿恍＿)(兮＿)	
21.050HG	(忽＿＿)(兮＿)(怳＿＿＿)(兮＿)	
21.030FY	(＿芴＿)(兮＿)(＿芒＿＿)(兮＿)	
65.030MA	(＿＿□)(＿□)(＿＿＿□)(＿呵)	
65.030MB	(＿＿惚)(＿呵)(＿＿＿望)(＿呵)	
00.000G-	(＿＿＿)(＿＿)(＿＿＿＿)(＿＿)	
00.000G-	(＿＿＿)(＿＿)(＿＿＿＿)(＿＿)	

21.040FE	Inside there are images.	
21.040SK	inside (there is) image —	
21.040SC	中有象呵	
21.040TK	its inside ((there is) > and)) image —	
21.040TC	其中((有又))象呵	
21.040WB	其中((有＿))象＿	
21.060HG	其中((有＿))象＿	
21.040FY	其中((有＿))象＿	
65.040MA	＿中((有＿))象呵	
65.040MB	＿中((＿又))象呵	
00.000G-	＿＿((＿＿))＿＿	
00.000G-	＿＿((＿＿))＿＿	

21.050FE	Elusive. Dim.[97]	
21.050SK	elusive — dim —	
21.050SC	恍呵惚呵	
21.050TK	(blurred > blurred > elusive > gaze) (— > —) (overlook > dim > dim) (— > —)	
21.050TC	(怳芒恍望)(兮呵)(忽芴惚)(兮呵)	
21.050WB	(＿＿恍＿)(兮＿)(＿＿惚)(兮＿)	
21.030HG	(怳＿＿＿)(兮＿)(忽＿＿)(兮＿)	
21.050FY	(＿芒＿＿)(兮＿)(＿芴＿)(兮＿)	
65.050MA	(＿＿＿望)(＿呵)(忽＿＿)(＿呵)	
65.050MB	(＿＿＿望)(＿呵)(＿＿惚)(＿呵)	
00.000G–	(＿＿＿＿)(＿＿)(＿＿＿)(＿＿)	
00.000G–	(＿＿＿＿)(＿＿)(＿＿＿)(＿＿)	

21.060FE	Inside there are things.	
21.060SK	inside (there is) thing —	
21.060SC	中有物呵	
21.060TK	its inside (there is) thing (— > —)	
21.060TC	其中有物(呵 ■)	
21.060WB	其中有物(＿＿)	
21.040HG	其中有物(＿＿)	
21.060FY	其中有物(＿＿)	
65.060MA	＿中有物(呵 ■)	
65.060MB	＿中有物(呵＿)	
00.000G–	＿＿＿＿＿(＿＿)	
00.000G–	＿＿＿＿＿(＿＿)	

21.07aFE	Hidden. Obscure.
21.07aSK	hidden — obscure —
21.07aSC	幽呵冥呵
21.07aTK	(tranquil > hidden > young) (— > —) (obscure > express) (— > —)
21.07aTC	(窈幽幼)(兮呵)(冥鸣)(兮呵)
21.07aWB	(窈＿＿＿)(兮＿＿)(冥＿＿)(兮＿＿)
21.07aHG	(窈＿＿＿)(兮＿＿)(冥＿＿)(兮＿＿)
21.07aFY	(＿幽＿＿)(兮＿＿)(冥＿＿)(兮＿＿)
65.07aMA	(＿幽＿＿)(＿呵)(＿鸣)(＿呵)
65.07aMB	(＿＿＿幼)(＿呵)(冥＿＿)(＿呵)
00.000G-	(＿＿＿＿＿)(＿＿＿)(＿＿＿)(＿＿＿)
00.000G-	(＿＿＿＿＿)(＿＿＿)(＿＿＿)(＿＿＿)

21.07bFE	Its centre has energy.
21.07bSK	its centre (there is) energy —
21.07bSC	其中有精呵
21.07bTK	its centre (there is) (energy > invite) (— > — > —)
21.07bTC	(其中有(精请)(呵吔■)
21.07bWB	(其中有(精＿＿)(＿＿＿＿＿＿)
21.07bHG	(其中有(精＿＿)(＿＿＿＿＿＿)
21.07bFY	(其中有(精＿＿)(＿＿＿＿＿＿)
65.07bMA	(＿中有(＿请)(＿吔■)
65.07bMB	(其中有(＿请)(呵＿＿＿＿)
00.000G-	(＿＿＿＿＿＿ (＿＿＿)(＿＿＿＿)
00.000G-	(＿＿＿＿＿＿ (＿＿＿)(＿＿＿＿)

21. 080FE	Its energy is very real.
21. 080SK	its energy very real
21. 080SC	其精什真
21. 080TK	its (energy > invite) (very) real
21. 080TC	其(精请)(什[__])真
21. 080WB	其(精__)(什[甚])真
21. 080HG	其(精__)(什[甚])真
21. 080FY	其(精__)(什[甚])真
65. 080MA	其(__请)(什[甚])真
65. 080MB	其(__请)(什[甚])真
00. 000G–	__ (__ __) (__ [__]) __
00. 000G–	__ (__ __) (__ [__]) __

21. 090FE	Inside it, there is information.
21. 090SK	it inside (there is) truth
21. 090SC	其中有信
21. 090TK	it inside (there is) truth
21. 090TC	其中有信
21. 090WB	其中有信
21. 090HG	其中有信
21. 090FY	其中有信
65. 090MA	其中□□
65. 090MB	其中有信
00. 000G–	-- -- -- --
00. 000G–	-- -- -- --

21.100FE   From past to present times, its name was never
            erased.
21.100SK   from (ancient times) since present its name
            not remove
21.100SC   自古及今其名不去
21.100TK   from ((ancient times); since; present) >
            (present; since; ancient times)) its name not
            remove
21.100TC   自(古及今)(今及古)其名不去
21.100WB   自(古及今)(______)其名不去
21.100HG   自(古及今)(______)其名不去
21.100FY   自(______)(今及古)其名不去
65.100MA   自(______)(今及古)其名不去
65.100MB   自(______)(今及古)其名不去
00.000G-   ___(______)(______)___ ___ ___
00.000G-   ___(______)(______)___ ___ ___

21.110FE   Therefore, align with the *Father of the
            Multitude.*[98]
21.110SK   according align multitude father
21.110SC   以顺众父
21.110TK   according (inspect > align) multitude (father
            > father) —
21.110TC   以(阅顺)众(甫父)■
21.110WB   以(阅___)众(甫___)___
21.110HG   以(阅___)众(甫___)___
21.110FY   以(阅___)众(甫___)___
65.110MA   以(___顺)众(___父)■
65.110MB   以(___顺)众(___父)___
00.000G-   ___(______)___(______)___
00.000G-   ___(______)___(______)___

21.120FE   How do I know that the *Father of the Multitude* is like this?[99]

21.120SK   I how consider know multitude father ('s) (like that) —

21.120SC   吾何以知众父之然也

21.120TK   I (how > how) consider know multitude (father > father)('s) ((like that) > (state of affairs)) (— > —)

21.120TC   吾(何奚)以知众(甫父)之(然状)(哉也)

21.120WB   吾(何＿)以知众(甫＿)之(＿状)(哉＿)

21.120HG   吾(何＿)以知众(甫＿)之(然＿)(哉＿)

21.120FY   吾(＿奚)以知众(甫＿)之(然＿)(哉＿)

65.120MA   吾(何＿)以知众(＿父)之(然＿)(＿＿)

65.120MB   吾(何＿)以知众(＿父)之(然＿)(＿也)

00.000G-   ＿(＿＿)＿＿＿(＿＿)＿(＿＿)(＿＿)

00.000G-   ＿(＿＿)＿＿＿(＿＿)＿(＿＿)(＿＿)

21.130FE   From this account.

21.130SK   (on this account)

21.130SC   (以此)

21.130TK   (on this account) —

21.130TC   (以此)■

21.130WB   (以此)＿

21.130HG   (以此)＿

21.130FY   (以此)＿

65.130MA   (以此)■

65.130MB   (以此)＿

00.000G-   (＿＿)＿

00.000G-   (＿＿)＿

Chapter 22

22. 010FE	Bend then be preserved.
22. 010SK	bend then preserve
22. 010SC	曲则全
22. 010TK	bend then (preserve > gold)
22. 010TC	曲则(全金)
22. 010WB	曲则(全___)
22. 010HG	曲则(全___)
22. 010FY	曲则(全___)
67. 010MA	曲则(___金)
67. 010MB	曲则(全___)
00. 000G-	___ ___ (___ ___)
00. 000G-	___ ___ (___ ___)

22. 020FE	Twist then be straightened.
22. 020SK	twist then straight
22. 020SC	枉则正
22. 020TK	twist then (straight > straight > order) —
22. 020TC	枉则(直正定) ∎
22. 020WB	枉则(直___ ___) ___
22. 020HG	枉则(直___ ___) ___
22. 020FY	枉则(___正___) ___
67. 020MA	枉则(___ ___定) ∎
67. 020MB	枉则(___正___) ___
00. 000G-	___ ___ (___ ___ ___) ___
00. 000G-	___ ___ (___ ___ ___) ___

22.030FE	Empty then be filled.	
22.030SK	hollow then fill	
22.030SC	洼则盈	
22.030TK	hollow then fill	
22.030TC	洼则盈	
22.030WB	洼则盈	
22.030HG	洼则盈	
22.030FY	洼则盈	
67.030MA	洼则盈	
67.030MB	洼则盈	
00.000G-	--- --- ---	
00.000G-	--- --- ---	

22.040FE	Exhaust then be renewed.	
22.040SK	exhaust then new	
22.040SC	敝则新	
22.040TK	(harm > exhaust) then new 一	
22.040TC	(弊敝) 则新 ■	
22.040WB	(___敝) 则新 ___	
22.040HG	(弊___) 则新 ___	
22.040FY	(___敝) 则新 ___	
67.040MA	(___敝) 则新 ■	
67.040MB	(___敝) 则新 ___	
00.000G-	(___ ___) --- --- ---	
00.000G-	(___ ___) --- --- ---	

22.050FE   Lack then receive.
22.050SK   lack then receive
22.050SC   少则得
22.050TK   lack then receive 一
22.050TC   少则得■
22.050WB   少则得...
22.050HG   少则得...
22.050FY   少则得...
67.050MA   少则得■
67.050MB   少则得...
00.000G-   --- --- --- ---
00.000G-   --- --- --- ---

22.060FE   Have surplus then be confused.
22.060SK   much then confuse
22.060SC   多则惑
22.060TK   much then confuse
22.060TC   多则惑
22.060WB   多则惑
22.060HG   多则惑
22.060FY   多则惑
67.060MA   多则惑
67.060MB   多则惑
00.000G-   --- --- ---
00.000G-   --- --- ---

22.07aFE	Therefore, sages hold on to the *One*.[100]
22.07aSK	therefore sage hold one
22.07aSC	(是以)(圣人)执一
22.07aTK	(therefore)((sage) > (reputable person))(hold > hold > hold) one
22.07aTC	(是以)((圣人)(声人))(抱裹执)一
22.07aWB	(是以)((圣人)(___))(抱___)一
22.07aHG	(是以)((圣人)(___))(抱___)一
22.07aFY	(___)((圣人)(___))(__裹__)一
67.07aMA	(是以)((___)(声人))(___执)一
67.07aMB	(是以)((圣人)(___))(___执)一
00.000G-	(___)((___)(___))(___)__
00.000G-	(___)((___)(___))(___)__

22.07bFE	Accordingly, they are the shepherds of the world.[101]
22.07bSK	according are world shepherd
22.07bSC	以为(天下)牧
22.07bTK	((are > (according; are))(world)((example > shepherd))
22.07bTC	((为(以为))(天下)式牧
22.07bWB	((为(___))(天下)式__
22.07bHG	((为(___))(天下)式__
22.07bFY	((__(以为))(天下)式__
67.07bMA	((__(以为))(天下)__牧
67.07bMB	((__(以为))(天下)__牧
00.000G-	((__(___))(___)__ __
00.000G-	((__(___))(___)__ __

22.080FE	They do not display themselves. Therefore, they are brilliant.
22.080SK	not themselves display — therefore brilliant
22.080SC	不自见也故明
22.080TK	not themselves (display > watch) — therefore brilliant
22.080TC	不自（见视）也故明
22.080WB	不自（见＿）＿故明
22.080HG	不自（见＿）＿故明
22.080FY	不自（见＿）＿故明
67.080MA	不□（＿视）＿故明
67.090MB	不自（见＿）也故明
00.000G–	＿＿（＿＿）＿＿＿
00.000G–	＿＿（＿＿）＿＿＿

22.090FE	They do not regard themselves. Therefore, they are honoured.
22.090SK	not themselves regard therefore honoured
22.090SC	不自视故章
22.090TK	not themselves (correct > display > regard) therefore (praise > honoured)
22.090TC	不自（是见视）故（彰章）
22.090WB	不自（是＿＿）故（彰＿）
22.090HG	不自（是＿＿）故（彰＿）
22.090FY	不自（是＿＿）故（彰＿）
67.090MA	不自（＿见＿）故（＿章）
67.080MB	不自（＿＿视）故（＿章）
00.000G–	＿＿（＿＿＿）＿（＿＿）
00.000G–	＿＿（＿＿＿）＿（＿＿）

22.100FE	They do not boast about themselves. Therefore, they have merit.
22.100SK	not themselves boast therefore have merit
22.100SC	不自伐故有功
22.100TK	not themselves boast therefore have merit —
22.100TC	不自伐故有功■
22.100WB	不自伐故有功...
22.100HG	不自伐故有功...
22.100FY	不自伐故有功...
67.100MA	不自伐故有功■
67.100MB	不自伐故有功...
00.000G-	--- --- --- --- --- ---
00.000G-	--- --- --- --- --- ---

22.110FE	They are not arrogant. Therefore, they will develop.
22.110SK	not arrogant therefore can develop
22.110SC	弗矜故能长
22.110TK	(not > not) themselves arrogant therefore can develop —
22.110TC	(不弗)自矜故能长■
22.110WB	(不...)自矜故...长...
22.110HG	(不...)自矜故...长...
22.110FY	(不...)自矜故...长...
67.110MA	(...弗)...矜故能长■
67.110MB	(...弗)...矜故能长...
00.000G-	(... ...) --- --- --- --- ---
00.000G-	(... ...) --- --- --- --- ---

22.120FE	They do not strive. Therefore, no one can strive with them.
22.120SK	those only not compete therefore world cannot able with their compete
22.120SC	夫唯不争故(天下)莫能与之争
22.120TK	those (only > only) not compete therefore (world) cannot able with their compete
22.120TC	夫(惟唯)不争故(天下)莫能与之争
22.120WB	夫(＿唯)不争故(天下)莫能与之争
22.120HG	夫(惟＿)不争故(天下)莫能与之争
22.120FY	夫(惟＿)不争故(天下)莫能与之争
67.120MA	夫(＿唯)不争故(＿＿)莫能与之争
67.120MB	夫(＿唯)不争故(＿＿)莫能与之争
00.000G-	＿(＿＿)＿＿＿(＿＿)＿＿＿＿
00.000G-	＿(＿＿)＿＿＿(＿＿)＿＿＿＿

22.130FE	The ones called the 'Ancients' said: "Those who bend will be preserved."
22.130SK	ancient ('s) (so called) bend will preserve those
22.130SC	古之(所谓)曲则全者
22.130TK	ancient ('s) (so called) bend will preserve those
22.130TC	古之(所谓)曲则全者
22.130WB	古之(所谓)曲则全者
22.130HG	古之(所谓)曲则全者
22.130FY	古之(所谓)曲则全者
67.130MA	古□(□□)□＿□□
67.130MB	古之(所谓)曲＿全者
00.000G-	＿＿(＿＿)＿＿＿＿
00.000G-	＿＿(＿＿)＿＿＿＿

22.140FE	Is that saying insignificant?	
22.140SK	insignificant saying 一	
22.140SC	几语也	
22.140TK	how (empty > insignificant) (saying > saying) (一 > 一)	
22.140TC	岂（虚几）（言语）（也哉）	
22.140WB	岂（虚＿）（言＿）（＿哉）	
22.140HG	岂（虚＿）（言＿）（＿哉）	
22.140FY	岂（虚＿）（言＿）（也哉）	
67.140MA	＿（＿□）（＿语）（＿＿）	
67.140MB	＿（＿几）（＿语）（＿＿）	
00.000G-	＿（＿＿）（＿＿）（＿＿）	
00.000G-	＿（＿＿）（＿＿）（＿＿）	

22.150FE	However, true preservation was their return.	
22.150SK	only true preserve return their	
22.150SC	才诚全归之	
22.150TK	(only > therefore) true preserve and return their	
22.150TC	（才故）诚全而归之	
22.150WB	（＿＿）诚全而归之	
22.150HG	（＿故）诚全而归之	
22.150FY	（＿＿）诚全而归之	
67.150MA	（才＿）诚全＿归之	
67.150MB	（才＿）诚全＿归之	
00.000G-	（＿＿）＿＿＿＿＿	
00.000G-	（＿＿）＿＿＿＿＿	

Chapter 23

23.010FE	Speaking seldom is natural.
23.010SK	seldom speak nature
23.010SC	希言（自然）
23.010TK	(seldom > seldom) speak (nature)
23.010TC	（希稀）言（自然）
23.010WB	（希___）言（自然）
23.010HG	（希___）言（自然）
23.010FY	（___稀）言（自然）
68.010MA	（希___）言（自然）
68.010MB	（希___）言（自然）
00.000G-	（______）___（______）
00.000G-	（______）___（______）

23.020FE	Strong storms do not drum all morning.
23.020SK	strong storm not drumming morning
23.020SC	飘风不冬朝
23.020TK	therefore ((strong)) storm not (all > high > drumming) morning
23.020TC	故（（飘[___]））风不（终崇冬）朝
23.020WB	故（（飘[___]））风不（终______）朝
23.020HG	___（（飘[___]））风不（终______）朝
23.020FY	故（（飘[飘]））风不（___崇___）朝
68.020MA	___（（飘[___]））风不（______冬）朝
68.020MB	___（（飘[___]））风不（______冬）朝
00.000G-	___（（___[___]））______（________）___
00.000G-	___（（___[___]））______（________）___

23. 030FE	Violent rains do not drum all day.
23. 030SK	violent rain not drumming day
23. 030SC	暴雨不冬日
23. 030TK	(sudden > violent) rain not (all > high > drumming) day
23. 030TC	(骤暴) 雨不 (终崇冬) 日
23. 030WB	(骤＿) 雨不 (终＿＿) 日
23. 030HG	(骤＿) 雨不 (终＿＿) 日
23. 030FY	(骤＿) 雨不 (＿崇＿) 日
68. 030MA	(＿暴) 雨不 (＿＿冬) 日
68. 030MB	(＿暴) 雨不 (＿＿冬) 日
00. 000G–	(＿＿) ＿＿ (＿＿＿) ＿
00. 000G–	(＿＿) ＿＿ (＿＿＿) ＿

23. 040FE	Who serves them?　The *Sky* and the *Earth*.[102]
23. 040SK	who (serve as) those *Sky Earth*
23. 040SC	孰为此天地
23. 040TK	who (serve as) those thing — *Sky Earth* —
23. 040TC	孰为此者天地也
23. 040WB	孰为此者天地＿
23. 040HG	孰为此者天地＿
23. 040FY	孰为此者天地也
68. 040MA	孰为此＿天地＿
68. 040MB	孰为此＿天地＿
00. 000G–	＿＿＿＿＿＿
00. 000G–	＿＿＿＿＿＿

23. 050FE   Yet, they cannot go on forever.

23. 050SK   yet not can forever

23. 050SC   而弗能久

23. 050TK   *Sky Earth* (yet > yet) (not > not) can forever

23. 050TC   天地（尚而）（不弗）能久

23. 050WB   天地（尚＿）（不＿）能久

23. 050HG   天地（尚＿）（不＿）能久

23. 050FY   天地（尚＿）（不＿）能久

68. 050MA   ＿＿（＿□）（＿□）□□

68. 050MB   ＿＿（＿而）（＿弗）能久

00. 000G−   ＿＿（＿＿）（＿＿）＿＿

00. 000G−   ＿＿（＿＿）（＿＿）＿＿

23. 060FE   So how about people?[103]

23. 060SK   have brother people —

23. 060SC   有兄人乎

23. 060TK   (and > have) ((moreover) brother people (— > —)

23. 060TC   （而有）（況［＿＿］）兄人（于乎）

23. 060WB   （而　）（況「　」）　人（于乎）

23. 060HG   （而＿）（況［況］）＿人（于乎）

23. 060FY   （而＿）（況［況］）＿人（于乎）

68. 060MA   （＿□）（＿［＿＿］）□人（于乎）

68. 060MB   （＿有）（＿［＿＿］）兄人（于乎）

00. 000G−   （＿＿）（＿［＿＿］）＿＿（＿＿）

00. 000G−   （＿＿）（＿［＿＿］）＿＿（＿＿）

23. 070FE	Therefore, those who submit their affairs to the *Way* will merge with the *Way*.
23. 070SK	therefore submit affair to *Way* those merge to *Way*
23. 070SC	故从事而道者同于道
23. 070TK	therefore submit affair (to > to) *Way* those *Way* those merge to *Way*
23. 070TC	故从事（于而）道者道者同于道
23. 070WB	故从事（于＿）道者道者同于道
23. 070HG	故从事（于＿）道者道者同于道
23. 070FY	故从事（于＿）道者道者同于道
68. 070MA	故从事（＿而）道者＿＿同于道
68. 070MB	故从事（＿而）道者＿＿同于道
00. 000G-	＿＿＿（＿＿）＿＿＿＿＿＿
00. 000G-	＿＿＿（＿＿）＿＿＿＿＿＿

23. 080FE	Those who submit their affairs to virtue will merge with virtue.
23. 080SK	submit affair to virtue those merge to virtue
23. 080SC	从事于德者同于德
23. 080TK	submit affair to (virtue > obtain) those obtain those merge to (virtue > obtain)
23. 080TC	从事于（德得）者得者同于（德得）
23. 080WB	＿＿＿（德＿）者＿＿同于（德＿）
23. 080HG	＿＿＿（德＿）者＿＿同于（德＿）
23. 080FY	从事于（＿得）者得者同于（＿得）
68. 080MA	＿＿＿（德＿）者＿＿同于（德＿）
68. 080MB	＿＿＿（德＿）者＿＿同于（德＿）
00. 000G-	＿＿＿（＿＿）＿＿＿＿＿（＿＿）
00. 000G-	＿＿＿（＿＿）＿＿＿＿＿（＿＿）

23.090FE   Those who submit their affairs to loss will merge with loss.

23.090SK   submit affair to lose those merge to lose

23.090SC   从事于失者同于失

23.090TK   submit affair to lose those those merge to lose those

23.090TC   从事于失者者同于失者

23.090WB   ﹍﹍﹍失者﹍同于失﹍

23.090HG   ﹍﹍﹍失者﹍同于失﹍

23.090FY   从事于失者﹍﹍﹍失者

68.090MA   ﹍﹍﹍﹍者者同于失﹍

68.090MB   ﹍﹍﹍失者﹍同于失﹍

00.000G-   ﹍﹍﹍﹍﹍﹍﹍﹍

00.000G-   ﹍﹍﹍﹍﹍﹍﹍﹍

23.100FE   Those who merge with virtue will also gain the Way.[104]

23.100SK   merge to virtue those *Way* also favour their

23.100SC   同于德者道亦德之

23.100TK   merge to lose to (*Way* > virtue) those *Way* also — happy (gain > favour) their

23.100TC   同于失于(道德)者道亦也乐(得德)之

23.100WB   同于﹍﹍(道﹍)者道亦﹍乐(得﹍)之

23.100HG   同于﹍﹍(道﹍)者道亦﹍乐(得﹍)之

23.100FY   同于失于(道﹍)者道亦﹍﹍(得﹍)之

68.100MA   同于﹍﹍(﹍德)□道亦﹍﹍(﹍德)之

68.100MB   同于﹍﹍(﹍德)者道亦﹍﹍(﹍德)之

00.000G-   ﹍﹍﹍(﹍﹍)﹍﹍﹍(﹍﹍)﹍

00.000G-   ﹍﹍﹍(﹍﹍)﹍﹍﹍(﹍﹍)﹍

23.110FE	Those who merge with loss will also lose the *Way*.
23.110SK	merge to loss *Way* also lose their
23.110SC	同于失道亦失之
23.110TK	merge to (virtue > obtain > loss) those (virtue > obtain > *Way*) also happy (obtain > lose) their
23.110TC	同于(德得失)者(德得道)亦乐(得失)之
23.110WB	同于(德＿＿)者(德＿＿)亦乐(得＿)之
23.110HG	同于(德＿＿)者(德＿＿)亦乐(得＿)之
23.110FY	＿于(＿得＿)者(＿得＿)亦＿(得＿)之
68.110MA	同于(＿＿□)者(＿＿道)亦＿(＿失)之
68.110MB	同于(＿＿失)者(＿＿道)亦＿(＿失)之
00.000G-	＿＿(＿＿＿)＿(＿＿＿)＿＿(＿＿)＿
00.000G-	＿＿(＿＿＿)＿(＿＿＿)＿＿(＿＿)＿

23.120FE	Those merging with loss will also lose their happiness.[105]
23.120SK	merge to lose those lose also happy obtain their
23.120SC	同于失者失亦乐得之
23.120TK	merge to lose those lose also happy obtain their
23.120TC	同于失者失亦乐得之
23.120WB	同于失者失亦乐得之
23.120HG	同于失者失亦乐得之
23.120FY	＿于失者失亦＿得之
00.000MA	＿＿＿＿＿＿＿＿＿＿
00.000MB	＿＿＿＿＿＿＿＿＿＿
00.000G-	＿＿＿＿＿＿＿＿＿＿
00.000G-	＿＿＿＿＿＿＿＿＿＿

23.130FE	If there is not enough truth then there will be distrust.[106]	
23.130SK	truth not enough then have (no trust) how	
23.130SC	信不足焉有(不信)焉	
23.130TK	truth not enough then have (no trust) how	
23.130TC	信不足焉有(不信)焉	
23.130WB	信不足焉有(不信)焉	
23.130HG	信不足焉有(不信)焉	
23.130FY	信不足焉有(不信)___	
00.000MA	___ ___ ___ ___ ___ (___ ___) ___	
00.000MB	___ ___ ___ ___ ___ (___ ___) ___	
00.000G-	___ ___ ___ ___ ___ (___ ___) ___	
00.000G-	___ ___ ___ ___ ___ (___ ___) ___	

Chapter 24

24. 010FE	Those who stand on tiptoe do not stand firm. [107]
24. 010SK	(stand on tiptoe) those not (stand up)
24. 010SC	跂者不立
24. 010TK	((look forward) > (stand on tiptoe) > cook)) those not (stand up)
24. 010TC	((企跂炊))者不立
24. 010WB	((企＿＿＿))者不立
24. 010HG	((＿跂＿))者不立
24. 010FY	((企＿＿＿))者不立
66. 010MA	((＿＿炊))者不立
66. 010MB	((＿＿炊))者不立
00. 000G-	((＿＿＿)) ＿＿＿
00. 000G-	((＿＿＿)) ＿＿＿

24. 020FE	Those who stride do not move. [108]
24. 020SK	stride those not move
24. 020SC	跨者不行
24. 020TK	stride those not move
24. 020TC	跨者不行
24. 020WB	跨者不行
24. 020HG	跨者不行
24. 020FY	跨者不行
00. 000MA	＿＿＿
00. 000MB	＿＿＿
00. 000G-	＿＿＿
00. 000G-	＿＿＿

24.030FE	Those who display themselves are without brilliance.
24.030SK	themselves display those without brilliant
24.030SC	自见者不明
24.030TK	themselves display those without brilliant 一
24.030TC	自见者不明■
24.030WB	自见者不明__
24.030HG	自见者不明__
24.030FY	自见者不明__
66.030MA	□见者不明■
66.030MB	自见者不明__
00.000G-	--- --- --- --- --- ---
00.000G-	--- --- --- --- --- ---

24.040FE	Those who regard themselves are without honour.
24.040SK	themselves regard those without honour
24.040SC	自是者不章
24.040TK	themselves (justify > regard) those without (praise > honour)
24.040TC	自(是视)者不(彰章)
24.040WB	自(是__)者不(彰__)
24.040HG	自(是__)者不(彰__)
24.040FY	自(是__)者不(彰__)
66.020MA	自(__视)__不(__章)
66.020MB	自(__视)者不(__章)
00.000G-	__(__ __) __ __ (__ __)
00.000G-	__(__ __) __ __ (__ __)

24.050FE	Those who boast about themselves are without merit.
24.050SK	themselves boast those without merit
24.050SC	自伐者无功
24.050TK	themselves boast those without merit
24.050TC	自伐者无功
24.050WB	自伐者无功
24.050HG	自伐者无功
24.050FY	自伐者无功
66.040MA	自伐者无功
66.040MB	自伐者无功
00.000G-	--- --- --- --- ---
00.000G-	--- --- --- --- ---

24.060FE	Those who are arrogant are without development.
24.060SK	themselves boast those not develop
24.060SC	自矜者不长
24.060TK	themselves boast those not develop
24.060TC	自矜者不长
24.060WB	自矜者不长
24.060HG	自矜者不长
24.060FY	自矜者不长
66.050MA	自矜者不长
66.050MB	自矜者不长
00.000G-	--- --- --- --- ---
00.000G-	--- --- --- --- ---

24.07aFE   Their *Way* is called:
24.07aSK   that is *Way* — call
24.07aSC   其在道也曰
24.07aTK   that (from > is) *Way* — call
24.07aTC   其(于在)道也曰
24.07aWB   其(＿在)道也曰
24.07aHG   其(于＿)道也曰
24.07aFY   其(＿在)道也曰
66.06aMA   其(＿在)道＿曰
66.06aMB   其(＿在)道也曰
00.000G-   ＿(＿＿)＿＿＿
00.000G-   ＿(＿＿)＿＿＿

24.07bFE   "Leftover food and unnecessary action."
24.07bSK   leftover food unnecessary act
24.07bSC   余食贅行
24.07bTK   (leftover > 粮) food unnecessary act —
24.07bTC   (余粮)食贅行■
24.07bWB   (余＿)食贅行＿
24.07bHG   (余＿)食贅行＿
24.07bFY   (余＿)食贅行＿
66.06bMA   (＿粮)食贅行■
66.06bMB   (＿粮)食贅行＿
00.000G-   (＿＿)＿＿＿＿
00.000G-   (＿＿)＿＿＿＿

24. 080FE	These things are disgusting. [109]
24. 080SK	thing (may be) disgust ('s)
24. 080SC	物或恶之
24. 080TK	thing (may be) (disgust > inferior) ('s)
24. 080TC	物或(恶亚)之
24. 080WB	物或(恶＿＿)之
24. 080HG	物或(恶＿＿)之
24. 080FY	物或(恶＿＿)之
66. 070MA	物或(恶＿＿)之
66. 070MB	物或(＿＿亚)之
00. 000G-	＿＿＿＿(＿＿＿＿)＿＿
00. 000G-	＿＿＿＿(＿＿＿＿)＿＿

24. 090FE	Therefore, those who have desires will not succeed. [110]
24. 090SK	therefore have desire those not profit 一
24. 090SC	故有欲者弗处也
24. 090TK	therefore have (*Way* > desire) those (not > not) ((profit) > store up) (一 > 一)
24. 090TC	故有(道欲)者(不弗)(处居)(也■)
24. 090WB	故有(道＿＿)者(不＿＿)(处＿＿)(＿＿＿＿)
24. 090HG	故有(道＿＿)者(不＿＿)(处＿＿)(＿＿＿＿)
24. 090FY	故有(道＿＿)者(不＿＿)(处＿＿)(也＿＿)
66. 080MA	故有(＿＿欲)者(＿＿□)(＿＿居)(＿＿■)
66. 080MB	故有(＿＿欲)者(＿＿弗)(＿＿居)(＿＿＿＿)
00. 000G-	＿＿＿＿(＿＿＿＿)＿＿(＿＿＿＿)(＿＿＿＿)(＿＿＿＿)
00. 000G-	＿＿＿＿(＿＿＿＿)＿＿(＿＿＿＿)(＿＿＿＿)(＿＿＿＿)

Chapter 25

25.010FE	There was a thing *Undivided* and complete before the *Sky* and the *Earth* were born.[111]
25.010SK	(there was) thing undivided complete before *Sky Earth* born
25.010SC	有物昆成先天地生
25.010TK	(there was) (thing > shape) (merge > undivided) complete before *Sky Earth* born
25.010TC	有(物状)(混昆)成先天地生
25.010WB	有(物＿＿)(混＿＿)成先天地生
25.010HG	有(物＿＿)(混＿＿)成先天地生
25.010FY	有(物＿＿)(混＿＿)成先天地生
69.010MA	有(物＿＿)(＿＿昆)成先天地生
69.010MB	有(物＿＿)(＿＿昆)成先天地生
11.010GA	有(＿＿状)(混＿＿)成先天地生
00.000G-	＿＿(＿＿＿＿)(＿＿＿＿) ＿＿ ＿＿ ＿＿ ＿＿ ＿＿

25.020FE	Desolate. Empty.
25.020SK	desolate — empty —
25.020SC	萧呵参呵
25.020TK	(desolate > desolate) (— > —) ((empty > lonely > (distinct) > confuse)) (— > —)
25.020TC	(寂萧)(兮呵)((寥寞(缪[＿＿])谬))(兮呵)
25.020WB	(寂＿＿)(兮＿＿)((寥＿＿(＿＿[＿＿])＿＿))(兮＿＿)
25.020HG	(寂＿＿)(兮＿＿)((寥＿＿(＿＿[＿＿])＿＿))(兮＿＿)
25.020FY	(寂＿＿)(兮＿＿)((＿＿寞(＿＿[＿＿])＿＿))(兮＿＿)
69.020MA	(＿＿萧)(＿＿呵)((＿＿＿＿(缪[繆])＿＿))(＿＿呵)
69.020MB	(＿＿萧)(＿＿呵)((＿＿＿＿(＿＿[＿＿])谬))(＿＿呵)
00.000G-	(＿＿＿＿)(＿＿＿＿)((＿＿＿＿(＿＿[＿＿])＿＿))(＿＿＿＿)
00.000G-	(＿＿＿＿)(＿＿＿＿)((＿＿＿＿(＿＿[＿＿])＿＿))(＿＿＿＿)

25. 03aFE	Independent and unchanging.
25. 03aSK	independent and not change
25. 03aSC	（独立）而不改
25. 03aTK	(solitary)(independent) and not change
25. 03aTC	（寂寥）（独立）而不改
25. 03aWB	（＿＿）（独立）＿不改
25. 03aHG	（＿＿）（独立）而不改
25. 03aFY	（＿＿）（独立）而不改
69. 03aMA	（＿＿）（独立）□□□
69. 03aMB	（＿＿）（独立）而不改
11. 02aGA	（寂寥）（独立）＿不改
00. 000G-	（＿＿）（＿＿）＿＿＿

25. 03bFE	Acting thoroughly without danger.[112]
25. 03bSK	thorough act and not danger
25. 03bSC	周行而不殆
25. 03bTK	thorough act and not danger
25. 03bTC	周行而不殆
25. 03bWB	周行而不殆
25. 03bHG	周行而不殆
25. 03bFY	周行而不殆
00. 00bMA	＿＿＿＿＿
00. 00bMB	＿＿＿＿＿
00. 000G-	＿＿＿＿＿
00. 000G-	＿＿＿＿＿

25.03cFE   Yet, it acts as the origin of the world.[113]
25.03cSK   yet act as world origin
25.03cSC   可以为(天地)母
25.03cTK   yet act as ((world) > (world)) origin
25.03cTC   可以为((天下)(天地))母
25.03cWB   可以为((天下)(___))母
25.03cHG   可以为((天下)(___))母
25.03cFY   可以为((天下)(___))母
69.03cMA   可以为((___)(天地))母
69.03cMB   可以为((___)(天地))母
11.02cGA   可以为((天下)(___))母
00.000G-   ___((___)(___))___

25.040FE   I do not know how its name is pronounced,[114]
            but I call it the *Way*.
25.040SK   I not know its name pronounce its call *Way*
25.040SC   吾未知其名字之曰道
25.040TK   I (not > not) know its name — therefore
            difficult pronounce its call *Way*
25.040TC   吾(不未)知其名也故彌字之曰道
25.040WB   吾(不___)知其名___字之曰道
25.040HG   吾(不___)知其名___字之曰道
25.040FY   吾(不___)知其名___故彌字之曰道
69.040MA   吾(___未)知其名___字之曰道
69.040MB   吾(___未)知其名也___字之曰道
11.030GA   ___(___未)知其名___字之曰道
00.000G-   ___(___)___ ___ ___ ___ ___ ___

25. 050FE	If I were forced to describe it, then I would call it great.
25. 050SK	I force were its name call great
25. 050SC	吾强为之名曰大
25. 050TK	I (force > force) were ((name; its) > (its; name)) call great
25. 050TC	吾(强彊)为((名之)(之名)曰大
25. 050WB	＿(强＿)为((＿＿)(之名)曰大
25. 050HG	＿(强＿)＿((名之)(＿＿)曰大
25. 050FY	＿(＿彊)为((＿＿)(之名)曰大
69. 050MA	吾(强＿)为((＿＿)(之名)曰大
69. 050MB	吾(强＿)为((＿＿)(之名)曰大
11. 040GA	吾(强＿)为((＿＿)(之名)曰大
00. 000G-	＿(＿＿)＿((＿＿)(＿＿)＿＿

25. 06aFE	Great means continuous.
25. 06aSK	great means (passing time)
25. 06aSC	大曰逝
25. 06aTK	great means ((passing time) > divining > defeat)
25. 06aTC	大曰(逝筮溃)
25. 06aWB	大曰(逝＿＿)
25. 06aHG	大曰(逝＿＿)
25. 06aFY	大曰(逝＿＿)
69. 06aMA	□曰(＿筮＿)
69. 06aMB	大曰(＿筮＿)
11. 05aGA	大曰(＿＿溃)
00. 000G-	＿＿(＿＿)

25.06bFE   Continuous means forever.
25.06bSK   (passing of time) means forever
25.06bSC   逝曰远
25.06bTK   ((passing of time) > divining > defeat) means forever
25.06bTC   (逝筮溃)曰远
25.06bWB   (逝＿＿)曰远
25.06bHG   (逝＿＿)曰远
25.06bFY   (逝＿＿)曰远
69.06bMA   (＿筮＿)曰远
69.06bMB   (＿筮＿)曰远
11.05bGA   (＿＿溃)曰远
00.000G-   (＿＿＿)＿＿

25.06cFE   Forever means returning.
25.06cSK   forever means return
25.06cSC   远曰反
25.06cTK   forever means (return > return)
25.06cTC   远曰(反返)
25.06cWB   远曰(反＿)
25.06cHG   远曰(反＿)
25.06cFY   远曰(＿返)
69.06cMA   □□(□＿)
69.06cMB   远曰(反＿)
11.05cGA   远曰(反＿)
00.000G-   ＿＿(＿＿)

25. 07aFE   Therefore, the *Way* is great;
25. 07aSK   therefore *Way* great
25. 07aSC   故道大
25. 07aTK   therefore *Way* great
25. 07aTC   故道大
25. 07aWB   故道大
25. 07aHG   故道大
25. 07aFY   ___道大
69. 07aMA   □□□
69. 07aMB   ___道大
11. 06cGA   ___道大
00. 000G-   --- --- ---

25. 07bFE   the *Sky* is great;[115]
25. 07bSK   *Sky* great
25. 07bSC   天大
25. 07bTK   *Sky* great
25. 07bTC   天大
25. 07bWB   天大
25. 07bHG   天大
25. 07bFY   天大
69. 07bMA   天大
69. 07bMB   天大
11. 06aGA   天大
00. 000G-   --- ---

    25. 07cFE   the *Earth* is great;
    25. 07cSK   *Earth* great
    25. 07cSC   地大
    25. 07cTK   *Earth* great
    25. 07cTC   地大
    25. 07cWB   地大
    25. 07cHG   地大
    25. 07cFY   地大
    69. 07cMA   地大
    69. 06bMB   地大
    11. 06bGA   地大
    00. 000G-   ‒‒ ‒‒

    25. 07dFE   and the King is also great.
    25. 07dSK   King also great
    25. 07dSC   王亦大
    25. 07dTK   (King > people) also great
    25. 07dTC   王人亦大
    25. 07dWB   王＿＿亦大
    25. 07dHG   王　亦大
    25. 07dFY   ＿＿人亦大
    69. 07dMA   王＿＿亦大
    69. 07dMB   王＿＿亦大
    11. 06dGA   王＿＿亦大
    00. 000G-   ‒‒ ‒‒ ‒‒

25.080FE	Inside the universe there are four *Greatnesses* and the King is one.[116]
25.080SK	(dominant country) inside (there are) four great and King claim one
25.080SC	国中有四大而王居一
25.080TK	((realm > (dominant country)) inside (there are) four great (and > then) King (claim > occupy) his one
25.080TC	((域国))中有四大(而焉)王(居处)其一
25.080WB	((域＿＿))中有四大(而＿＿)王(居＿＿)其一
25.080HG	((域＿＿))中有四大(＿＿＿＿)王(居＿＿)其一
25.080FY	((域＿＿))中有四大(而＿＿)王(＿＿处)其一
69.080MA	((＿＿国))中有四大(而＿＿)王(居＿＿)＿＿一
69.080MB	((＿＿国))中有四大(而＿＿)王(居＿＿)＿＿一
11.070GA	((＿＿国))中有四大(＿＿焉)王(居＿＿)＿＿一
00.000G-	((＿＿＿＿))＿＿＿＿＿＿(＿＿＿＿)＿＿(＿＿＿＿)＿＿＿＿

25.090FE	Therefore, people follow the *Earth*;
25.090SK	therefore people follow *Earth*
25.090SC	焉人法地
25.090TK	(therefore > respect) people follow *Earth*
25.090TC	(焉尊)人法地
25.090WB	(焉＿＿)人法地
25.090HG	(焉＿＿)人法地
25.090FY	(＿＿尊)人法地
69.090MA	(焉＿＿)人法地
69.090MB	(焉＿＿)人法地
11.080GA	(焉＿＿)人法地
00.000G-	(＿＿＿＿)＿＿＿＿＿＿

25.10aFE	the *Earth* follows the *Sky*;[117]
25.10aSK	*Earth* follow *Sky*
25.10aSC	地法天
25.10aTK	*Earth* follow *Sky*
25.10aTC	地法天
25.10aWB	地法天
25.10aHG	地法天
25.10aFY	地法天
69.10aMA	□法□
69.10aMB	地法天
11.09aGA	地法天
00.000G-	--- --- ---

25.10bFE	the *Sky* follows the *Way*;[118]
25.10bSK	*Sky* follow *Way*
25.10bSC	天法道
25.10bTK	*Sky* follow *Way*
25.10bTC	天法道
25.10bWB	天法道
25.10bHG	天法道
25.10bFY	天法道
69.10bMA	天法□
69.10bMB	天法道
11.09bGA	天法道
00.000G-	--- --- ---

25.10cFE   and the *Way* follows nature.
25.10cSK   *Way* follow nature
25.10cSC   道法（自然）
25.10cTK   *Way* follow nature —
25.10cTC   道法（自然）■
25.10cWB   道法（自然）＿＿
25.10cHG   道法（自然）＿＿
25.10cFY   道法（自然）＿＿
69.10cMA   □法（□□）＿＿
69.10cMB   道法（自然）＿＿
11.09cGA   道法（自然）■
00.000G-   ＿＿＿（＿＿＿）＿＿

Chapter 26

26.010FE	Heaviness is the foundation of lightness.
26.010SK	heavy is light foundation
26.010SC	重为轻根
26.010TK	heavy is (light > fluid)(foundation > foundation)
26.010TC	重为(轻䡉)(根据)
26.010WB	重为(轻___)(根___)
26.010HG	重为(轻___)(根___)
26.010FY	重为(轻___)(根___)
70.010MA	□为(___䡉)(___据)
70.010MB	重为(轻___)(根___)
00.000G-	___ ___ (___ ___)(___ ___)
00.000G-	___ ___ (___ ___)(___ ___)

26.020FE	Tranquillity is the sovereign of rashness.
26.020SK	tranquil is rash sovereign
26.020SC	静为趮君
26.020TK	((tranquil) > tranquil > pure)) is (rash > rash) sovereign
26.020TC	((静[___])靖清))为(躁趮)君
26.020WB	((静[___])___ ___))为(躁___)君
26.020HG	((静[靜])___ ___))为(躁___)君
26.020FY	((___[___])靖___))为(躁___)君
70.020MA	((___[___])___清))为(___趮)君
70.020MB	((静[___])___ ___))为(___趮)君
00.000G-	((___[___])___ ___)) ___ (___ ___) ___
00.000G-	((___[___])___ ___)) ___ (___ ___) ___

26. 03aFE Therefore, great men who travel all day
26. 03aSK (therefore) (great man) all day travel
26. 03aSC (是以)(君子)终日行
26. 03aTK (therefore) ((sage) > (great man)) (all > numerous) day travel
26. 03aTC (是以)((圣人)(君子))(终众)日行
26. 03aWB (是以)((圣人)(＿＿))(终＿)日行
26. 03aHG (是以)((圣人)(＿＿))(终＿)日行
26. 03aFY (是以)((＿＿)(君子))(终＿)日行
70. 03aMA (是以)((＿＿)(君子))(＿众)日行
70. 03aMB (是以)((＿＿)(君子))(终＿)日行
00. 000G- (＿＿)((＿＿)(＿＿))(＿＿)＿＿
00. 000G- (＿＿)((＿＿)(＿＿))(＿＿)＿＿

26. 03bFE will not leave their heavy wagons.
26. 03bSK not leave their wagon heavy
26. 03bSC 不离其辎重
26. 03bTK not (leave > distance) their (wagon > jar) heavy
26. 03bTC 不(离远)其(辎甾)重
26. 03bWB 不(离＿)＿(辎＿)重
26. 03bHG 不(离＿)＿(辎＿)重
26. 03bFY 不(离＿)其(辎＿)重
70. 03bMA 不(离＿)其(＿甾)重
70. 03bMB 不(＿远)其(＿甾)重
00. 000G- ＿(＿＿)＿(＿＿)＿
00. 000G- ＿(＿＿)＿(＿＿)＿

26. 04aFE	Although, there is a walled guest house
26. 04aSK	although (there is) encircle (guest house)
26. 04aSC	虽有环馆
26. 04aTK	(although > only) (there is) ((glory; watchtower) > (encircle; guest house) > (encircle; military official))
26. 04aTC	(虽唯)有((荣观)(环馆)(环官))
26. 04aWB	(虽__)有((荣观)(____)(____))
26. 04aHG	(虽__)有((荣观)(____)(____))
26. 04aFY	(虽__)有((荣观)(____)(____))
70. 04aMX	(虽__)有((____)(环馆)(____))
70. 04aMA	(__唯)有((____)(____)(环官))
70. 04aMB	(虽__)有((____)(____)(环官))
00. 000G-	(____)__((____)(____)(____))
00. 000G-	(____)__((____)(____)(____))

26. 04bFE	in a quiet place nearby,
26. 04bSK	quiet place nearby
26. 04bSC	燕处则
26. 04bTK	(quiet > relax > quiet) place nearby
26. 04bTC	(燕宴燕)处则
26. 04bWB	(____燕)处__
26. 04bHG	(燕____)处__
26. 04bFY	(__宴__)处__
70. 04bMA	(____燕)处□
70. 04bMB	(____燕)处则
00. 000G-	(____)____
00. 000G-	(____)____

26.04cFE	they remain aloof.
26.04cSK	(aloof)
26.04cSC	超然
26.04cTK	((aloof) > (distinct; just like))
26.04cTC	((超然)(昭若))
26.04cWB	((超然)(__ __))
26.04cHG	((超然)(__ __))
26.04cFY	((超然)(__ __))
70.04cMA	((__ __)(□若))
70.04cMB	((__ __)(昭若))
00.000G-	((__ __)(__ __))
00.000G-	((__ __)(__ __))

26.05aFE	Just like a lord with ten thousand chariots
26.05aSK	(just like) how (ten thousand) chariot ('s) lord
26.05aSC	若何万乘之主
26.05aTK	((deal with) > (just like) > (just like)) its how (ten thousand) chariot ('s) lord
26.05aTC	(奈如若)之何万乘之主
26.05aWB	(奈__ __)__何万乘之主
26.05aHG	(奈__ __)__何万乘之主
26.05aFY	(__如__)之何万乘之主
70.05aMA	(__ __若)__何万乘之主
70.05aMB	(__ __若)__何万乘之主
00.000G-	(__ __ __)__ __ __ __ __ __
00.000G-	(__ __ __)__ __ __ __ __ __

26. 05bFE   who considers himself less important than the State.[119]

26. 05bSK   yet consider himself unimportant than state

26. 05bSC   而以身轻于(天下)

26. 05bTK   yet consider himself (unimportant > fluid) than (state)

26. 05bTC   而以身(轻巠)于(天下)

26. 05bWB   而以身(轻___)___(天下)

26. 05bHG   而以身(轻___)___(天下)

26. 05bFY   而以身(轻___)___(天下)

70. 05bMA   而以身(___巠)于(天下)

70. 05bMB   而以身(轻___)于(天下)

00. 000G-   ___ ___ ___ (___ ___) ___ (___ ___)

00. 000G-   ___ ___ ___ (___ ___) ___ (___ ___)

26. 060FE   Lightness will lose the foundation.

26. 060SK   light will lose foundation

26. 060SC   轻则失本

26. 060TK   low (light > fluid) will lose (officials > foundation)

26. 060TC   下(轻巠)则失(臣本)

26. 060WB   ___(轻___)则失(___本)

26. 060HG   下(轻___)则失(臣___)

26. 060FY   ___(轻___)则失(___本)

70. 060MA   ___(___巠)则失(___本)

70. 060MB   ___(轻___)则失(___本)

00. 000G-   ___ (___ ___) ___ ___ (___ ___)

00. 000G-   ___ (___ ___) ___ ___ (___ ___)

26. 070FE	Rashness will lose the sovereign.
26. 070SK	rash will lose sovereign
26. 070SC	趮則失君
26. 070TK	(rash > rash) will lose sovereign
26. 070TC	(躁趮)則失君
26. 070WB	(躁___)則失君
26. 070HG	(躁___)則失君
26. 070FY	(躁___)則失君
70. 070MA	(___趮)則失君
70. 070MB	(___趮)則失君
00. 000G–	(______) _________
00. 000G–	(______) _________

Chapter 27

27.010FE	Competent travellers leave no trail.
27.010SK	competent traveller no trail
27.010SC	善(行者)无(辙迹)
27.010TK	competent (traveller) act no ((trail) > (make; footprint))
27.010TC	善(行者)行无((辙迹)(达迹))
27.010WB	善(＿＿)行无((辙迹)(＿＿))
27.010HG	善(行者)＿无((辙迹)(＿＿))
27.010FY	善(行者)＿无((辙迹)(＿＿))
71.010MA	善(行者)＿无((辙迹)(＿＿))
71.010MB	善(行者)＿无((＿＿)(达迹))
00.000G-	＿(＿＿)＿＿((＿＿)(＿＿))
00.000G-	＿(＿＿)＿＿((＿＿)(＿＿))

27.020FE	Competent speakers pursue no flaws.
27.020SK	competent speaker no flaw pursue
27.020SC	善(言者)无瑕适
27.020TK	competent ((speaker) speak)) no flaw (banish > pursue)
27.020TC	善((言者)言))无瑕(谪适)
27.020WB	善((＿＿)言))无瑕(谪＿)
27.020HG	善((＿＿)言))无瑕(谪＿)
27.020FY	善((言者)＿))无瑕(谪＿)
71.020MA	□((言者)＿))无瑕(＿适)
71.020MB	善((言者)＿))无瑕(＿适)
00.000G-	＿((＿＿)＿))＿＿(＿＿)
00.000G-	＿((＿＿)＿))＿＿(＿＿)

27. 030FE   Competent accountants do not use bamboo counting sticks.

27. 030SK   competent accountant not use (token for counting) (bamboo slip)

27. 030SC   善(数者)不用筹策

27. 030TK   competent ((count > (accountant) > count)) (not > not) (use > use) ((token for counting) > stupid)) (bamboo slip)

27. 030TC   善((计(数者)数))(不无)(用以)((筹[___])梼))策

27. 030WB   善((___(______)数))(不___)(用___)((筹[___])___))策

27. 030HG   善((计(______)___))(不___)(用___)((筹[___])___))策

27. 030FY   善((___(数者)___))(___无)(______)((筹[籇])___))策

71. 030MA   善((___(数者)___))(不___)(___以)((___[___])梼))策

71. 030MB   善((___(数者)___))(不___)(用___)((___[___])梼))策

00. 000G-   ___((___(______)___))(______)(______)((___[___])___))___

00. 000G-   ___((___(______)___))(______)(______)((___[___])___))___

27. 04aFE   Competent wardens lock without keys.

27. 04aSK   competent warden without lock key

27. 04aSC   善(闭者)无关篇

27. 04aTK   competent — ((warden) > close)) without lock (bolt > key)

27. 04aTC   善■((闭者)闭))无关(楗篇)

27. 04aWB   善___((______)闭))无关(楗___)

27. 04aHG   善___((闭者)___))无关(楗___)

27. 04aFY   善___((闭者)___))无关(楗___)

71. 04aMA   善___((闭者)___))无关(___篇)

71. 04aMB   善■((闭者)___))无关(___篇)

00. 000G-   ______((______)___))______(______)

00. 000G-   ______((______)___))______(______)

27.04bFE   Yet, it cannot be opened.
27.04bSK   yet cannot open 一
27.04bSC   而不可启也
27.04bTK   yet (cannot)(open > open) 一
27.04bTC   而(不可)(开启)也
27.04bWB   而(不可)(开＿＿)＿＿
27.04bHG   而(不可)(开＿＿)＿＿
27.04bFY   而(不可)(开＿＿)＿＿
71.04bMA   而(不可)(＿＿启)也
71.04bMB   而(不可)(＿＿启)也
00.000G-   ＿＿(＿＿＿＿)(＿＿＿＿)＿＿
00.000G-   ＿＿(＿＿＿＿)(＿＿＿＿)＿＿

27.05aFE   Competent weavers arrange without strings.
27.05aSK   competent weaver without string arrange
27.05aSC   善(结者)无绳约
27.05aTK   competent ((weaver) > weave)) without string arrange
27.05aTC   善((结者)结))无绳约
27.05aWB   善((＿＿＿＿)结))无绳约
27.05aHG   善((结者)＿＿))无绳约
27.05aFY   善((结者)＿＿))无绳约
71.05aMA   善((结者)＿＿))□□约
71.05aMB   善((结者)＿＿))无绳约
00.000G-   ＿＿((＿＿＿＿)＿＿))＿＿＿＿＿＿
00.000G-   ＿＿((＿＿＿＿)＿＿))＿＿＿＿＿＿

27.05bFE	Yet, it cannot be untied.
27.05bSK	yet (cannot) untie 一
27.05bSC	而(不可)解也
27.05bTK	yet (cannot) untie 一
27.05bTC	而(不可)解也
27.05bWB	而(不可)解___
27.05bHG	而(不可)解___
27.05bFY	而(不可)解___
71.05bMA	而(不可)解也
71.05bMB	而(不可)解也
00.000G-	___ (______) ______
00.000G-	___ (______) ______

27.06aFE	Therefore, sages save people always competently[120]
27.06aSK	therefore sage always competent save people
27.06aSC	(是以)(圣人)恒善救人
27.06aTK	(therefore)((sage) > (reputable person))(always > always) competent save people
27.06aTC	(是以)((圣人)(声人))(常恒)善救人
27.06aWB	(是以)((圣人)(______))(常__)善救人
27.06aHG	(是以)((圣人)(______))(常__)善救人
27.06aFY	(是以)((圣人)(______))(常__)善救人
71.06aMA	(是以)((______)(声人))(__恒)善救人
71.06aMB	(是以)((圣人)(______))(__恒)善救人
00.000G-	(______)((______)(______))(______)______
00.000G-	(______)((______)(______))(______)______

27. 06bFE   by not rejecting them.
27. 06bSK   and not reject people
27. 06bSC   而无弃人
27. 06bTK   therefore (other people) and not reject people
27. 06bTC   故人而无弃人
27. 06bWB   故＿＿＿无弃人
27. 06bHG   故＿＿＿无弃人
27. 06bFY   故人＿无弃人
71. 06bMA   ＿＿＿而无弃人
71. 06bMB   ＿＿＿而无弃人
00. 000G-   ＿＿＿＿＿＿＿＿
00. 000G-   ＿＿＿＿＿＿＿＿

27. 070FE   Always save competently things. [121]
27. 070SK   always competent save thing
27. 070SC   常善救物
27. 070TK   always competent save thing
27. 070TC   常善救物
27. 070WB   常善救物
27. 070HG   常善救物
27. 070FY   常善救物
00. 000MA   ＿＿＿＿＿
00. 000MB   ＿＿＿＿＿
00. 000G-   ＿＿＿＿＿
00. 000G-   ＿＿＿＿＿

27. 080FE   Not rejected things are resources.
27. 080SK   thing not reject resource
27. 080SC   物无弃财
27. 080TK   therefore thing not reject (thing > resource)
27. 080TC   故物无弃(物财)
27. 080WB   故＿无弃(物＿)
27. 080HG   故＿无弃(物＿)
27. 080FY   故物无弃(物＿)
71. 070MA   ＿物无弃(＿财)
71. 070MB   ＿物无弃(＿财)
00. 000G-   ＿＿＿＿(＿＿)
00. 000G-   ＿＿＿＿(＿＿)

27. 090FE   Accordingly, that is called brilliant.
27. 090SK   is call according brilliant
27. 090SC   是谓袭明
27. 090TK   is (call) (according > pull > stated) brilliant
27. 090TC   是(谓[＿])(袭曳申)明
27. 090WB   是(谓[＿])(袭＿＿)明
27. 090HG   是(谓[＿])(袭＿＿)明
27. 090FY   是(谓[＿])(袭＿＿)明
71. 080MA   是(谓[胃])(＿＿申)明
71. 080MB   是(谓[胃])(＿曳＿)明
00. 000G-   ＿(＿[＿])(＿＿)＿
00. 000G-   ＿(＿[＿])(＿＿)＿

27.100FE   Therefore, competent people are the teachers
           of incompetent people.
27.100SK   therefore competent people those (incompetent)
           people ('s) teacher
27.100SC   故善人者(不善)人之师
27.100TK   therefore competent people those (incompetent)
           people ('s) teacher
27.100TC   故善人者(不善)人之师
27.100WB   故善人者(不善)人之师
27.100HG   故善人者(不善)人之师
27.100FY   故善人者(不善)人之师
71.090MA   故善□…(…□)□之师
71.090MB   故善人…(…善)人之师
00.000G-   ……………(……)………
00.000G-   ……………(……)………

27.110FE   Incompetent people are the resources of
           competent people.
27.110SK   incompetent people competent people ('s)
           resource 一
27.110SC   (不善)人善人之资也
27.110TK   (incompetent) people those competent people
           ('s) resource people 一
27.110TC   (不善)人者善人之资人也
27.110WB   (不善)人者善人之资……
27.110HG   (不善)人者善人之资……
27.110FY   (不善)人者善人之资……
71.100MA   (不善)人…善人之资…也
71.100MB   (不善)人…善人之资人也
00.000G-   (……)………………………
00.000G-   (……)………………………

27.120FE	Those who do not value their teachers,
27.120SK	not value his teacher
27.120SC	不贵其师
27.120TK	not value his teacher
27.120TC	不贵其师
27.120WB	不贵其师
27.120HG	不贵其师
27.120FY	不贵其师
71.110MA	不贵其师
71.110MB	不贵其师
00.000G-	--- --- --- ---
00.000G-	--- --- --- ---

27.130FE	or do not love their resources, although knowledgeable, are greatly confused.
27.130SK	not love his resource although know — great confuse
27.130SC	不爱其资虽知乎大迷
27.130TK	not love his resource (although > only) (know > know) — great (confuse > blinded)
27.130TC	不爱其资(虽唯)(知智)乎大(迷眯)
27.130WB	不爱其资(虽__)(__智)__大(迷__)
27.130HG	不爱其资(虽__)(知__)__大(迷__)
27.130FY	不爱其资(虽__)(知__)__大(迷__)
71.120MA	不爱其资(__唯)(知__)乎大(__眯)
71.120MB	不爱其资(虽__)(知__)乎大(迷__)
00.000G-	--- --- --- --- (__ __)(__ __)--- --- (__ __)
00.000G-	--- --- --- --- (__ __)(__ __)--- --- (__ __)

27.140FE	This is called the essential detail.[122]
27.140SK	this call detail essential
27.140SC	是谓眇要
27.140TK	(this > this) (call) ((essential; mystery) > (mystery; essential) > (detail; essential))
27.140TC	(是此) (谓[___]) ((要妙) (妙要) (眇要))
27.140WB	(是___) (谓[___]) ((要妙) (___ ___) (___ ___))
27.140HG	(是___) (谓[___]) ((要妙) (___ ___) (___ ___))
27.140FY	(___此) (谓[___]) ((要妙) (___ ___) (___ ___))
71.130MA	(是___) (谓[胃]) ((___ ___) (___ ___)) 眇要))
71.130MB	(是___) (谓[胃]) ((___ ___) (___ ___) (眇要))
00.000G-	(___ ___) (___[___]) ((___ ___) (___ ___) (___ ___))
00.000G-	(___ ___) (___[___]) ((___ ___) (___ ___) (___ ___))

Chapter 28

28.01aFE	Know the male and observe the female[123]
28.01aSK	know its male observe its female
28.01aSC	知其雄守其雌
28.01aTK	know its male observe its female
28.01aTC	知其雄守其雌
28.01aWB	知其雄守其雌
28.01aHG	知其雄守其雌
28.01aFY	知其雄守其雌
72.01aMA	知其雄守其雌
72.01aMB	知其雄守其雌
00.000G-	--- --- --- --- --- ---
00.000G-	--- --- --- --- --- ---

28.01bFE	and become the stream of the world.[124]
28.01bSK	become world stream
28.01bSC	为(天下)溪
28.01bTK	become (world) (stream > cock)
28.01bTC	为(天下)(溪鸡)
28.01bWB	为(天下)(溪___)
28.01bHG	为(天下)(溪___)
28.01bFY	为(天下)(溪___)
72.01bMA	为(天下)(溪___)
72.01bMB	为(天下)(___鸡)
00.000G-	___ (___ ___) (___ ___)
00.000G-	___ (___ ___) (___ ___)

28.02aFE	Be the stream of the world[125]
28.02aSK	be world stream
28.02aSC	为(天下)(溪
28.02aTK	be (world) (stream > cock)
28.02aTC	为(天下)(溪鸡)
28.02aWB	为(天下)(溪＿)
28.02aHG	为(天下)(溪＿)
28.02aFY	为(天下)(溪＿)
72.02aMA	为(天下)(溪＿)
72.02aMB	为(天下)(＿鸡)
00.000G-	＿(＿＿)(＿＿)
00.000G-	＿(＿＿)(＿＿)

28.02bFE	and the eternal virtue never leaves.
28.02bSK	eternal virtue not leave
28.02bSC	恒德不离
28.02bTK	(constant > eternal) virtue not (leave > cock)
28.02bTC	(常恒)德不(离鸡)
28.02bWB	(常＿)德不(离＿)
28.02bHG	(常＿)德不(离＿)
28.02bFY	(常＿)德不(离＿)
72.02bMA	(＿恒)德不(＿鸡)
72.02bMB	(＿恒)德不(离＿)
00.000G-	(＿＿)＿＿(＿＿)
00.000G-	(＿＿)＿＿(＿＿)

28.03aFE	If the eternal virtue never leaves,	
28.03aSK	eternal virtue not leave	
28.03aSC	恒德不离	
28.03aTK	eternal virtue not (leave > cock)	
28.03aTC	恒德不离鸡	
00.000WB	--- --- --- --- ---	
00.000HG	--- --- --- --- ---	
00.000FY	--- --- --- --- ---	
72.03aMA	恒德不＿＿鸡	
72.03aMB	恒德不离＿＿	
00.000G-	--- --- --- --- ---	
00.000G-	--- --- --- --- ---	

28.03bFE	then you will return to infancy.	
28.03bSK	again return to infancy	
28.03bSC	复归于(婴儿)	
28.03bTK	again return to (infancy)	
28.03bTC	复归于(婴儿)	
28.030WB	复归于(婴儿)	
28.030HG	复归于(婴儿)	
28.030FY	复归于(婴儿)	
72.03bMA	复归＿＿(婴儿)	
72.03bMB	复□□(□□)	
00.000G-	--- --- --- (--- ---)	
00.000G-	--- --- --- (--- ---)	

28. 04aFE   Know the white and observe the black[126]
28. 04aSK   know its white observe its black
28. 04aSC   知其白守其黑
28. 04aTK   know its white observe its black
28. 04aTC   知其白守其黑
28. 04aWB   知其白守其黑
28. 04aHG   知其白守其黑
28. 04aFY   知其白守其黑
72. 07aMA   知其＿守其黑
72. 07aMB   知其白守其黑
00. 000G-   ___ ___ ___ ___ ___ ___
00. 000G-   ___ ___ ___ ___ ___ ___

28. 04bFE   and be the example for the world.[127]
28. 04bSK   be world example
28. 04bSC   为(天下)式
28. 04bTK   be (world) example
28. 04bTC   为(天下)式
28. 04bWB   为(天下)式
28. 04bHG   为(天下)式
28. 04bFY   为(天下)式
72. 07bMA   为(天下)式
72. 07bMB   为(天下)式
00. 000G-   ___ (___ ___) ___
00. 000G-   ___ (___ ___) ___

28. 05aFE	Be the example for the world[128]
28. 05aSK	be (world) example
28. 05aSC	为(天下)式
28. 05aTK	be (world) example
28. 05aTC	为(天下)式
28. 05aWB	为(天下)式
28. 05aHG	为(天下)式
28. 05aFY	为(天下)式
72. 08aMA	为(天下)式
72. 08aMB	为(天下)式
00. 000G-	＿＿(＿＿＿)＿＿
00. 000G-	＿＿(＿＿＿)＿＿

28. 05bFE	and the eternal virtue never errs.
28. 05bSK	eternal virtue not err
28. 05bSC	恒德不忒
28. 05bTK	(constant > eternal) virtue not err (borrow)
28. 05bTC	(常恒)德不忒(贷[＿＿＿])
28. 05bWB	(常＿＿)德不忒(＿＿[＿＿＿])
28. 05bHG	(常＿＿)德不忒(＿＿[＿＿＿])
28. 05bFY	(常＿＿)德不忒(贷[貸])
72. 08bMA	(＿＿恒)德不忒(＿＿[＿＿＿])
72. 08bMB	(＿＿恒)德不忒(＿＿[＿＿＿])
00. 000G-	(＿＿＿＿)＿＿＿＿＿＿(＿＿[＿＿＿])
00. 000G-	(＿＿＿＿)＿＿＿＿＿＿(＿＿[＿＿＿])

28. 06aFE   If the eternal virtue never errs,[129]
28. 06aSK   eternal virtue not err
28. 06aSC   恒德不忒
28. 06aTK   eternal virtue not err
28. 06aTC   恒德不忒
00. 000WB   --- --- --- ---
00. 000HG   --- --- --- ---
00. 000FY   --- --- --- ---
72. 09aMA   ___德不忒
72. 09aMB   恒德不忒
00. 000G-   --- --- --- ---
00. 000G-   --- --- --- ---

28. 06bFE   then it returns to moderation.
28. 06bSK   again return to (moderate)
28. 06bSC   复归于(无极)
28. 06bTK   again return to (moderate)
28. 06bTC   复归于(无极)
28. 060WB   复归于(无极)
28. 060HG   复归于(无极)
28. 060FY   ___归于(无极)
72. 09bMA   复归于(无极)
72. 09bMB   复归于(无极)
00. 000G-   --- --- --- (--- ---)
00. 000G-   --- --- --- (--- ---)

28. 07aFE	Know the pure and observe the disgrace[130]
28. 07aSK	know its pure observe its disgrace
28. 07aSC	知其白守其辱
28. 07aTK	know its (glory > pure) observe its disgrace
28. 07aTC	知其(荣白)守其辱
28. 07aWB	知其(荣⋯)守其辱
28. 07aHG	知其(荣⋯)守其辱
28. 07aFY	知其(荣⋯)守其辱
72. 04aMA	知其(⋯白)守其辱
72. 04aMB	□其(⋯白)守其辱
00. 000G–	⸺ ⸺ (⸺ ⸺) ⸺ ⸺ ⸺
00. 000G–	⸺ ⸺ (⸺ ⸺) ⸺ ⸺ ⸺

28. 07bFE	and be the valley of the world.[131]
28. 07bSK	become world valley
28. 07bSC	为(天下)浴
28. 07bTK	become (world) 一 (valley > valley)
28. 07bTC	为(天下)■(谷浴)
28. 07bWB	为(天下)⋯(谷⋯)
28. 07bHG	为(天下)⋯(谷⋯)
28. 07bFY	为(天下)⋯(谷⋯)
72. 04bMA	为(天下)⋯(⋯浴)
72. 04bMB	为(天下)■(⋯浴)
00. 000G–	⋯ (⋯ ⋯) ⋯ (⋯ ⋯)
00. 000G–	⋯ (⋯ ⋯) ⋯ (⋯ ⋯)

28. 08aFE   Be the valley of the world[132]
28. 08aSK   be world valley
28. 08aSC   为(天下)浴
28. 08aTK   be (world)(valley > valley)
28. 08aTC   为(天下)(谷浴)
28. 08aWB   为(天下)(谷___)
28. 08aHG   为(天下)(谷___)
28. 08aFY   为(天下)(谷___)
72. 05aMA   为(天下)(___□)
72. 05aMB   为(天下)(___浴)
00. 000G-   ___ (______) (______)
00. 000G-   ___ (______) (______)

28. 08bFE   and the eternal virtue will be always enough.
28. 08bSK   eternal virtue be enough
28. 08bSC   恒德乃足
28. 08bTK   (constant > eternal) virtue be enough
28. 08bTC   (常恒)德乃足
28. 08bWB   (常___)德乃足
28. 08bHG   (常___)德乃足
28. 08bFY   (常___)德乃足
72. 05bMA   (___恒)德乃□
72. 05bMB   (___恒)德乃足
00. 000G-   (______) ___ ___ ___
00. 000G-   (______) ___ ___ ___

28. 09aFE	If the eternal virtue is always enough,
28. 09aSK	eternal virtue be enough
28. 09aSC	恒德乃足
28. 09aTK	eternal virtue be enough
28. 09aTC	恒德乃足
00. 000WB	--- --- --- ---
00. 000HG	--- --- --- ---
00. 000FY	--- --- --- ---
72. 06aMA	___德乃□
72. 06aMB	恒德乃足
00. 000G-	--- --- --- ---
00. 000G-	--- --- --- ---

28. 09bFE	then you will return to simplicity.
28. 09bSK	again return to simple
28. 09bSC	复归于朴
28. 09bTK	again return to simple
28. 09bTC	复归于朴
28. 090WB	复归于朴
28. 090HG	复归于朴
28. 090FY	复归于朴
72. 06bMA	□□□□
72. 06bMB	复归于朴
00. 000G-	--- --- --- ---
00. 000G-	--- --- --- ---

28.100FE	Simplicity breaks up and then it becomes tools.[133]	
28.100SK	simple (break up) then become tool	
28.100SC	朴散则为器	
28.100TK	(simple > master)(break up) then become tool	
28.100TC	(朴榷)散则为器	
28.100WB	(朴＿＿)散则为器	
28.100HG	(朴＿＿)散则为器	
28.100FY	(朴＿＿)散则为器	
72.100MA	(＿＿榷)散□□□	
72.100MB	(朴＿＿)散则为器	
00.000G-	(＿＿＿＿)＿＿＿＿＿＿＿＿	
00.000G-	(＿＿＿＿)＿＿＿＿＿＿＿＿	

28.11aFE	Sages use them[134]	
28.11aSK	sage use them	
28.11aSC	(圣人)用之	
28.11aTK	(sage) use them	
28.11aTC	(圣人)用之	
28.11aWB	(圣人)用之	
28.11aHG	(圣人)用之	
28.11aFY	(圣人)用之	
72.11aMA	(□人)用＿	
72.11aMB	(圣人)用＿	
00.000G-	(＿＿＿＿)＿＿＿＿	
00.000G-	(＿＿＿＿)＿＿＿＿	

28. 11bFE	and become official leaders.
28. 11bSK	then become official leader
28. 11bSC	则为官长
28. 11bTK	then become official leader
28. 11bTC	则为官长
28. 11bWB	则为官长
28. 11bHG	则为官长
28. 11bFY	则为官长
72. 11bMA	则为官长
72. 11bMB	则为官长
00. 000G-	--- --- --- ---
00. 000G-	--- --- --- ---

28. 120FE	They will not divide great organisations.
28. 120SK	they great organisation not divide
28. 120SC	夫大制无割
28. 120TK	(therefore > they) great organisation (not > not) divide
28. 120TC	(故夫)大制(不无)割
28. 120WB	(故__)大制(不__)割
28. 120HG	(故__)大制(不__)割
28. 120FY	(__ __)大制(__ 无)割
72. 120MA	(__ 夫)大制(__ 无)割
72. 120MB	(__ 夫)大制(__ 无)割
00. 000G-	(__ __) __ __ (__ __) __
00. 000G-	(__ __) __ __ (__ __) __

Chapter 29

29.01aFE	If people desire to take the world and interfere with it,[135]
29.01aSK	will desire take world and interfere ('s)
29.01aSC	将欲取(天下)而为之
29.01aTK	will desire take (world) and interfere ('s) it
29.01aTC	将欲取(天下)而为之者
29.01aWB	将欲取(天下)而为之﹍
29.01aHG	将欲取(天下)而为之﹍
29.01aFY	将欲取(天下)而为之者
73.01aMA	将欲取(天下)而为之﹍
73.01aMB	将欲取(□□)□□□﹍
00.000G-	﹍﹍﹍(﹍﹍)﹍﹍﹍
00.000G-	﹍﹍﹍(﹍﹍)﹍﹍﹍

29.01bFE	I see that they have no alternative.[136]
29.01bSK	I see they (have no alternative)
29.01bSC	吾见其(不得已)
29.01bTK	I see they ((have no alternative) > (not; □; □))
29.01bTC	吾见其((不得已)弗□□))
29.01bWB	吾见其((不得已)﹍﹍))
29.01bHG	吾见其((不得已)﹍﹍))
29.01bFY	吾见其((不得已)﹍﹍))
73.01bMA	吾见其((﹍﹍)弗□□))
73.01bMB	□□□((□得已)﹍﹍))
00.000G-	﹍﹍﹍((﹍﹍)﹍﹍))
00.000G-	﹍﹍﹍((﹍﹍)﹍﹍))

29. 02aFE	The world is a container of energy[137]
29. 02aSK	(world) energy container 一
29. 02aSC	（天下）神器也
29. 02aTK	this (world) energy container 一
29. 02aTC	夫（天下）神器也
29. 02aWB	...（天下）神器...
29. 02aHG	...（天下）神器...
29. 02aFY	夫（天下）神器...
73. 02aMA	...（□□）□器也
73. 02aMB	夫（天下）神器也
00. 000G-	...（......）......
00. 000G-	...（......）......

29. 02bFE	that cannot be interfered with.
29. 02bSK	cannot interfere it 一
29. 02bSC	（非可）为者也
29. 02bTK	((cannot) > (cannot)) interfere it 一
29. 02bTC	((不可)(非可))为者也
29. 02bWB	((不可)(......))为...也
29. 02bHG	((不可)(......))为...也
29. 02bFY	((不可)(......))为...也
73. 02bMA	((......)(非可))为者也
73. 02bMB	((......)(非可))为者也
00. 000G-	((......)(......))......
00. 000G-	((......)(......))......

29.03aFE   Those who act will fail.[138]
29.03aSK   act ('s) those fail ('s)
29.03aSC   为之者败之
29.03aTK   act ('s) those fail ('s)
29.03aTC   为之者败之
29.03aWB   为＿者败之
29.03aHG   为＿者败之
29.03aFY   为＿者败之
73.03aMA   为＿者败之
73.03aMB   为之者败之
00.000G-   ＿＿ ＿＿ ＿＿ ＿＿ ＿＿
00.000G-   ＿＿ ＿＿ ＿＿ ＿＿ ＿＿

29.03bFE   Those who hold will lose.[139]
29.03bSK   hold ('s) those lose ('s)
29.03bSC   执之者失之
29.03bTK   hold ('s) those lose ('s) 一
29.03bTC   执之者失之■
29.03bWB   执＿者失之＿
29.03bHG   执＿者失之＿
29.03bFY   执＿者失之＿
73.03bMA   执＿者失之＿
73.03bMB   执之者失之■
00.000G-   ＿＿ ＿＿ ＿＿ ＿＿ ＿＿
00.000G-   ＿＿ ＿＿ ＿＿ ＿＿ ＿＿

29. 040FE	Things may succeed or may fail.
29. 040SK	thing (may be) succeed (may be) fail
29. 040SC	物或行或隋
29. 040TK	therefore all thing (may be) succeed (may be) (follow > fail > offal)
29. 040TC	故凡物或行或(随隋)
29. 040WB	故＿物或行或(随＿)
29. 040HG	故＿物或行或(随＿)
29. 040FY	＿凡物或行或(随＿)
73. 040MA	＿＿物或行或(随＿)
73. 040MB	＿＿物或行或(＿隋)
00. 000G-	＿＿＿＿＿＿＿＿ (＿＿)
00. 000G-	＿＿＿＿＿＿＿＿ (＿＿)

29. 050FE	They may be hot or may be cold. [140]
29. 050SK	(may be) hot (may be) subside
29. 050SC	或热或坐
29. 050TK	(may be) (roar > shiver > blow > easy > hot) (may be) (blow > subside)
29. 050TC	或(呴噤歔灵热)或(吹坐)
29. 050WB	或(＿＿＿歔＿＿)或(吹＿)
29. 050HG	或(呴＿＿＿＿)或(吹＿)
29. 050FY	或(＿噤＿＿＿)或(吹＿)
73. 050MA	或(＿＿＿灵＿)或(□＿)
73. 050MB	或(＿＿＿＿热)或(＿坐)
00. 000G-	＿ (＿＿＿＿＿＿) ＿ (＿＿)
00. 000G-	＿ (＿＿＿＿＿＿) ＿ (＿＿)

29. 060FE	They may be strong or may be weak.
29. 060SK	(may be) strong (may be) weak
29. 060SC	或强或赢
29. 060TK	(may be)(strong > strong)(may be)(weak > file)
29. 060TC	或(强彊)或(赢锉)
29. 060WB	或(强＿)或(赢＿)
29. 060HG	或(强＿)或(赢＿)
29. 060FY	或(＿彊)或(＿锉)
73. 060MA	□(□＿)□(＿□)
00. 000MB	＿(＿＿)＿(＿＿)
00. 000G-	＿(＿＿)＿(＿＿)
00. 000G-	＿(＿＿)＿(＿＿)

29. 070FE	They may grow or may decay.
29. 070SK	(may be) grow (may be) decay
29. 070SC	或培或堕
29. 070TK	(may be)(carry > grow > file > spoil > serve)(may be)(decay > decay)
29. 070TC	或(载培挫坏陪)或(隳堕)
29. 070WB	或(　挫　)或(隳　)
29. 070HG	或(载＿＿＿)或(隳＿)
29. 070FY	或(＿培＿＿)或(＿堕)
73. 070MA	或(＿＿＿坏＿)或(＿堕)
73. 060MB	或(＿＿＿＿陪)或(＿堕)
00. 000G-	＿(＿＿＿＿)＿(＿＿)
00. 000G-	＿(＿＿＿＿＿)＿(＿＿)

29. 08aFE	Therefore, sages reject extremes, [141]
29. 08aSK	therefore sage reject extreme
29. 08aSC	（是以）（圣人）去什
29. 08aTK	(therefore)((sage) > (reputable person)) reject (extreme)
29. 08aTC	（是以）（（圣人）（声人））去（什［＿］）
29. 08aWB	（是以）（（圣人）（＿＿））去（什［甚］）
29. 08aHG	（是以）（（圣人）（＿＿））去（什［甚］）
29. 08aFY	（是以）（（圣人）（＿＿））去（什［甚］）
73. 08aMA	（是以）（（＿＿）（声人））去（什［甚］）
73. 07aMB	（是以）（（圣人）（＿＿））去（什［甚］）
00. 000G-	（＿＿）（（＿＿）（＿＿））＿（＿［＿］）
00. 000G-	（＿＿）（（＿＿）（＿＿））＿（＿［＿］）

29. 08bFE	reject grandeur, and reject extravagance.
29. 08bSK	reject grandeur reject extravagance
29. 08bSC	去大去诸
29. 08bTK	reject (extravagance > grandeur) reject (great > extravagance > book > all)
29. 08bTC	去（奢大）去（泰奢楮诸）
29. 08bWB	去（奢＿）去（泰＿＿＿）
29. 08bHG	去（奢＿）去（泰＿＿＿）
29. 08bFY	去（奢＿）去（泰＿＿＿）
73. 08bMA	去（＿大）去（＿＿楮＿）
73. 07bMB	去（＿大）去（＿＿＿诸）
00. 000G-	＿（＿＿）＿（＿＿＿）
00. 000G-	＿（＿＿）＿（＿＿＿＿）

Chapter 30

30. 01aFE	Use the *Way* to assist the leaders of people.
30. 01aSK	use *Way* assist people leader those
30. 01aSC	以道佐人主者
30. 01aTK	use *Way* (assist > left) people leader those
30. 01aTC	以道(佐左)人主者
30. 01aWB	以道(佐＿)人主者
30. 01aHG	以道(佐＿)人主者
30. 01aFY	以道(佐＿)人主者
74. 01aMA	以道(＿左)人主＿
74. 01aMB	以道(佐＿)人主＿
04. 01aGA	以道(佐＿)人主者
00. 000G-	＿＿(＿＿)＿＿＿

30. 01bFE	Do not use soldiers to force the world.[142]
30. 01bSK	not desire use soldier force to world
30. 01bSC	不欲以兵强于(天下)
30. 01bTK	not desire use soldier (force > force) to (world)
30. 01bTC	不欲以兵(强彊)丁(天下)
30. 01bWB	不＿以兵(强＿)＿(天下)
30. 01bHG	不＿以兵(强＿)于(天下)
30. 01bFY	不＿以兵(＿彊)＿(天下)
74. 01bMA	不＿以兵(强＿)□(天下)
74. 01bMB	不＿以兵(强＿)于(天下)
04. 01bGA	不欲以兵(强＿)于(天下)
00. 000G-	＿＿＿＿＿(＿＿＿)＿(＿＿＿)

30. 020FE   Such actions are likely to rebound.

30. 020SK   such affair like rebound

30. 020SC   其事好还

30. 020TK   such affair like 一 (rebound > escalate)

30. 020TC   其事好■还长

30. 020WB   其事好___还___

30. 020HG   其事好___还___

30. 020FY   其事好___还___

74. 020MA   □□□___□___

74. 020MB   其□□___□___

04. 080GA   其事好■___长

00. 000G-   ___ ___ ___ ___ ___ ___

30. 030FE   Where armies have camped only thorny bushes will grow.[143]

30. 030SK   army ('s) place stay bush thorn grow ('s)

30. 030SC   师之所居楚朸生之

30. 030TK   army ('s) place (occupy > stay) ((bramble; thorn) > (bush; thorn) > thorn)) grow (('s) > then)

30. 030TC   师之所(处居)((荆棘)(楚朸)棘))生(之焉)

30. 030WB   师之所(处___)((荆棘)(___ ___)___))生(___焉)

30. 030HG   师之所(处___)((荆棘)(___ ___)___))生(___焉)

30. 030FY   师之所(处___)((荆棘)(___ ___)___))生(___焉)

74. 030MA   □□所(___居)((___ ___)(楚朸)___))生(之___)

74. 030MB   □□□(___□)((□___)(___ ___)棘))生(之___)

00. 000G-   ___ ___ ___ (___ ___)((___ ___)(___ ___)___))___(___ ___)

00. 000G-   ___ ___ ___ (___ ___)((___ ___)(___ ___)___))___(___ ___)

30. 040FE   Big armies leave bad harvests behind.[144]

30. 040SK   big army ('s) behind certainly happen bad harvest

30. 040SC   大军之后必有凶年

30. 040TK   big army ('s) behind certainly happen bad harvest

30. 040TC   大军之后必有凶年

30. 040WB   大军之后必有凶年

30. 040HG   大军之后必有凶年

30. 040FY   大军之后必有凶年

00. 000MA   --- --- --- --- --- --- --- ---

00. 000MB   --- --- --- --- --- --- --- ---

00. 000G-   --- --- --- --- --- --- --- ---

00. 000G-   --- --- --- --- --- --- --- ---

30. 050FE   Those who are competent succeed and stop in time.

30. 050SK   competent those succeed and stop 一

30. 050SC   善者果而已矣

30. 050TK   therefore competent those succeed and stop 一

30. 050TC   故善者果而已矣

30. 050WB   ___善者果而已___

30. 050HG   ___善者果而已___

30. 050FY   故善者果而已矣

74. 040MA   ___善者果而已矣

74. 040MB   ___善者果而已矣

04. 020GA   ___善者果而已___

00. 000G-   --- --- --- --- --- --- ---

30. 060FE   Do not dare to take power.
30. 060SK   not dare use take power then
30. 060SC   毋敢以取強焉
30. 060TK   (not > not) dare use take (power > power) then
             —
30. 060TC   (不毋)敢以取(強彊)焉 ■
30. 060WB   (不＿)敢以取(強＿)＿＿
30. 060HG   (不＿)敢以取(強＿)＿＿
30. 060FY   (不＿)敢以取(＿彊)焉＿
74. 050MA   (＿毋)＿以取(強＿)焉＿
74. 050MB   (＿毋)＿以取(強＿)焉＿
04. 030GA   (不＿)＿以取(強＿)＿ ■
00. 000G–   (＿＿)＿＿＿(＿＿)＿＿

30. 070FE   Succeed without boasting.
30. 070SK   succeed but not boast
30. 070SC   果而弗矜
30. 070TK   succeed but (not > not) boast —
30. 070TC   果而(勿弗)矜 ■
30. 070WB   果而(勿＿)矜＿
30. 070HG   果而(勿＿)矜＿
30. 070FY   果而(勿＿)矜＿
74. 070MA   果而(勿＿)矜＿
74. 070MB   果而(勿＿)矜＿
04. 060GA   果而(＿弗)矜 ■
00. 000G–   ＿＿(＿＿)＿＿

30. 080FE   Succeed without attacking.
30. 080SK   succeed but without attack
30. 080SC   果而弗伐
30. 080TK   succeed but (without > without > without)
             attack
30. 080TC   果而(勿毋弗)伐
30. 080WB   果而(勿__ __)伐
30. 080HG   果而(勿__ __)伐
30. 080FY   果而(勿__ __)伐
74. 080MA   果而(__ □__)□
74. 080MB   果□(__ □__)伐
04. 040GA   果而(__ __弗)伐
00. 000G-   __ __(__ __ __)__

30. 090FE   Succeed without arrogance.
30. 090SK   succeed but without arrogance
30. 090SC   果而毋骄
30. 090TK   succeed but (without > without) arrogance
30. 090TC   果而(勿毋)骄
30. 090WB   果而(勿__)骄
30. 090HG   果而(勿__)骄
30. 090FY   果而(勿__)骄
74. 060MA   果而(__毋)骄
74. 060MB   果而(__毋)骄
04. 050GA   果而(__毋)骄
00. 000G-   __ __(__ __)__

30. 100FE	Succeed without excess.
30. 100SK	succeed but without gain (too much)
30. 100SC	果而毋得已
30. 100TK	succeed but (without > without) gain (too much)
30. 100TC	果而(不毋)得已
30. 100WB	果而(不＿＿)得已
30. 100HG	果而(不＿＿)得已
30. 100FY	果而(不＿＿)得已
74. 090MA	果而(＿＿毋)得已
74. 090MB	果而(＿＿毋)得已
00. 000G–	＿＿＿＿ (＿＿＿＿) ＿＿＿＿
00. 000G–	＿＿＿＿ (＿＿＿＿) ＿＿＿＿

30. 110FE	That is called succeeding without force.
30. 110SK	claim is call succeed but without force
30. 110SC	居是谓果而不强
30. 110TK	claim is (call) succeed but (without > without) (force > force)
30. 110TC	居是(谓[＿＿])果而(勿不)(强彊)
30. 110WB	＿＿＿＿ (＿＿[＿＿])果而(勿＿＿)(强＿＿)
30. 110HG	＿＿＿＿ (＿＿[＿＿])果而(勿＿＿)(强＿＿)
30. 110FY	＿＿是(＿＿[＿＿])果而(勿＿＿)(＿＿彊)
74. 100MA	居是(谓[胃])□而(＿＿不)(强＿＿)
74. 100MB	居是(谓[胃])果而(＿＿＿＿)(强＿＿)
04. 070GA	＿＿是(谓[＿＿])果而(＿＿不)(强＿＿)
00. 000G–	＿＿＿＿ (＿＿[＿＿]) ＿＿＿＿ (＿＿＿＿) (＿＿＿＿)

30. 120FE	Strong things will become weak.[145]
30. 120SK	thing strong yet weak
30. 120SC	物壮而老
30. 120TK	thing strong (then > yet) weak
30. 120TC	物壮(则而)老
30. 120WB	物壮(则 ___)老
30. 120HG	物壮(则 ___)老
30. 120FY	物壮(则 ___)老
74. 110MA	物壮(___ 而)老
74. 110MB	物壮(___ 而)老
00. 000G-	___ ___ (___ ___) ___
00. 000G-	___ ___ (___ ___) ___

30. 130FE	They are not called the *Way*.[146]
30. 130SK	are call they not *Way*
30. 130SC	是谓之不道
30. 130TK	are (call) their (not > not) *Way*
30. 130TC	是(谓[___])之(不非)道
30. 130WB	是(谓[___]) ___ (不 ___)道
30. 130HG	是(谓[___]) ___ (不 ___)道
30. 130FY	是(谓[___]) ___ (___ 非)道
74. 120MA	是(谓[胃])之(不 ___)道
74. 120MB	___ (谓[胃])之(不 ___)道
00. 000G-	___ (___ [___]) ___ (___ ___) ___
00. 000G-	___ (___ [___]) ___ (___ ___) ___

30.140FE	What is not the *Way* will perish soon.[147]
30.140SK	not *Way* early perish
30.140SC	不道早已
30.140TK	(not > not) *Way* (early > flea) perish
30.140TC	(不非)道(早蚤)已
30.140WB	(不__)道(早__)已
30.140HG	(不__)道(早__)已
30.140FY	(__非)道(早__)已
74.130MA	(不__)道(__蚤)已
74.130MB	(不__)道(__蚤)已
00.000G-	(__ __) __ (__ __) __
00.000G-	(__ __) __ (__ __) __

Chapter 31

31.010FE	Armies are the tools of misfortune.
31.010SK	those army those (misfortune) ('s) tool —
31.010SC	夫兵者(不祥)之器也
31.010TK	those (satisfy > satisfy) army those (misfortune) ('s) tool —
31.010TC	夫(佳美)兵者(不祥)之器也
31.010WB	夫(佳__)兵者(不祥)之器__
31.010HG	夫(佳__)兵者(不祥)之器__
31.010FY	夫(__美)兵者(不祥)之器__
75.010MA	夫(______)兵者(不祥)之器□
75.010MB	夫(______)兵者(不祥)之器也
00.000G-	___(______) ______ (______) ___ ___ ___
00.000G-	___(______) ______ (______) ___ ___ ___

31.020FE	They are disgusting.[148]
31.020SK	thing (may be) disgust ('s)
31.020SC	物或恶之
31.020TK	thing (may be) disgust ('s)
31.020TC	物或恶之
31.020WB	物或恶之
31.020HG	物或恶之
31.020FY	物或恶之
75.020MA	物或恶之
75.020MB	物或恶□
00.000G-	___ ___ ___ ___
00.000G-	___ ___ ___ ___

31. 030FE   Therefore, those who possess the *Way* will not
             claim them.[149]
31. 030SK   therefore possess *Way* those not claim
31. 030SC   故有道者弗居
31. 030TK   therefore ((possess; *Way*) > (possess; desire))
             those (not > not) ((deal with) > claim)
31. 030TC   故((有道)(有欲))者(不弗)(处居)
31. 030WB   故((有道)(＿＿))者(不＿)(处＿)
31. 030HG   故((有道)(＿＿))者(不＿)(处＿)
31. 030FY   故((有道)(＿＿))者(不＿)(处＿)
75. 030MA   故((＿＿)(有欲))者(＿弗)(＿居)
75. 030MB   □((＿＿)(□□))□(＿□)(＿□)
00. 000G-   ＿((＿＿)(＿＿))＿(＿＿)(＿＿)
00. 000G-   ＿((＿＿)(＿＿))＿(＿＿)(＿＿)

31. 040FE   Great men will occupy and value the
             unorthodox.
31. 040SK   (great man) occupy will value left
31. 040SC   (君子)居则贵左
31. 040TK   (therefore) (great man) occupy will value left
31. 040TC   (是以)(君子)居则贵左
31. 040WB   (＿＿)(君子)居则贵左
31. 040HG   (＿＿)(君子)居则贵左
31. 040FY   (是以)(君子)居则贵左
75. 040MA   (＿＿)(君子)居则贵左
75. 040MB   (＿＿)(□子)居则贵左
00. 000G-   (＿＿)(＿＿)＿＿＿＿＿
32. 010GC   (＿＿)(君子)居则贵左

31.050FE	They will use soldiers who value the orthodox.
31.050SK	use soldier will value right
31.050SC	用兵則貴右
31.050TK	use soldier will value right
31.050TC	用兵則貴右
31.050WB	用兵則貴右
31.050HG	用兵則貴右
31.050FY	用兵則貴右
75.050MA	用兵則貴右
75.050MB	用兵則貴右
00.000G-	--- --- --- ---
32.020GC	用兵則貴右

31.060FE	Armies are the tools of misfortune.
31.060SK	army those (misfortune) ('s) tool 一
31.060SC	兵者(不祥)之器也
31.060TK	army those (misfortune) ('s) tool 一
31.060TC	兵者(不祥)之器也
31.060WB	兵者(不祥)之器 ___
31.060HG	兵者(不祥)之器 ___
31.060FY	兵者(不祥)之器 ___
75.070MA	□□(不祥)之器也
75.070MB	兵者(不祥)□器也
00.000G-	--- --- (--- ---) --- --- ---
32.040GC	--- --- (□□)□□□

31. 070FE   Therefore, armies are not the tools of great men.

31. 070SK   therefore army those not (great man) ('s) tool —

31. 070SC   故兵者非(君子)之器也

31. 070TK   therefore call army those not (((great man); ('s)) ((sovereign; ('s); person))) tool —

31. 070TC   故曰兵者非(((君子)之))((君之子)))器也

31. 070WB   ＿＿＿＿＿非(((君子)之))((＿＿＿＿)))器＿

31. 070HG   ＿＿＿＿＿非(((君子)之))((＿＿＿＿)))器＿

31. 070FY   ＿＿＿＿＿非(((君子)之))((＿＿＿＿)))器＿

75. 060MA   故＿兵者非(((＿＿)＿))((君之子)))器也

75. 060MB   故＿兵者非(((君子)之))((＿＿＿)))器＿

00. 000G–   ＿＿＿＿＿＿(((＿＿)＿))((＿＿＿)))＿＿

32. 030GC   故曰兵者＿(((＿＿)＿))((＿＿＿)))＿＿

31. 08aFE   When there is no alternative then use them.

31. 08aSK   (have no alternative) and use their

31. 08aSC   (不得已)而用之

31. 08aTK   (have no alternative) and use their

31. 08aTC   (不得已)而用之

31. 08aWB   (不得已)而用之

31. 08aHG   (不得已)而用之

31. 08aFY   (不得已)而用之

75. 08aMA   (不得已)而用之

75. 08aMB   (不得已)而用之

00. 000G–   (＿＿＿)＿＿＿

32. 05aGC   (不得已)而用之

31.08bFE   Attack with sharp weapons to become victorious,
31.08bSK   (sharp weapon) attack become victor
31.08bSC   铦袭为上
31.08bTK   use ((no; desire) > (quiet; calm) > (sharp weapon); attack) > (sharp weapon); vigorous)) become victor
31.08bTC   以((恬淡)(恬憺)(铦袭)(铦(龙[＿＿])))为上
31.08bWB   ＿＿((恬淡)(＿＿＿＿)(＿＿＿＿)(＿＿(＿＿[＿＿])))为上
31.08bHG   ＿＿((恬淡)(＿＿＿＿)(＿＿＿＿)(＿＿(＿＿[＿＿])))为上
31.08bFY   以((＿＿＿＿)(恬憺)(＿＿＿＿)(＿＿(＿＿[＿＿])))为上
75.08bMA   ＿＿((＿＿＿＿)(＿＿＿＿)(铦袭)(＿＿(＿＿[＿＿])))为上
75.08bMB   ＿＿((＿＿＿＿)(＿＿＿＿)(＿＿＿＿)(铦(龙[龍])))为上
00.000G-   ＿＿((＿＿＿＿)(＿＿＿＿)(＿＿＿＿)(＿＿(＿＿[＿＿])))＿＿＿＿
32.05bGC   ＿＿((恬淡)(＿＿＿＿)(＿＿＿＿)(＿＿(＿＿[＿＿])))为上

31.08cFE   but use them without satisfaction.
31.08cSK   without satisfy 一
31.08cSC   勿美也
31.08cTK   victory (therefore > and) (without > without > without) satisfy 一
31.08cTC   胜(故而)(不勿弗)美也
31.08cWB   胜(＿＿而)(不＿＿＿＿)美＿＿
31.08cHG   胜(＿＿而)(不＿＿＿＿)美＿＿
31.08cFY   ＿＿(故＿＿)(不＿＿＿＿)美也
75.08cMA   ＿＿(＿＿＿＿)(＿＿勿＿＿)美也
75.08cMB   ＿＿(＿＿＿＿)(＿＿勿＿＿)美也
00.000G-   ＿＿(＿＿＿＿)(＿＿＿＿＿＿)＿＿＿＿
32.05cGC   ＿＿(＿＿＿＿)(＿＿＿＿弗)美也

31. 09aFE	Those who are satisfied by them,
31. 09aSK	if satisfy ('s)
31. 09aSC	若美之
31. 09aTK	(if > if) satisfy certainly happy their happy ('s) it
31. 09aTC	(而若)美必乐之乐之者
31. 09aWB	(而＿)美＿＿＿之者
31. 09aHG	(而＿)美＿＿＿之者
31. 09aFY	(＿若)美必乐之乐之者
75. 09aMA	(＿若)美＿＿＿之＿
75. 09aMB	(＿若)美＿＿＿之＿
00. 000G-	(＿＿)＿＿＿＿＿
32. 06aGC	(＿＿)美＿＿＿之＿

31. 09bFE	like to kill people.
31. 09bSK	be like kill people —
31. 09bSC	是乐杀人也
31. 09bTK	be like kill people —
31. 09bTC	是乐杀人也
31. 09bWB	是乐杀人＿
31. 09bHG	是乐杀人＿
31. 09bFY	是乐杀人也
75. 09bMA	是乐杀人也
75. 09bMB	是乐杀人也
00. 000G-	＿＿＿＿＿
32. 06bGC	是乐杀人＿

31.10aFE   Those who like to kill people
31.10aSK   those like kill people
31.10aSC   夫乐杀人
31.10aTK   those like ((kill; people) > (people; kill; people)) those
31.10aTC   夫乐((杀人)(人杀人))者
31.10aWB   夫乐((杀人)(＿＿＿))者
31.10aHG   夫乐((杀人)(＿＿＿))者
31.10aFY   夫乐((＿＿)(人杀人))者
75.10aMA   夫乐((杀人)(＿＿＿))＿
75.10aMB   夫乐((杀人)(＿＿＿))＿
00.000G-   ＿＿((＿＿)(＿＿＿))＿
32.07aGC   夫乐((□＿)(＿＿＿))＿

31.10bFE   cannot achieve the goals of the State.[150]
31.10bSK   (cannot) according achieve goal to (state) 一
31.10bSC   (不可)以得志于(天下)矣
31.10bTK   will (cannot) according achieve goal to (state) 一
31.10bTC   则(不可)以得志于(天下)矣
31.10bWB   则(不可)以得志于(天下)矣
31.10bHG   则(不可)以得志于(天下)矣
31.10bFY   ＿(不可)以得志于(天下)矣
75.10bMA   ＿(不可)以得志于(天下)矣
75.10bMB   ＿(不可)以得志于(天下)矣
00.000G-   ＿(＿＿)＿＿＿＿(＿＿)＿
32.07bGC   ＿(□□)以得志于(天下)＿

31. 110FE   Therefore, during fortunate events, the left
             side is honoured.[151]
31. 110SK   therefore fortunate event honoured (left side)
31. 110SC   (是以)吉事上左
31. 110TK   (therefore > (therefore)) fortunate event
             (respect > honoured) (left side)
31. 110TC   ((故(是以))吉事(尚上)左
31. 110WB   ((___(______))吉事(尚___)左
31. 110HG   ((故(______))吉事(尚___)左
31. 110FY   ((故(______))吉事(尚___)左
75. 110MA   ((___(是以))吉事(___上)左
75. 110MB   ((___(是以))吉事(___□)□
00. 000G-   ((___(______))______(______)___
32. 080GC   ((故(______))吉事(___上)左

31. 120FE   During funerals, the right side is honoured.[152]
31. 120SK   funeral event honoured (right side)
31. 120SC   喪事上右
31. 120TK   (serious > funeral) event (respect > honoured)
             (right side)
31. 120TC   (凶喪)事(尚上)右
31. 120WB   (凶___)事(尚___)右
31. 120HG   (凶___)事(尚___)右
31. 120FY   (凶___)事(尚___)右
75. 120MA   (___喪)事(___上)右
75. 120MB   (___□)□(___□)□
00. 000G-   (______)___(______)___
32. 090GC   (___喪)事(___上)右

31.13aFE	Therefore, junior generals occupy the left side,
31.13aSK	therefore junior general occupy (left side)
31.13aSC	（是以）便（将军）居左
31.13aTK	(therefore) (prejudiced > junior) (general) (occupy > occupy) (left side)
31.13aTC	（是以）（偏便）（将军）（处居）左
31.13aWB	（＿＿）（偏＿）（将军）（＿居）左
31.13aHG	（＿＿）（偏＿）（将军）（处＿）左
31.13aFY	（是以）（偏＿）（将军）（处＿）左
75.13aMA	（是以）（＿便）（将军）（＿居）左
75.13aMB	（是以）（偏＿）（将军）（＿居）左
00.000G-	（＿＿）（＿＿）（＿＿）（＿＿）＿
32.10aGC	（是以）（偏＿）（将军）（＿居）左

31.13bFE	while senior generals occupy the right side.
31.13bSK	and senior (general) occupy (right side)
31.13bSC	而上（将军）居右
31.13bTK	and senior (general) (occupy > occupy) (right side)
31.13bTC	而上（将军）（处居）右
31.13bWB	＿上（将军）（＿居）右
31.13bHG	＿上（将军）（处＿）右
31.13bFY	＿上（将军）（处＿）右
75.13bMA	＿上（将军）（＿居）右
75.13bMB	而上（将军）（＿居）右
00.000G-	＿＿（＿＿）（＿＿）＿
32.10bGC	＿上（将军）（＿居）右

31. 140FE　Their places are determined in accord with funeral ceremonies.

31. 140SK　Declare according funeral ceremony occupy their —

31. 140SC　言以丧礼居之也

31. 140TK　Declare place high (force) then according funeral ceremony ((deal with) > occupy) their —

31. 140TC　言居上(势[＿])则以丧礼(处居)之也

31. 140WB　言＿＿＿(＿[＿])＿以丧礼(处＿)之＿

31. 140HG　言＿＿＿(＿[＿])＿以丧礼(处＿)之＿

31. 140FY　言居上(势[势])则以丧礼(处＿)之＿

75. 140MA　言＿＿＿(＿[＿])＿以丧礼(＿居)之也

75. 140MB　言＿＿＿(＿[＿])＿以丧礼(＿居)之也

00. 000G-　＿＿＿＿＿＿(＿[＿])＿＿＿＿＿＿＿＿(＿＿＿)＿＿＿

32. 110GC　言＿＿＿(＿[＿])＿以丧礼(＿居)之也

31. 15aFE　If people were killed,

31. 15aSK　kill people ('s)

31. 15aSC　杀人之

31. 15aTK　((kill; people) > (wilful; murder)) ('s)

31. 15aTC　((杀人)(故杀))之

31. 15aWB　((杀人)(＿＿＿＿))之

31. 15aHG　((杀人)(＿＿＿＿))之

31. 15aFY　((杀人)(＿＿＿＿))＿

75. 15aMA　((杀人)(＿＿＿＿))＿

75. 15aMB　((杀□)(＿＿＿＿))＿

00. 000G-　((＿＿＿＿)(＿＿＿＿))＿

32. 12aGC　((＿＿＿＿)(故杀))□

31. 15bFE   then many will
31. 15bSK   many will
31. 15bSC   众则
31. 15bTK   ((numerous) > many)) will
31. 15bTC   ((众多)众))则
31. 15bWB   ((＿＿)众))＿
31. 15bHG   ((众多)众))＿
31. 15bFY   ((众多)＿))则
75. 15bMA   ((＿＿)众))＿
75. 15bMB   ((＿＿)□))＿
00. 000G-   ((＿＿)＿))＿
32. 12bGC   ((＿＿)□))则

31. 15cFE   attend with sadness.
31. 15cSK   with sadness attend their
31. 15cSC   以(哀悲)莅之
31. 15cTK   with ((sad; compassion) > (mood; sad) > (sad;
             comply) (weep)) (attend > stand) their
31. 15cTC   以((悲哀)(哀悲)(悲依)(泣))莅立)之
31. 15cWB   以((＿＿)(哀悲)(＿＿)(泣))＿＿)之
31. 15cHG   以((悲哀)(＿＿)(＿＿)(泣))＿＿)之
31. 15cFY   以((悲哀)(＿＿)(＿＿)(泣))＿＿)之
75. 15cMA   以((＿＿)(＿＿)(悲依)(＿))＿立)之
75. 15cMB   □((＿＿)(＿＿)(□□)(＿))＿立)□
00. 000G-   ＿((＿＿)(＿＿)(＿＿)(＿))＿＿)＿
32. 12cGC   以((悲哀)(＿＿)(＿＿)(＿))位＿)之

31. 16aFE	Hence, treat battle victories
31. 16aSK	battle victory
31. 16aSC	战胜
31. 16aTK	battle victory those
31. 16aTC	战胜者
31. 16aWB	战胜...
31. 16aHG	战胜...
31. 16aFY	战胜者
75. 16aMA	战胜...
75. 16aMB	□胜...
00. 000G-	--- --- ---
32. 13aGC	战胜...

31. 16bFE	as funeral ceremonies.
31. 16bSK	as with funeral ceremonies treat its
31. 16bSC	而以丧礼处之
31. 16bTK	(as > as) with funeral ceremonies treat claim its —
31. 16bTC	(则而)以丧礼处居之■
31. 16bWB	(___ ___)以丧礼处...之...
31. 16bHG	(则...)以丧礼处...之...
31. 16bFY	(则...)以丧礼处...之...
75. 16bMA	(___ ___)以丧礼处...之...
75. 16bMB	(...而)以丧礼处...之...
00. 000G-	(___ ___) --- --- --- --- --- ---
32. 13bGC	(则...)以丧礼...居之■

Chapter 32

32.010FE	The *Way* is forever *Nameless*.[153]
32.010SK	*Way* forever (*Nameless*)
32.010SC	道恒(无名)
32.010TK	*Way* (constant > forever) ((have not; name) > (missing; name))
32.010TC	道(常恒)((无名)(__ __))
32.010WB	道(常__)((无名)(__ __))
32.100HG	道(常__)((无名)(__ __))`
32.010FY	道(常__)((无名)(__ __))
76.010MA	道(__恒)((无名)(__ __))
76.010MB	道(__恒)((无名)(__ __))
10.010GA	道(__恒)((__ __)(亡名))
00.000G-	__(__ __)((__ __)(__ __))

32.02aFE	It is so simple.
32.02aSK	simple just
32.02aSC	朴唯
32.02aTK	((simple; although) > (master; just) > (simple; just))(small > small)
32.02aTC	((朴虽)(楃唯)(朴唯))(小微)
32.02aWB	((朴虽)(__ __)(__ __))(小__)
32.02aHG	((朴虽)(__ __)(__ __))(小__)
32.02aFY	((朴虽)(__ __)(__ __))(小__)
76.02aMA	((__ __)(楃唯)(__ __))(□__)
76.02aMB	((__ __)(__ __)(朴唯))(小__)
10.02aGA	((朴虽)(__ __)(__ __))(__微)
00.000G-	((__ __)(__ __)(__ __))(__ __)

32.02bFE	Yet, the world should not dare to control it.[154]
32.02bSK	yet (world) not dare control 一
32.02bSC	而（天下）弗敢臣也
32.02bTK	yet ((world) > (world)) (not; dare) > (not; can) > (not; dare)) control 一
32.02bTC	而（天下）（（天地）（不敢）（莫能）（弗敢））臣也
32.02bWB	＿＿（天下）（（＿＿＿）（＿＿＿）（莫能）（＿＿＿））臣也
32.02bHG	＿＿（天下）（（＿＿＿）（不敢）（＿＿＿）（＿＿＿））臣也
32.02bFY	＿＿（天下）（（＿＿＿）（＿＿＿）（莫能）（＿＿＿））臣＿
76.02bMA	□（□□）（（＿＿＿）（＿＿＿）（□＿）（＿＿＿））□□
76.02bMB	而（天下）（（＿＿＿）（＿＿＿）（＿＿＿）（弗敢））臣＿
10.02bGA	＿＿（＿＿＿）（（天地）（＿＿＿）（＿＿＿）（弗敢））臣＿
00.000G-	＿＿（＿＿＿）（（＿＿＿）（＿＿＿）（＿＿＿）（＿＿＿）） ＿＿ ＿＿

32.03aFE	If Marquises and Kings would follow it,[155]
32.03aSK	marquise king if can follow its
32.03aSC	侯王若能守之
32.03aTK	((marquise; king) (king; marquise)) (if > if) can follow its
32.03aTC	（（侯王）（王侯））（若如）能守之
32.03aWB	（（侯王）（＿＿＿））（若＿）能守之
32.03aHG	（（侯王）（＿＿＿））（若＿）能守之
32.03aFY	（（＿＿＿）（王侯））（若＿）能守＿
76.03aMA	（（□王）（＿＿＿））（若＿）能守之
76.03aMB	（（侯王）（＿＿＿））（若＿）能守之
10.03aGA	（（侯王）（＿＿＿））（＿＿如）能守之
00.000G-	（（＿＿＿）（＿＿＿））（＿＿＿） ＿＿ ＿＿

32. 03bFE	then *All-things* would submit themselves.
32. 03bSK	(*All-things*) will themselves submit
32. 03bSC	(万物)将自宾
32. 03bTK	(*All-things*) will themselves submit —
32. 03bTC	(万物)将自宾■
32. 03bWB	(万物)将自宾⎯⎯
32. 03bHG	(万物)将自宾⎯⎯
32. 03bFY	(万物)将自宾⎯⎯
76. 03bMA	(万物)将自宾⎯⎯
76. 03bMB	(万物)将自宾⎯⎯
10. 03bGA	(万物)将自宾■
00. 000G-	(⎯⎯ ⎯⎯)⎯⎯ ⎯⎯ ⎯⎯

32. 040FE	If the *Sky* and the *Earth* would unite with each other,[156]
32. 040SK	*Sky Earth* (each other) unite —
32. 040SC	天地相合也
32. 040TK	*Sky Earth* (each other) (unite > unite) —
32. 040TC	天地相(合谷)也
32. 040WB	天地相(合⎯⎯)⎯⎯
32. 040HG	天地相(合⎯⎯)⎯⎯
32. 040FY	天地相(合⎯⎯)⎯⎯
76. 040MA	天地相(⎯⎯谷)⎯⎯
76. 040MB	天地相(合⎯⎯)⎯⎯
10. 040GA	天地相(合⎯⎯)也
00. 000G-	⎯⎯ ⎯⎯ ⎯⎯(⎯⎯ ⎯⎯)⎯⎯

32. 050FE   then it would rain sweet dew.
32. 050SK   according drop sweet dew
32. 050SC   以降甘露
32. 050TK   according (drop > more > exceed) sweet (dew >
              洛)
32. 050TC   以(降俞逾)甘(露洛)
32. 050WB   以(降＿＿)甘(露＿)
32. 050HG   以(降＿＿)甘(露＿)
32. 050FY   以(降＿＿)甘(露＿)
76. 050MA   以(＿俞＿)甘(＿洛)
76. 050MB   以(＿俞＿)甘(＿洛)
10. 050GA   以(＿＿逾)甘(露＿)
00. 000G-   ＿(＿＿＿) ＿(＿＿)

32. 060FE   People would not have to be ordered, but they
              would balance themselves.
32. 060SK   people not their order but themselves balance
              then
32. 060SC   民莫之令而自均焉
32. 060TK   people not their order but themselves balance
              then
32. 060TC   民莫之令而自均焉
32. 060WB   民莫之令而自均＿
32. 060HG   民莫之令而自均＿
32. 060FY   民莫之令而自均焉
76. 060MA   民莫之□□□□□焉
76. 060MB   □□□令而自均焉
10. 060GA   民莫之令而自均焉
00. 000G-   ＿＿＿＿＿＿＿＿＿＿＿

32.070FE	In an established organisation, titles will appear.
32.070SK	establish organisation appear name
32.070SC	始制有名
32.070TK	establish organisation appear name
32.070TC	始制有名
32.070WB	始制有名
32.070HG	始制有名
32.070FY	始制有名
76.070MA	始制有□
76.070MB	始制有名
10.070GA	始制有名
00.000G-	--- --- --- ---

32.080FE	If titles appear, then know that it is time to stop.
32.080SK	name also already appear those also will know stop
32.080SC	名亦既有夫亦將知止
32.080TK	name also already appear those also will know its stop
32.080TC	名亦既有夫亦將知之止
32.080WB	名亦既有夫亦將知⋯止
32.080HG	名亦既有夫亦將知之⋯
32.080FY	名亦既有夫亦將知⋯止
76.080MA	□□□有夫□□□⋯□
76.080MB	名亦既有夫亦將知⋯止
10.080G-	名亦既有夫亦將知⋯止
00.000G-	--- --- --- --- --- --- --- --- --- ---

32. 090FE Know when to stop and there will be no danger.[157]

32. 090SK know stop (why) not danger

32. 090SC 知止(所以)不殆

32. 090TK know its stop (why) can use not danger

32. 090TC 知之止(所以)可以不殆

32. 090WB 知＿＿止(＿＿＿＿)可以不殆

32. 090HG 知之＿＿(所以)＿＿＿＿不殆

32. 090FY 知＿＿止(所以)＿＿＿＿不殆

76. 090MA □＿＿□(所以)＿＿＿＿不□

76. 090MB 知＿＿止(所以)＿＿＿＿不殆

10. 090GA 知＿＿止(所以)＿＿＿＿不殆

00. 000G- ＿＿＿＿＿＿(＿＿＿＿)＿＿＿＿＿＿＿＿

32. 10aFE The *Way* is to the world,[158]

32. 10aSK like *Way* ('s) at (world) —

32. 10aSC 譬道之在(天下)也

32. 10aTK ((like > (so that) > humble)) *Way* ('s) at (world) —

32. 10aTC ((譬俾卑))道之在(天下)也

32. 10aWB ((譬＿＿＿＿))道之在(天下)＿＿

32. 10aHG ((譬＿＿＿＿))道之在(天下)＿＿

32. 10aFY ((譬＿＿＿＿))道之在(天下)＿＿

76. 10aMA ((＿＿俾＿＿))道之在(□□)□

76. 10aMB ((＿＿＿＿卑))□□在(天下)也

10. 10aGA ((譬＿＿＿＿))道之在(天下)也

00. 000G- ((＿＿＿＿＿＿))＿＿＿＿＿＿(＿＿＿＿)＿＿

32.10bFE	what a valley is to a river,[159]	
32.10bSK	like river valley ('s)	
32.10bSC	犹川浴之	
32.10bTK	(like > □)(river > small)(valley > valley) ('s)	
32.10bTC	(犹□)(川小)(谷浴)之	
32.10bWB	(犹__)(川__)(谷__)之	
32.10bHG	(犹__)(川__)(谷__)之	
32.10bFY	(犹__)(川__)(谷__)之	
76.10bMA	(__□)(__□)(__浴)之	
76.10bMB	(__□)(__小)(__浴)之	
10.10bGA	(犹__)(__小)(__谷)之	
00.000G-	(____)(____)(____)__	

32.10cFE	and what a river is to the sea.[160]	
32.10cSK	and river sea 一	
32.10cSC	与江海也	
32.10cTK	(and > to) river sea (一 > 一)	
32.10cTC	(与于)江海(也■)	
32.10cWB	(__于)江海( )	
32.10cHG	(与__)江海(____)	
32.10cFY	(与__)江海(也__)	
76.10cMA	(与__)江海(也__)	
76.10cMB	(与__)江海(也__)	
10.10cGA	(与__)江海(__■)	
00.000G-	(____)____(____)	

Chapter 33

33.010FE	Those who know other people are wise.
33.010SK	know (other people) those known 一
33.010SC	知人者智也
33.010TK	know (other people) those known 一
33.010TC	知人者智也
33.010WB	知人者智...
33.010HG	知人者智...
33.010FY	知人者智也
77.010MA	知人者知也
77.010MB	知人者知也
00.000G-	--- --- --- --- ---
00.000G-	--- --- --- --- ---

33.020FE	Those who know themselves are brilliant.
33.020SK	themselves know those brilliant 一
33.020SC	自知者明也
33.020TK	themselves know those brilliant 一
33.020TC	自知者明也
33.020WB	自知者明...
33.020HG	自知者明...
33.020FY	自知者明也
77.020MA	自知□□□
77.020MB	自知...明也
00.000G-	--- --- --- --- ---
00.000G-	--- --- --- --- ---

33.030FE	Those who overcome other people have power.
33.030SK	overcome (other people) those have power —
33.030SC	胜人者有力也
33.030TK	overcome (other people) those have power —
33.030TC	胜人者有力也
33.030WB	胜人者有力...
33.030HG	胜人者有力...
33.030FY	胜人者有力也
77.030MA	□□者有力也
77.030MB	胜人者有力也
00.000G-	--- --- --- --- --- ---
00.000G-	--- --- --- --- --- ---

33.040FE	Those who overcome themselves are strong.
33.040SK	themselves overcome those strong —
33.040SC	自胜者强也
33.040TK	themselves overcome those (strong > strong) —
33.040TC	自胜者(强彊)也
33.040WB	自胜者(强...)...
33.040HG	自胜者(强...)...
33.040FY	自胜者(...彊)也
77.040MA	自胜者(□...)□
77.040MB	自胜者(强...)也
00.000G-	--- --- --- (--- ---) ---
00.000G-	--- --- --- (--- ---) ---

33. 050FE	Those who know what is enough are rich. [161]
33. 050SK	know enough those rich —
33. 050SC	知足者富也
33. 050TK	know enough those rich —
33. 050TC	知足者富也
33. 050WB	知足者富__
33. 050HG	知足者富__
33. 050FY	知足者富也
77. 050MA	□□□□也
77. 050MB	知足者富也
00. 000G–	--- --- --- --- ---
00. 000G–	--- --- --- --- ---

33. 060FE	Those who are strong pioneers have ambition.
33. 060SK	strong pioneer have ambition —
33. 060SC	强(行者)有志也
33. 060TK	(strong > strong)(pioneer) have ambition —
33. 060TC	(强彊)(行者)有志也
33. 060WB	(强__)(行者)有志__
33. 060HG	(强__)(行者)有志__
33. 060FY	(__彊)(行者)有志也
77. 060MA	(强__)(行者)有志也
77. 060MB	(强__)(行者)有志也
00. 000G–	(__ __)(__ __) --- --- ---
00. 000G–	(__ __)(__ __) --- --- ---

33. 070FE   Those who do not lose their institutions will last long.

33. 070SK   not lose their institute those (last long) —

33. 070SC   不失其所者久也

33. 070TK   not lose their institute those (last long) —

33. 070TC   不失其所者久也

33. 070WB   不失其所者久＿＿

33. 070HG   不失其所者久＿＿

33. 070FY   不失其所者久也

77. 070MA   不失其所者久也

77. 070MB   不失其所者久也

00. 000G-   ＿＿ ＿＿ ＿＿ ＿＿ ＿＿

00. 000G-   ＿＿ ＿＿ ＿＿ ＿＿ ＿＿

33. 080FE   Those who die, but are not forgotten, will live on.

33. 080SK   die but not (forget those) live —

33. 080SC   死而不(忘者)寿也

33. 080TK   die but not ((missing in battle) (forget those)) live —

33. 080TC   死而不((亡者)(忘者))寿也

33. 080WB   死而不((亡者)(＿＿＿))寿＿＿

33. 080HG   死而不((亡者)(＿＿＿))寿＿＿

33. 080FY   死而不((亡者)(＿＿＿))寿也

77. 080MA   死＿＿不((＿＿＿)(忘者))寿也

77. 080MB   死而不((＿＿＿)(忘者))寿也

00. 000G-   ＿＿＿＿＿ ((＿＿＿)(＿＿＿)) ＿＿＿＿

00. 000G-   ＿＿＿＿＿ ((＿＿＿)(＿＿＿)) ＿＿＿＿

Chapter 34

34. 010FE	The *Way* floats.
34. 010SK	*Way* float —
34. 010SC	道汎呵
34. 010TK	great *Way* (float > float > float) (— > —)
34. 010TC	大道(汎汜渢)(兮呵)
34. 010WB	大道(___氾___)(兮___)
34. 010HG	大道(汎______)(兮___)
34. 010FY	大道(汎______)(兮___)
78. 010MA	___道(______□)(___□)
78. 010MB	___道(______渢)(___呵)
00. 000G-	______ (_________) (______)
00. 000G-	______ (_________) (______)

34. 020FE	It can be unorthodox or orthodox.
34. 020SK	it can left right —
34. 020SC	其可左右也
34. 020TK	it can left right —
34. 020TC	其可左右也
34. 020WB	其可左右___
34. 020HG	其可左右___
34. 020FY	其可左右___
78. 020MA	□□□□□
78. 020MB	其可左右也
00. 000G-	____________
00. 000G-	____________

34.030FE	It completes its affairs successfully.
34.030SK	succeed complete its affair
34.030SC	(成功)遂之事
34.030TK	(*All-things*) (succeed) (rely; complete) its (and > with > affair) live
34.030TC	(万物)(成功)(恃遂)之(而以事)生
34.030WB	(万物)(＿＿)(恃＿)之(而＿＿)生
34.030HG	(万物)(＿＿)(恃＿)之(而＿＿)生
34.030FY	(万物)(＿＿)(恃＿)之(＿以＿)生
78.030MA	(＿＿)(□□)(＿遂)＿(＿＿事)＿
78.030MB	(＿＿)(成功)(＿遂)＿(＿＿□)＿
00.000G-	(＿＿)(＿＿)(＿＿)＿(＿＿)＿
00.000G-	(＿＿)(＿＿)(＿＿)＿(＿＿)＿

34.040FE	Yet, it is not a famous being.
34.040SK	yet not famous being —
34.040SC	而弗名有也
34.040TK	yet (not > not) dismiss (succeed) and not (famous > claim) being —
34.040TC	而(不弗)辞(功成)而不(名居)有也
34.040WB	而(不＿)辞(功成)＿不(名＿)有＿
34.040HG	而(不＿)辞(功成)而不(名＿)有＿
34.040FY	而(不＿)辞(功成)而不(＿居)＿＿
78.040MA	而(＿弗)＿(＿＿)＿＿(名＿)有也
78.040MB	□(＿弗)＿(＿＿)＿＿(名＿)有也
00.000G-	＿(＿＿)＿(＿＿)＿＿(＿＿)＿＿
00.000G-	＿(＿＿)＿(＿＿)＿＿(＿＿)＿＿

34. 05aFE	*All-things* return to it.[162]
34. 05aSK	(*All-things*) return then
34. 05aSC	(万物)归焉
34. 05aTK	((love); support) > (cover; guilt; serve) > (cover; support)) (*All-things*) return then
34. 05aTC	(爱[___])养衣被服衣养(万物)归焉
34. 05aWB	(___[___])_________衣养(万物)_____
34. 05aHG	(爱[愛])养_________(万物)_____
34. 05aFY	(___[___])___衣被服_____(万物)_____
78. 05aMA	(___[___])_____________(万物)归焉
78. 05aMB	(___[___])_____________(万物)归焉
00. 000G-	(___[___])_____________(_____)_____
00. 000G-	(___[___])_____________(_____)_____

34. 05bFE	Yet, it does not act as their master.[163]
34. 05bSK	yet not act master
34. 05bSC	而弗为主
34. 05bTK	yet (not > not) act master
34. 05bTC	而(不弗)为主
34. 05bWB	而(不___)为主
34. 05bHG	而(不___)为主
34. 05bFY	而(不___)为主
78. 05bMA	而(___弗)为主
78. 05bMB	而(___弗)为主
00. 000G-	___(_____)_____
00. 000G-	___(_____)_____

34.060FE   It is always without desire.[164]
34.060SK   will always without desire 一
34.060SC   则恒无欲也
34.060TK   (therefore > will)(always > always) without
            desire 一
34.060TC   (故则)(常恒)无欲也
34.060WB   (＿＿)(常＿)无欲＿
34.060HG   (＿＿)(常＿)无欲＿
34.060FY   (故＿)(常＿)无欲＿
78.060MA   (＿则)(＿恒)无欲也
78.060MB   (＿则)(＿恒)无欲也
00.000G-   (＿＿)(＿＿)＿＿＿
00.000G-   (＿＿)(＿＿)＿＿＿

34.070FE   Hence, it could be named small.
34.070SK   can named as small 一
34.070SC   可名于小矣
34.070TK   can named as small 一
34.070TC   可名于小矣
34.070WD   可名于小＿
34.070HG   可名于小矣
34.070FY   可名于小矣
78.070MA   可名于小＿
78.070MB   可名于小＿
00.000G-   ＿＿＿＿＿
00.000G-   ＿＿＿＿＿

34. 08aFE *All-things* return to it.[165]
34. 08aSK (*All-things*) return then
34. 08aSC （万物）归焉
34. 08aTK (*All-things*) return its then
34. 08aTC （万物）归之焉
34. 08aWB （万物）归＿焉
34. 08aHG （万物）归＿焉
34. 08aFY （万物）归之＿
78. 08aMA （万物）归＿焉
78. 08aMB （万物）归＿焉
00. 000G– （＿＿）＿＿＿
00. 000G– （＿＿）＿＿＿

34. 08bFE Yet, it does not act as their master.[166]
34. 08bSK yet not act master
34. 08bSC 而弗为主
34. 08bTK yet (not > not)(act > know) master
34. 08bTC 而（不弗）（为知）主
34. 08bWB 而（不＿）（为＿）主
34. 08bHG 而（不＿）（为＿）主
34. 08bFY 而（不＿）（＿知）主
78. 08bMA □（＿□）（为＿）主
78. 08bMB 而（＿弗）（为＿）主
00. 000G– ＿（＿＿）（＿＿）＿
00. 000G– ＿（＿＿）（＿＿）＿

34. 090FE   Hence, it could be named great.
34. 090SK   can call as great 一
34. 090SC   可名于大矣
34. 090TK   can ((call; as) > (call; as) > (call; as))
             great 一
34. 090TC   可((名于)(名为)(命于))大矣
34. 090WB   可((＿＿)(名为)(＿＿))大＿
34. 090HG   可((名于)(＿＿)(＿＿))大矣
34. 090FY   可((名于)(＿＿)(＿＿))大矣
78. 090MA   可((名于)(＿＿)(＿＿))大＿
78. 090MB   可((＿＿)(＿＿)(命于))大＿
00. 000G-   ＿((＿＿)(＿＿)(＿＿))＿＿
00. 000G-   ＿((＿＿)(＿＿)(＿＿))＿＿

34. 10aFE   Therefore, sages can achieve greatness,[167]
34. 10aSK   therefore sage can achieve great 一
34. 10aSC   (是以)(圣人)能成大也
34. 10aTK   (therefore)((sage) > (reputable person))('s)
             can achieve they great 一
34. 10aTC   (是以)((圣人)(声人))之能成其大也
00. 000WB   (＿＿)((＿＿)(＿＿))＿＿＿＿
34. 10aHG   (是以)((圣人)(＿＿))＿＿＿＿
34. 10aFY   (是以)((圣人)(＿＿))＿能成其大也
78. 10aMA   (是□)((＿＿)(声人))之能成＿大也
78. 10aMB   (是以)((圣人)(＿＿))之能成＿大也
00. 000G-   (＿＿)((＿＿)(＿＿))＿＿＿＿
00. 000G-   (＿＿)((＿＿)(＿＿))＿＿＿＿

34. 10bFE	because they do not act great.
34. 10bSK	because they not act great —
34. 10bSC	以其不为大也
34. 10bTK	because they all not naturally act great —
34. 10bTC	以其终不自为大也
34. 100WB	以其终不自为大...
34. 10bHG	... ... 终不...为大...
34. 10bFY	以其终不自...大...
78. 10bMA	以其...不...为大也
78. 10bMB	以其...不...为大也
00. 000G-	... ...
00. 000G-	... ...

34. 110FE	Therefore, they can achieve greatness.
34. 110SK	therefore can achieve they great
34. 110SC	故能成其大
34. 110TK	therefore can achieve they great
34. 110TC	故能成其大
34. 110WB	故能成其大
34. 110HG	故能成其大
34. 110FY	故能成其大
78. 110MA	故能成...大
78. 110MB	故能成...大
00. 000G-	... ...
00. 000G-	... ...

Chapter 35

35.010FE	Hold on to the *Great Image* and the world will come.[168]
35.010SK	hold great image (world) come
35.010SC	执大象(天下)往
35.010TK	(hold > plan) great image it (world) come
35.010TC	(执设)大象者(天下)往
35.010WB	(执＿)大象＿(天下)往
35.010HG	(执＿)大象＿(天下)往
35.010FY	(执＿)大象者(天下)往
79.010MA	(执＿)大象＿(□□)往
79.010MB	(执＿)大象＿(天下)往
00.000G-	(＿＿)＿＿＿(＿＿)＿
31.010GC	(＿设)大象＿(天下)往

35.020FE	It will come without harm and with great calm.
35.020SK	come and without harm calm great
35.020SC	往而不害平大
35.020TK	come and without harm 安 calm (great > great > great)
35.020TC	往而不害安平(泰太大)
35.020WB	往而不害安平(＿太＿)
35.020HG	往而不害安平(泰＿＿)
35.020FY	往而不害安平(泰＿＿)
79.020MA	往而不害安平(＿＿大)
79.020MB	往而不害安平(＿＿大)
00.000G-	＿＿＿＿＿＿(＿＿＿)
31.020GC	往而不害安平(＿＿大)

35. 030FE	Music and food will stop passing travellers.
35. 030SK	happy and food pass traveller stop
35. 030SC	乐与饵过客止
35. 030TK	happy and food pass (traveller > arrival) stop
35. 030TC	乐与饵过(客格)止
35. 030WB	乐与饵过(客__)止
35. 030HG	乐与饵过(客__)止
35. 030FY	乐与饵过(客__)止
79. 030MA	乐与饵过(__格)止
79. 030MB	乐与□过(__格)止
00. 000G-	__ __ __ __ (__ __) __
31. 030GC	乐与饵过(客__)止

35. 04aFE	However, words describing the *Way*
35. 04aSK	therefore *Way* ('s) emerge words —
35. 04aSC	故道之出言也
35. 04aTK	therefore *Way* ('s) emerge (mouth > words) —
35. 04aTC	故道之出(口言)也
35. 04aWB	__道之出(口__)__
35. 04aHG	__道之出(口__)__
35. 04aFY	__道之出(__言)__
79. 04aMA	故道之出(__言)也
79. 04aMB	故道之出(__言)也
00. 000G-	__ __ __ __ (__ __) __
31. 04aGC	故□□□(__□)__

35. 04bFE   are called: bland and without taste.
35. 04bSK   call bland — they without taste —
35. 04bSC   曰淡呵其无味也
35. 04bTK   call (discuss > bland) (— > — > —) they
             without taste —
35. 04bTC   曰(谈淡)(乎兮呵)其无味也
35. 04bWB   ...(...淡)(乎......)其无味...
35. 04bHG   ...(...淡)(乎......)其无味...
35. 04bFY   ...(...淡)(...兮...)其无味...
79. 04bMA   曰(谈...)(......呵)其无味也
79. 04bMB   曰(...淡)(......呵)其无味也
00. 000G-   ...(......)(......)..............
31. 04bGC   ...(...淡)(......呵)其无味也

35. 050FE   Look at it, and there is not enough to see.
35. 050SK   look its not enough see —
35. 050SC   视之不足见也
35. 050TK   look its not enough see —
35. 050TC   视之不足见也
35. 050WD   视之不足见...
35. 050HG   视之不足见...
35. 050FY   视之不足见...
79. 050MA   □□不足见也
79. 050MB   视之不足见也
00. 000G-   ....
31. 050GC   视之不足见...

35. 060FE	Listen to it, and there is not enough to hear.
35. 060SK	listen its not enough hear 一
35. 060SC	听之不足闻也
35. 060TK	listen its not enough hear 一
35. 060TC	听之不足闻也
35. 060WB	听之不足闻___
35. 060HG	听之不足闻___
35. 060FY	听之不足闻___
79. 060MA	听之不足闻也
79. 060MB	听之不足闻也
00. 000G-	___ ___ ___ ___ ___ ___
31. 060GC	听之不足闻___

35. 070FE	However, use it and it cannot be depleted.[169]
35. 070SK	use its cannot already 一
35. 070SC	用之(不可)既也
35. 070TK	use its but (cannot) already (一 > 一)
35. 070TC	用之而(不可)既(也■)
35. 070WB	用之___(不可)既(___ ___)
35. 070HG	用之___(不可)既(___ ___)
35. 070FY	用之___(不可)既(___ ___)
79. 070MA	用之___(不可)既(也___)
79. 070MB	用之___(不可)既(也___)
00. 000G-	___ ___ ___(___ ___)___(___ ___)
31. 070GC	___ ___而(不可)既(也■)

Chapter 36

36.01aFE	To fold something,
36.01aSK	will want fold its
36.01aSC	将欲翕之
36.01aTK	will want (fold > fold > collect) its
36.01aTC	将欲(翕歙拾)之
36.01aWB	将欲(＿歙＿)之
36.01aHG	将欲(翕＿＿)之
36.01aFY	将欲(翕＿＿)之
80.01aMA	将欲(＿＿拾)之
80.01aMB	将欲(翕＿＿)之
00.000G–	＿＿(＿＿＿)＿
00.000G–	＿＿(＿＿＿)＿

36.01bFE	it must have been unfolded before.[170]
36.01bSK	must ancient unfold its
36.01bSC	必古张之
36.01bTK	must ((original) > ancient)) unfold its
36.01bTC	必((固古))张之
36.01bWB	必((固＿))张之
36.01bHG	必((固＿))张之
36.01bFY	必((固＿))张之
80.01bMA	必((＿古))张之
80.01bMB	必((＿古))张之
00.000G–	＿((＿＿))＿＿
00.000G–	＿((＿＿))＿＿

36.02aFE To weaken something,
36.02aSK will want weak its
36.02aSC 将欲弱之
36.02aTK will want weak its
36.02aTC 将欲弱之
36.02aWB 将欲弱之
36.02aHG 将欲弱之
36.02aFY 将欲弱之
80.02aMA 将欲弱之
80.02aMB 将欲弱之
00.000G- --- --- --- ---
00.000G- --- --- --- ---

36.02bFE it must have been strengthened before.[171]
36.02bSK must ancient strong its
36.02bSC 必古强之
36.02bTK must ((of course) > ancient)) — (strong > strong) its
36.02bTC 必((固古))■(强彊)之
36.02bWB 必((固⎽⎽))⎽⎽(强⎽⎽)之
36.02bHG 必((固⎽⎽))⎽⎽(强⎽⎽)之
36.02bFY 必((固⎽⎽))⎽⎽(⎽⎽彊)之
80.02bMA □((⎽⎽□))⎽⎽(强⎽⎽)之
80.02bMB 必((⎽⎽古))■(强⎽⎽)之
00.000G- ⎽⎽((⎽⎽⎽⎽))⎽⎽(⎽⎽⎽⎽)⎽⎽
00.000G- ⎽⎽((⎽⎽⎽⎽))⎽⎽(⎽⎽⎽⎽)⎽⎽

36.03aFE   To abandon something,
36.03aSK   will want reject its
36.03aSC   将欲去之
36.03aTK   will want (reject > reject) its
36.03aTC   将欲(废去)之
36.03aWB   将欲(废___)之
36.03aHG   将欲(废___)之
36.03aFY   将欲(废___)之
80.03aMA   将欲(___去)之
80.03aMB   将欲(___去)之
00.000G-   ___ ___ (___ ___) ___
00.000G-   ___ ___ (___ ___) ___

36.03bFE   it must have been attached before.
36.03bSK   must ancient together its
36.03bSC   必古与之
36.03bTK   must ((of course) > ancient))(prosper >
            together) its
36.03bTC   必((固古)(兴与))之
36.03bWB   必((固___)(兴___))之
36.03bHG   必((固___)(兴___))之
36.03bFY   必((固___)(兴___))之
80.03bMA   必((___古)(___与))之
80.03bMB   必((___古)(___与))之
00.000G-   ___ ((___ ___)(___ ___)) ___
00.000G-   ___ ((___ ___)(___ ___)) ___

36. 04aFE	To seize something,
36. 04aSK	will wants seize its
36. 04aSC	将欲夺之
36. 04aTK	will wants seize its
36. 04aTC	将欲夺之
36. 04aWB	将欲夺之
36. 04aHG	将欲夺之
36. 04aFY	将欲夺之
80. 04aMA	将欲夺之
80. 04aMB	将欲夺之
00. 000G-	--- --- ---
00. 000G-	--- --- ---

36. 04bFE	it must have been separated before.
36. 04bSK	must ancient give its
36. 04bSC	必古予之
36. 04bTK	must ((of course) > ancient)) (give > give) its
36. 04bTC	必((固古))(与予)之
36. 04bWB	必((固...))(与...)之
36. 04bHG	必((固...))(与...)之
36. 04bFY	必((固...))(与...)之
80. 04bMA	必((...古))(...予)之
80. 04bMB	必((...古))(...予)□
00. 000G-	---((... ---))(--- ---) ---
00. 000G-	---((... ---))(--- ---) ---

36.050FE   This is called profound brilliance.
36.050SK   is call profound brilliance
36.050SC   是谓微明
36.050TK   is (call) profound brilliance
36.050TC   是(谓[＿])微明
36.050WB   是(谓[＿])微明
36.050HG   是(谓[＿])微明
36.050FY   是(谓[＿])微明
80.050MA   是(谓[胃])微明
80.050MB   是(谓[胃])微明
00.000G-   ＿(＿[＿])＿＿
00.000G-   ＿(＿[＿])＿＿

36.060FE   The soft and weak will overcome the strong.
36.060SK   soft weak overcome strong
36.060SC   柔弱胜强
36.060TK   soft its (overcome) strong weak its overcome
            ((unyielding) > strong > strong)
36.060TC   柔之(胜[＿])刚弱之胜(刚强)(彊强)
36.060WB   柔＿(＿[＿])＿弱＿胜(刚强)(＿＿)
36.060HG   柔＿(＿[＿])＿弱＿胜(刚强)(＿＿)
36.060FY   柔之(胜[勝])刚弱之胜(＿＿)(彊＿)
80.060MA   友＿(＿[＿])＿弱＿胜(＿＿)(＿强)
80.060MB   柔＿(＿[＿])＿弱＿胜(＿＿)(＿强)
00.000G-   ＿＿(＿[＿])＿＿＿(＿＿)(＿＿)
00.000G-   ＿＿(＿[＿])＿＿＿(＿＿)(＿＿)

36.070FE	A fish should not leave the deep water.
36.070SK	fish (should not) leave from deep
36.070SC	鱼(不可)脱于渊
36.070TK	fish ((should not) > not)) (happy > leave > persuade) from deep
36.070TC	鱼((不可)不))(悦脱说)于渊
36.070WB	鱼((不可)＿＿))(＿＿脱＿＿)于渊
36.070HG	鱼((不可)＿＿))(悦＿＿＿＿)于渊
36.070FY	鱼((不可)＿＿))(悦＿＿＿＿)于渊
80.070MA	鱼((＿＿＿＿)不))(脱＿＿＿＿)于渊
80.070MB	鱼((不可)＿＿))(＿＿＿＿说)于渊
00.000G-	＿＿((＿＿＿＿)＿＿))(＿＿＿＿＿＿)＿＿＿＿
00.000G-	＿＿((＿＿＿＿)＿＿))(＿＿＿＿＿＿)＿＿＿＿

36.080FE	The sharp weapons of the State should not be used in view of the people.[172]
36.080SK	state ('s) (sharp weapon) (should not) use see people
36.080SC	邦之(利器)(不可)以示人
36.080TK	(state > state) ('s) (sharp weapon) (should not) use (show > see) people
36.080TC	(国邦)之(利器)(不可)以(示视)人
36.080WB	(国＿＿)之(利器)(不可)以(示＿＿)人
36.080HG	(国＿＿)之(利器)(不可)以(示＿＿)人
36.080FY	(＿＿邦)之(利器)(不可)以(示＿＿)人
80.080MA	(＿＿邦)＿＿(利器)(不可)以(＿＿视)人
80.080MB	(国＿＿)＿＿(利器)(不可)以(示＿＿)人
00.000G-	(＿＿＿＿)＿＿(＿＿＿＿)(＿＿＿＿＿＿)＿＿(＿＿＿＿)＿＿
00.000G-	(＿＿＿＿)＿＿(＿＿＿＿)(＿＿＿＿＿＿)＿＿(＿＿＿＿)＿＿

Chapter 37

37.01aFE	The *Way* is forever *Nameless*.[173]
37.01aSK	*Way* forever *Nameless* —
37.01aSC	道恒（无名）也
37.01aTK	*Way* (constant > forever) ((*Non-action*) > (*Nameless*) > (*Non-action*)) —
37.01aTC	道（常恒）（（无为）（无名）（亡为））也
37.01aWB	道（常＿）（（无为）（＿＿）（＿＿））＿
37.01aHG	道（常＿）（（无为）（＿＿）（＿＿））＿
37.01aFY	道（常＿）（（无为）（＿＿）（＿＿））＿
81.010MA	道（＿恒）（（＿＿）（无名）（＿＿））＿
81.010MB	道（＿恒）（（＿＿）（无名）（＿＿））＿
07.01aGA	道（＿恒）（（＿＿）（＿＿）（亡为））也
00.000G-	＿（＿＿）（（＿＿）（＿＿）（＿＿））＿

37.01bFE	*Non-existence* and *Non-action*.[174]
37.01bSK	and *Non-existence* (*Non-action*)
37.01bSC	而无（不为）
37.01bTK	and *Non-existence* (*Non-action*)
37.01bTC	而无（不为）
37.01bWB	而无（不为）
37.01bHG	而无（不为）
37.01bFY	而无（不为）
00.000MA	＿＿（＿＿）
00.000MB	＿＿（＿＿）
00.000G-	＿＿（＿＿）
00.000G-	＿＿（＿＿）

37.02aFE   If Marquises and Kings could follow it,[175]
37.02aSK   marquise King if can follow its
37.02aSC   侯王若能守之
37.02aTK   ((marquise; King) > (King; marquise)) if can
            follow its
37.02aTC   ((侯王)(王侯))若能守之
37.02aWB   ((侯王)(＿＿))若能守之
37.02aHG   ((侯王)(＿＿))若能守之
37.02aFY   ((＿＿)(王侯))若能守＿
81.02aMA   ((侯王)(＿＿))若＿守之
81.02aMB   ((侯王)(＿＿))若能守之
07.02aGA   ((侯王)(＿＿))＿能守之
00.000G-   ((＿＿)(＿＿))＿＿＿

37.02bFE   then *All-things* would transform themselves.
37.02bSK   then *All-things* would themselves reform
37.02bSC   而(万物)将自化
37.02bTK   then (*All-things*) would themselves reform
37.02bTC   而(万物)将自化
37.02bWB   ＿(万物)将自化
37.02bHG   ＿(万物)将自化
37.02bFY   ＿(万物)将自化
81.02bMA   ＿(万物)将自化
81.02bMB   ＿(万物)将自化
07.02bGA   而(万物)将自化
00.000G-   ＿(＿＿)＿＿

37.03aFE   If this transformation would cause desire,
37.03aSK   reform and desire cause
37.03aSC   化而欲作
37.03aTK   reform and desire cause □□□
37.03aTC   化而欲作□□□
37.03aWB   化而欲作﹍﹍﹍
37.03aHG   化而欲作﹍﹍﹍
37.03aFY   化而欲作﹍﹍﹍
81.03aMA   化而欲□□□□
81.03aMB   化而欲作﹍﹍﹍
07.03aGA   化而欲作﹍﹍﹍
00.000G-   ﹍﹍﹍﹍﹍﹍

37.03bFE   then I would suppress it by using the
            simplicity of the *Nameless*.[176]
37.03bSK   I will suppress its use *Nameless* ('s) simple
37.03bSC   吾将镇之以(无名)之朴
37.03bTK   I will (suppress > fill) its use ((*Nameless*) >
            (missing; name)) ('s) simple
37.03bTC   吾将(镇阗)之以(无名)亡名之朴
37.03bWB   吾将(镇﹍)之以(无名)﹍﹍之朴
37.03bHG   吾将(镇﹍)之以(无名)﹍﹍之朴
37.03bFY   吾将(镇﹍)之以(无名)﹍﹍之朴
81.03bMA   □□(﹍□)之以(无名)﹍﹍之﹍
81.03bMB   吾将(﹍阗)之以(无名)﹍﹍之朴
07.03bGA   ﹍将(镇﹍)之以(﹍﹍)亡名之朴
00.000G-   ﹍﹍(﹍﹍)﹍﹍(﹍﹍)﹍﹍﹍

37.04aFE	Suppressing it by using the simplicity of the *Nameless*[177]
37.04aSK	suppress its use (*Nameless*) ('s) (simple
37.04aSC	镇之以(无名)之朴
37.04aTK	((suppress > (fill; fill)) its use (*Nameless*) master ('s) (simple > master)
37.04aTC	((镇阗阗))之以(无名)椢之朴椢
37.04aWB	((___ ___))___ ___(无名)___之朴___
37.04aHG	((___ ___))___ ___(无名)___之朴___
37.04aFY	((___ ___))___ ___(无名)___之朴___
81.04aMA	((___ ___))___ ___(无名)椢之___椢
81.04aMX	((镇___ ___))之以(无名)___之朴___
81.04aMB	((___阗阗))___以(无名)___之朴___
00.000G	((___ ___))___ ___(___ ___)___ ___ ___
00.000G−	((___ ___))___ ___(___ ___)___ ___ ___

37.04bFE	will not disgrace them.
37.04bSK	them will not disgrace
37.04bSC	夫将不辱
37.04bTK	them also will (not > not > not)((desire > disgrace > (know; enough))
37.04bTC	夫亦将(不无不)((欲辱(知足))
37.04bWB	夫亦将(___无___)((欲___(___ ___))
37.04bHG	___亦将(不___ ___)((欲___(___ ___))
37.04bFY	夫亦将(不___ ___)((欲___(___ ___))
81.04bMA	夫___将(___ ___不)((___辱(___ ___))
81.04bMB	夫___将(___ ___不)((___辱(___ ___))
07.040GA	夫亦将(___ ___ ___)((___ ___(知足))
00.000G−	___ ___ ___(___ ___ ___)((___ ___(___ ___))

37. 05aFE	Use tranquillity without disgrace
37. 05aSK	without disgrace use tranquil
37. 05aSC	不辱以静
37. 05aTK	without (desire > disgrace > knowledge) use (tranquil > tranquil > passion)
37. 05aTC	不(欲辱智)以(静靖情)
37. 05aWB	不(欲＿＿)以(静＿＿)
37. 05aHG	不(欲＿＿)以(静＿＿)
37. 05aFY	不(欲＿＿)以(＿靖＿)
81. 05aMA	不(＿辱＿)以(＿＿情)
81. 05aMB	不(＿辱＿)以(静＿＿)
07. 05aGA	＿(＿＿智)以(静＿＿)
00. 000G–	＿(＿＿＿)＿(＿＿＿)

37. 05bFE	and the world will regulate itself.[178]
37. 05bSK	world will itself regulate
37. 05bSC	(天地)将自正
37. 05bTK	((world) > (world)) (*All-things*) will itself (regulate > order) —
37. 05bTC	((天下)(天地)(万物))将自(正定)■
37. 05bWB	((天下)(＿＿)(＿＿))将自(＿定)＿
37. 05bHG	((天下)(＿＿)(＿＿))将自(正＿)＿
37. 05bFY	((天下)(＿＿)(＿＿))将自(正＿)＿
81. 05bMA	((＿＿)(天地)(＿＿))将自(正＿)＿
81. 05bMB	((＿＿)(天地)(＿＿))将自(正＿)＿
07. 05bGA	((＿＿)(＿＿)(万物))将自(＿定)■
00. 000G–	((＿＿)(＿＿)(＿＿))＿＿(＿＿)＿

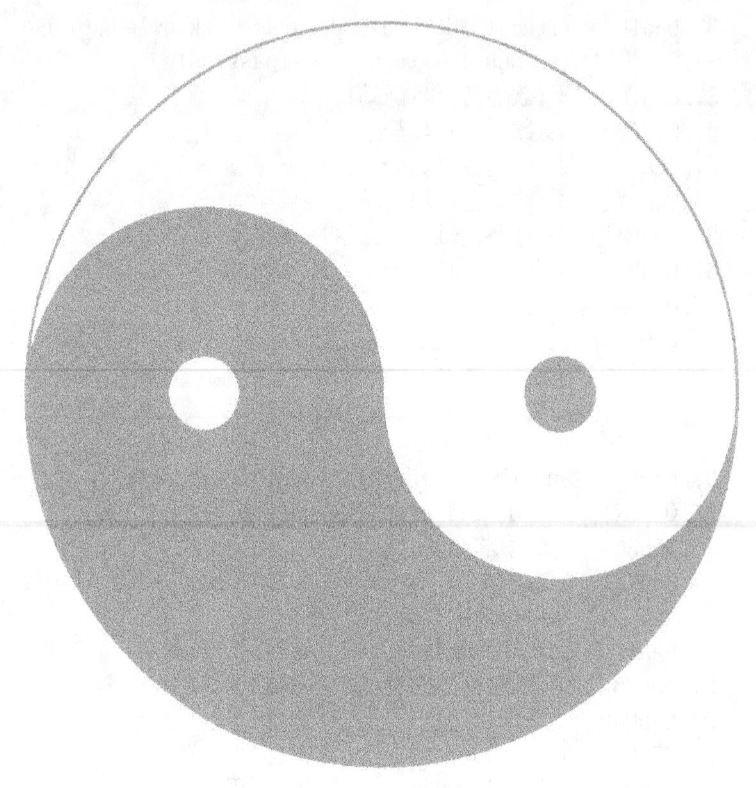

Yin-Yang

APPENDIX

INDEX

abandon..92, 273

above... 105

accept... 92

accountant.. 204

accumulate.. 73

achieve.. 77, 134, 243, 265, 266

action...38, 47, 54, 55, 71, 82, 83, 185, 188, 189, 203, 225, 230, 262, 264, 266, 321, 322

admire.. 42, 76

adoration..140, 324

affair..36, 134, 166, 178, 179, 261

after... 35

agreement..321, 323

alive... 119

All-things...19, 26, 37, 49, 54, 66, 122, 251, 261, 262, 264, 278, 281, 306

ambiguity.. 14, 16, 17, 20

ambition..45, 258

anarchy... 47

ancestor... 49

ancient....12, 14, 15, 16, 110, 112, 165, 173, 271, 272, 273, 274

Ancients..112, 173

arms are bared..321, 323

army... 230, 231, 237, 239, 240

arrogance.. 76, 126, 172, 184, 233

attach... 273

attack..233, 241

baby... 151

back... 109

bad..32, 231

bagpipe... 56

balance... 252

bamboo counting sticks.. 204

beauty... 31

before... 35

begin..324
behind.. 63, 231
bend... 167, 173
beneficial....................... 54, 55, 66, 69, 88, 136, 140, 141, 324
benevolence.................................. 320, 321, 323, 324
big.. 150, 231
black..215
blend...50
blind...89
boast...172, 184, 232
body... 93, 96, 97, 98, 99
bone...46
born...187
break...221
bright..89
brilliant....................... 125, 171, 183, 208, 256, 275
bureaucracy.. 139, 323
burglar...142
careful...114
carriage...85
caught... 103
certain..155
chariot..200
child..52, 151, 311
China......................................12, 327, 333, 335, 337
Chinese..................15, 16, 17, 20, 21, 24, 327, 329, 331, 358
Chu...12
claim...............36, 39, 67, 122, 194, 234, 238, 248, 261
clay..86
clear.. 118, 154
clever.. 137, 142
cleverness..323
cold...226
collective mindmode..325
colour...89
compassion................................ 138, 141, 247, 324

competent...75, 79, 112, 147, 203, 204, 205, 206, 207, 209, 231

complexity............ 15

computer-assisted... 21

Confucius 319

confused... ....139, 155, 156, 169, 210, 323

consistent... ....21, 22

constant... .... 25, 125, 126, 127, 213, 216, 219, 249, 277

context... .... 13, 17, 18, 20, 21, 22, 325

continuous............190, 191

control... ....70, 250

conundrum............ 18

corps de esprit... 78

cosmological... 327

country............80, 194

cup............ 86

cycle............ 18, 22

danger... .... 130, 188, 254

Dao De Jing...12, 13, 14, 15, 16, 17, 20, 21, 319, 327, 329, 331, 333, 335, 337, 338, 358

dare............ 47, 232, 250

deaf............ 89

decay... 227

deep............49, 68, 113, 276

defend... 75

deplete............ 270

desire...27, 28, 38, 43, 46, 119, 120, 145, 159, 186, 223, 229, 238, 241, 263, 279, 280, 281

desolate............ 187

detail............27, 30, 57, 112, 211

develop... .... 84, 172, 184

diamond............ 20

dictionary............ 21

die............259

different... ....29, 148, 159, 321

difficult... .... 33, 42, 91, 114, 116, 189

dim... ....108, 160, 161, 162

discard... 140, 141, 142, 146

disgrace... 93, 94, 95, 218, 280, 281

disharmony... 138

disorder... 50, 139, 323, 324

display... 43, 171, 183

dissatisfy... 147

dissipating... 116

distress... 93, 94, 95

distrust... 133, 181

divide... 222

door... 87

dust... 51

dwelling... 68

ear... 89

Earth...26, 54, 56, 59, 61, 176, 177, 187, 193, 194, 195, 251, 320

easy... 33, 226

elusive... 108, 160, 161, 162

Emperor... 53

empty... 44, 48, 56, 117, 121, 168, 174, 187

endure... 61

energy... 163, 164, 224

English... 3, 16, 17, 20, 21, 24, 327, 346, 347

enough... 133, 143, 152, 181, 219, 220, 258, 269, 270, 280, 321

escape... 19, 316

eternal... 25, 213, 214, 216, 217, 219, 220

excess... 234

exhausted... 56, 57, 120, 168

exist... 52, 60, 131

Existence... 19, 33, 88, 110, 306, 337

exploit... 84

extravagance... 228

extreme... 74, 121, 155, 228

eye... 89, 92

fail... 72, 225, 226

fame... 261

family... 138, 323

Father of the Multitude..165, 166
father...165, 166
favour...93, 94, 95, 179
fear...132, 148
female...59, 81, 212
filial piety...138, 141, 324
fill...45, 73, 75, 168
firm...182
first...63, 358
fish...276
flattery..146
flavour...90
fold...271
food..159, 185, 268
force.................................13, 190, 229, 234, 246, 318, 323
forever.........................35, 60, 129, 177, 191, 249, 277
formation..337
fortune...76
forward...182
foundation..197, 201
Fu Yi...21, 24, 331
fullness..119, 120
funeral...244, 246, 248
gates of nature...81
generals...245
generate...38, 82, 83
give..69, 274, 321
glare..51
gold...75, 167
good......................................32, 58, 66, 68, 69, 70, 71, 73
goods...42, 91
great...93, 96, 131, 136, 137, 160, 190, 192, 193, 194, 198, 210,
   222, 228, 238, 240, 260, 265, 266, 267, 323
Greatnesses...194
grow...227, 230
guest house...199
guest...115, 199

Guodian... .... 15, 21, 24, 337, 338

hammer... 74

happiness...180

hard... 60

harm 91, 120, 168, 267

harmony... 35

harvest... 231

head..109

hear... .... 102, 270

heart... 58

Heaven... 18

heavy..197

He-Shang Gong... 329

hesitant... 115

high... .... 34, 175, 176, 246

hold... .... 115, 170, 225, 267

holistic... .... 15, 20

home...59

honour...171, 183, 244

hot...226

household..323

hub... 85

hunting... 90

hypocrisy...137, 141, 323

I...52, 96, 97, 122, 151, 153, 154, 155, 156, 158, 159, 166, 189, 190, 223, 279, 311

image..161

inaudible...102

incompetent...209

independent...188

indifferent... 156

infant...79, 151, 214

inferior..321

infinite..106

information...164

initiate... 37

inkblot... 14

inside...................................58, 64, 161, 162, 164, 194
institution...144, 259
insubstantial... 103
insult... 132
interfere...223, 224
invisible...52, 101
jade.. 75
justice..............................136, 320, 321, 322, 323, 324
kaleidoscope.. 15
key... 204
keyword..21, 24
kill...242, 243, 246
kind.. 121
King Canute.. 325
King...128, 193, 194, 250, 278
know...41, 46, 47, 52, 80, 81, 82, 110, 112, 113, 125, 126, 127, 131, 137, 140, 146, 166, 189, 210, 212, 215, 218, 253, 254, 256, 258, 264, 280, 281, 311, 323, 324, 358
lack...145, 153, 169
Lao Zi...12, 13, 14, 15, 19, 20, 21, 306, 316, 319, 320, 323, 324, 325, 327, 329, 331, 333, 335, 337, 338
lead...131, 222, 229
left...229, 238, 244, 245, 260
Li Erh.. 12
life..62, 130
light...105, 197, 201
limit... 28
listen..57, 102, 270
live...62, 259, 261
location.. 68
long.. 34
look...101, 144, 182, 269
lord.. 200
loss.............................76, 95, 153, 179, 180, 201, 202, 225, 259
love..80, 99, 131, 210, 262, 320
low..34, 105, 132, 201
loyalty... 324

male...212

many... 30, 57, 67, 247

Marquis.. 250, 278

master................................ 116, 221, 249, 262, 264, 280

Mawangdui............................... 15, 21, 331, 333, 335, 358

memory..344

merge........................... 51, 85, 104, 117, 178, 179, 180, 187

merit.. 77, 134, 172, 184

meta-analysis..21

metaphor..14

metaphysical...327

meta-translation...20

mind...44, 90, 154

misfortune... 76, 126, 237, 239

moderate..217

modesty..144

Mother...26, 132, 159

move...57, 71, 182

much...147, 148, 152, 169, 234

mud... 117, 118

music..268

Mysterious Female..59

mystery... 30, 79

name...25, 26, 29, 101, 102, 103, 106, 165, 189, 190, 249, 253, 263, 265, 279

Nameless...26, 249, 277, 279, 280

nature............69, 77, 81, 128, 129, 135, 175, 196, 266, 320, 358

neighbour..115

nemonik thinking..325

Non-action.. 36, 47, 80, 277

Non-Existence...................... 19, 33, 85, 86, 87, 88, 277, 306, 337

Nothingness... 107, 108

objective mindmode..325

obscure..163

obtain.. 19, 42, 91, 178, 180, 316

One...................................19, 78, 104, 105, 170, 306, 337

order................................. 70, 87, 110, 124, 125, 167, 252, 281 organisation...222, 253

origin...13, 26, 59, 110, 189, 318, 337

orthodox...239, 260

outside... 64

overcome...257, 275

passion... 281

people...41, 42, 43, 44, 46, 55, 67, 69, 80, 89, 90, 91, 135, 140, 141, 144, 154, 155, 159, 177, 193, 194, 206, 207, 209, 229, 242, 243, 246, 252, 256, 257, 276, 358

perish... 236

physics... 13, 19, 20, 306, 325

pictograph... 14, 15, 16, 17, 18, 20, 21, 24, 333, 335

plan... 115, 134, 267

plenty... 321

possess...38, 83, 238, 323, 324

power...232, 257

praise... 131

predict... 151

prepare... 344

preserve... 167, 173, 174

principle... 13, 111, 318

profound virtue... 84

propriety... 320, 321, 322, 323, 324

psychology... 13

pure...197, 218

purpose...98, 99, 152, 158, 321, 322

rain... 176

rash...197, 202

rational... 15

rebuke... 146

receive...95, 169

refill... 48

regard...171, 183

reject...40, 92, 136, 140, 141, 142, 207, 208, 228, 273, 323, 324

religious... 327

rely...38, 83, 261

renew...120, 168

resource..208, 209, 210

respect... .... 194, 244

rest...157

return...107, 122, 123, 124, 125, 141, 152, 174, 191, 214, 217, 220, 262, 264, 324

revolt..43

rich..258

right.......................................139, 239, 244, 245, 260

righteousness................................... 141, 324

River Sage... 329

river... 114, 255

root... .... 123, 124

Rorschach test.....................................14

rule...44, 70, 80, 91

sacred..14

sacrificial feast... 150

sad...247

sage.............................36, 44, 55, 63, 91, 170, 206, 221, 228, 265

satisfaction...................................147, 241, 242

save... .... 206, 207

saying... ....94, 96, 174

sea... 157, 255

see..27, 28, 101, 109, 223, 269, 276

seek... .... 19, 316

seize... 103, 274

selfish... 65, 145

selfless...65

separate..274

sequence...........................15, 333, 335, 337, 358

shapeless..107

sharp... .... 50, 74, 241, 276

shepherd..170

short...34

simple... ....116, 144, 220, 221, 249, 279, 280

sincerity... 324

skill...70

Sky............26, 54, 56, 59, 61, 176, 177, 187, 192, 195, 251, 320

small...112, 249, 255, 263
smooth...50, 101
snow.. 116
Socrates.. 322
soft...51, 79, 275
soldier..229, 239
solemn.. 115
sovereign.. 197, 202, 240
speak...37, 69, 134, 175, 203
spoke.. 85
springtime.. 150
Ssu-ma Ch'ien.. 12
stage... 150
State.. 139, 201, 243, 276, 323
steal... 42
stir..118, 119
stomach.. 45, 91
stop.. 47, 73, 149, 231, 253, 254, 268
storm.. 175
straight... 167
straw dogs... 54, 55
stream...212, 213
strength... 46, 272, 344
stress 344
strict... 155
stride.. 182
string.. 205
strive... 41, 66, 71, 173
strong... 46, 227, 235, 257, 258, 272, 275
stubborn... 158
stupid fool... 154
subjectivity... 20
substance.. 13, 105, 318
success............................. 39, 134, 186, 226, 231, 232, 233, 234, 261
suffer... 19, 93, 95, 96, 97, 316
superior...66, 321, 322, 323
surplus...153, 169

synonym... 21
take... 223, 232
teach... 37, 209, 210
team spirit... 78
ten... 200
thief... 142
thin... 324
thinking... 68, 344
thorny bushes... 230
Three... 19, 306
timing... 71
tiptoe... 182
tired... 152
title... 253
tone... 35, 89
tool... 221, 237, 239, 240
tranquil... 66, 71, 118, 121, 124, 163, 197, 281
translation... 3, 16, 17, 18, 20, 21, 22, 327, 346, 347, 358
travel... 152, 198, 203, 268
trust... 98, 100, 133, 181
truth... 69, 164, 174, 181
twist... 167
Two... 19, 306, 337
ugly... 31
uncertain... 156
unchanging... 188
unfold... 271
universe... 12, 13, 194, 318, 320, 337
unorthodox... 238, 260
untangle... 50
use...48, 57, 60, 80, 82, 85, 86, 87, 88, 110, 118, 119, 143, 204, 221, 229, 232, 239, 240, 241, 254, 270, 276, 279, 280, 281, 321
vague... 116
Valley Spirit... 59
valley... 59, 117, 218, 219, 255
victory... 248

village... 150

violent... ....175, 176

virtue...160, 178, 179, 180, 213, 214, 216, 217, 219, 220, 320,
321, 322, 324

vital energy... 79

voice... .... 35, 140

void... 105

wagon... 198

Wang Bi... ....24, 327, 329, 333, 335, 337

warden... 204

water... .... 66, 114, 276

Way of Gentlemen... .... 319, 320, 321, 324, 325

Way of Nature... .... 13, 77, 319, 320, 321, 322, 323, 324, 325

Way of People... .... 13, 319, 320, 321, 324

Way...25, 48, 67, 77, 110, 111, 112, 119, 123, 129, 136, 160,
178, 179, 180, 185, 186, 189, 192, 195, 196, 229, 235, 236,
238, 249, 254, 260, 268, 277, 358

weak... .... 45, 227, 235, 272, 275

weakness... 344

wealth... 76

weapon... ....241, 276

weaver... 205

white... 215

window... 87

winter... 114

wisdom... 12

wise... 256

withdraw... 77

words... 268

working... ....60, 70, 337

world...31, 98, 99, 100, 170, 173, 189, 212, 213, 215, 216, 218,
219, 223, 224, 229, 250, 254, 267, 281

Yang... 358

Yellow River... 329

BIBLIOGRAPHY

Blakney, R. B. (1955). *The Way of Life—Lao Tzu.* Penguin Books Ltd., Ontario, Canada.

Breuilly, E. (1996). *See: Palmer, M.*

Bynner, W. (1986). *The Way of Life According to Lao Zi.* The Berkley Publishing Group, New York.

Carus, P. (1999). *The Teachings of Lao-Tzu: The Tao-Te Ching.* Random House. London.

Chan Wing-Tsit. (1988). *The Way of Lao Tzu (Tao-te ching).* New York: Macmillan Publishing Company.

Chen Zhu. (1929). *See: Zhu Chen.*

Cheng Gia-Fu and English, J. (1972). *Lao Tzu: Tao Te Ching.* New York: Vintage Books.

Cleary, T. (1998). *The Essential Tao.* Castle Books. New Jersey.

Confucius. (1979). *The Analects.* (B. Radice, Ed., & D. C. Lau, Trans.) Middlesex, England: Penguin Books.

Ding Yuanzhi. (1998). *Guodian zhujian Laozi shixi yu yanjiu.* Taibei: Wanjuanlou.

Donglaixiansheng. (1965). *Yin zhu he shang gong lao zi dao de jing.* Tai bei shi: Yi wen.

Duyvendak, J. J. L. (1954). *Tao Te Ching: The Book of the Way and Its Virtue.* London: John Murray.

English, J. (1972). *See: Cheng Gia-Fu.*

Feng Wu. (2012). *Wang Bi.* Kunming Shi: Yunnan jiao yu chu ban she.

Fu Huisheng. (1992). *Lao Zi.* Hunan Publishing House.

Fu Yi. (555-639 AD). *See: Appendix / Chinese versions Dao De Jing / Fu Yi.*

Fung Yu-lan. (1983). *See: Bodde, D.*

Gia-Fu Cheng. (1972). *See: Cheng Gia-Fu.*

Giles, H. A. (1886). *The Remains of Lao Tzu.* London: John Murray.

Gong He-Shang. (179-157 BC). *See: He-Shang Gong.*

Griffith, S. B. (1971). *Sun Tzu: The Art of War.* Oxford University Press.

Guanghui Jiang. (1999). *Guodian chujian yanjiu .* Shenyang Shi: Liaoning jiao yu chu ban she.

Guodian. (~300 BC). *See: Appendix / Chinese versions Dao De Jing / Guodian.*

Hao Peng. (1998). *Guodian-Chu-mu-zhujian.* Beijing: Wenwu Chubanshe.

Henricks, R. G. (1993). *Lao-Tzu: Te-Tao Ching.* The modern library, New York.

Henricks, R. G. (2000). *Lao Tzu's Tao Te Ching.* New York: Columbia University Press.

He-Shang Gong. (179-157 BC). *See: Appendix / Chinese versions Dao De Jing / He-Shang Gong.*

Holloway, K. W. (2009). *Guodian: the newly discovered seeds of Chinese religious and political philosophy.* New York: Oxford University Press.

Hubeisheng Jingmenshi bowuguan. (1998). *Guodian Chumu zhujian.* Beiing: Wenwu Press.

Huisheng Fu. (1992). *See: Fu Huisheng.*

Jianfeng Zhan. (1982). *See: Zhan Jianfeng.*

Jiang Guanghui. (1999). *See: Guanghui Jiang.*

Jingmen shi bo wu guan. (1998). *Guodian chu mu zhu jian.* Beijing: Wen wu chu ban she.

Ju-chou Yang. (1987). *See: Yang Ju-chou.*

Kangsheng Xu. (1985). *See: Xu Kangsheng.*

Kohn, L. and LaFarque, M. (1985). *Lao-tzu and the Tao-te-ching.* Albany: State University of New York Press.

Kwok Man-ho. (1990 and 1997). *See: Man-ho Kwok.*

LaFargue, M. (1985). *See: Kohn, L.*

Land, P. (1990). *Lao Tsu: My Tao.* Puriri Press. Auckland, New Zealand.

Lao Zi. (~200 BC / sealed 168 Bc to 1973). *Mawangdui version-A of Lao Zi's Dao De Jing.* See: Appendix / Chinese versions Dao De Jing / Mawangdui-A.

Lao Zi. (~200 BC / sealed 168 Bc to 1973). *Mawangdui version-B of Lao Zi's Dao De Jing.* See: Appendix / Chinese versions Dao De Jing / Mawangdui-B.

Lao Zi. (~300 BC / sealed to 1993). *Guodian version of Lao Zi's Dao De Jing*. See: Appendix / Chinese versions Dao De Jing / Guodian.

Lao Zi. (179-157 BC). *He-Shang Gong version of Lao Zi's Dao De Jing*. See: Appendix / Chinese versions Dao De Jing / He-Shang Gong.

Lao Zi. (226-249 AD). *Wang Bi version of Lao Zi's Dao De Jing*. See: Appendix / Chinese versions Dao De Jing / Wang Bi.

Lao Zi. (555-639 AD / sealed ~200 BC). *Fu Yi version of Lao Zi's Dao De Jing*. See: Appendix / Chinese versions Dao De Jing / Fu Yi.

Lao Zi. (80 BC-10 AD). *Yan Sun version of Lao Zi's Dao De Jing*. http://www.reference.com/browse/Tao_Te_Ching.

Lau, D. C. (1985). *Lao Tzu: Tao Te Ching*. Penguin Books Ltd., London, England.

Lau, D. C. (1989). *Tao Te Ching*. Hong Kong: The Chinese University Press.

Legge, J. (1997, first published in 1891). *Lao Tze The Tao Teh King*. Dover Publications, Inc., New York.

Lin Lizhen. (2008). *See: Lizhen Lin*.

Lin, D. (2006). *Tao Te Ching. Annotated and Explained*. Woodstock: SkyLights Paths Publisihing.

Lin, J. P. (1977). *A Translation of Lao Tzu's Tao Te Ching and Wang Pi's commentary*. The University of Michigan.

Ling-feng Yeng. (1976). *See: Yeng Ling-feng.*

Lizhen Lin. (2008). *Wang bi.* Tai bei shi: Dong da.

Lu Yusan. (1987). *See: Yusan Lu.*

Lu Zuqian. (1965). *See: Zuqian Lu.*

Luzuqian; Yanlingfeng. (1966). *Yin zhu he shang gong lao zi dao de jing.* Ban qiao shi: Yi wen.

Man-ho Kwok and O'Brien, J. (1990). *The Eight Immortals of Taoism.* London: Rider.

Man-ho Kwok; Palmer, M.; & Ramsay, J. (1997). *Lao Tzu: The Tao Te Ching.* Element Books. Australia.

Maurer, H. (1982). *Tao The Way of the Ways.* Cambridge: Cambridge University Press.

Mawangdui Han mu bo shu zheng li xiao zu. (1976). *Ma wang dui han mu bo shu " laozi ".* Bei jing: Wen wu chu ban she.

Mawangdui-A. (~200 BC). *See: Appendix / Chinese versions Dao De Jing / Mawangdui-A.*

Mawangdui-B. (~200 BC). *See: Appendix / Chinese versions Dao De Jing / Mawangdui-B.*

Ma-wang-tui Han mu po-shu Lao-tzu. (1976). Peking: Wen-wu.

Mencius. (1970). *The Works of Mencius.* (J. Legge, Trans.) New York: Dover Publications Inc.

Miles, T. H. (1992). *Tao te ching.* Avery Publishing Group Inc. USA.

Mitchell, S. (1999). *Lao Tzu: Tao Te Ching*. Harper Collins Publishers, New York.

O'Brien. (1990). *See: Man-ho Kwok.*

Palmer, M. (1997). *See: Man-ho Kwok.*

Palmer, M. and Breuilly, E. (1996). *The Book of Chuang Tzu*. Arkana; Penguin Books Ltd., London, England.

Peng Hao. (1998). *See: Hao Peng.*

Ramsay, J. (1997). *See: Man-ho Kwok.*

Research Group on Ancient Literary Sources of the Department of Education . (1980). *The silk manuscripts of the Han tombs at Mawangdui (vol. I)*. Wenwu Chubanshe, Zhejiang, China.

Rhett, Y. W. Y, and Ames, R. T. (1981). *Lao Zi*. Chinese Material Center.

Rump, A. and Wing-tsit Chan. (1979). *Commentary on the Lao-tzu by Wang Pi*. Honolulu: University of Hawaii Press.

Schade, A. (2016). *Dictionary Nemonik Thinking*. nemonik-thinking.org.

Schade, A. (2016). *Education Kills Humanity*. nemonik-thinking.org.

Schade, A. (2016). *Global Warming is the Solution*. nemonik-thinking.org.

Schade, A. (2016). *Glossary Nemonik Thinking*. nemonik-thinking.org.

Schade, A. (2016). *The Threat of Bilateral Climate Change.* nemonik-thinking.org.

Schade, A. (2016). *Think Smarter with Nemonik Thinking.* nemonik-thinking.org.

Schade, A. (2017). *Lao Tzu's Tao Te Ching* (2 ed.). nemonik-thinking.org.

Schade, A. (2017). *Lao Zi's Dao De Jing* (2 ed.). nemonik-thinking.org.

Schade, A. (2017). *Lao Zi's Dao De Jing Demystified* (2 ed., Vol. 4). nemonik-thinking.org.

Schade, A. (2017). *Lao Zi's Dao De Jing for Nemonik Thinkers* (1 ed.). nemonik-thinking.org.

Schade, A. (2017). *Stunning Revelations about Lao Zi's Dao De Jing* (2 ed., Vol. 5). nemonik-thinking.org.

Schade, A. (2018). *Dictionary Lao Zi's Dao De Jing* (1 ed., Vol. 1). nemonik-thinking.org.

Schade, A. (2018). *Meta-translation Lao Zi's Dao De Jing (1-37)* (2 ed., Vol. 2). nemonik-thinking.org.

Schade, A. (2018). *Meta-translation Lao Zi's Dao De Jing (38-81)* (2 ed., Vol. 3). nemonik-thinking.org.

Schade, A. (planned 2017). *Sun Zi's The Art of War.* nemonik-thinking.org.

Song-ru Zhang. (1981). *See: Zhang Song-ru.*

Tie-Ji Xiong. (1995). *See: Xiong Tie-Ji.*

Waley, A. (1934). *The Way and its Power: A Study of the Tao Te Ching.* London: George Allan and Unwin, Ltd.

Waley, A. (1968). *Lao Tzu: The Way and its Power.* Mandala Books, London.

Walker, B. (1995). *Hua Hu Ching: The Unknown Teachings of Lao Tzu.* Harper Collins Publishers, New York.

Walker, B. B. (1996). *The Tao Te Ching of Lao Tzu.* St. Martin's Press, New York.

Wang Bi. (226-249 AD). *See: Appendix / Chinese versions Dao De Jing / Wang Bi.*

Wang Pi. (226-249 AD). *See: Wang Bi.*

Wen Xing. (2005). *Guodian Laozi yu tai yi sheng shui.* Beijing Shi: Xue yuan chu ban she.

Willemsens, J. (1990). *De Weg van Lao-tse.* Bres, 145. Amsterdam, The Netherlands.

Wing, R. L. (1986). *Lao Tzu: The Tao of Power.* The Aquarian Press, London.

Wing-Tsit Chan. (1979). *See: Rump, A.*

Wing-Tsit Chan. (1988). *See: Chan Wing-Tsit.*

Wu Feng. (2012). *See: Feng Wu.*

Xing Wen. (2005). *See: Wen Xing.*

Xiong Tie-Ji. (1995). *A History of the Study of Laozi in China.* Fujian People Press, Fujian, China.

Xu Kangsheng. (1985). *Annotation and research of Boshu Laozi.* Zhejiang People Press, Zhejiang, China.

Xu Zuo-xin. (1981). *A New Annotation of Laozi.* New Century Press, Taiwan.

Yang Ju-chou. (1987). *Lao-Tze Tao Teh Ching: Chinese/English.* TaiBei, Taiwan.

Yanlingfeng. (1966). *See: Luzuqian; Yanlingfeng.*

Yeng Ling-feng. (1976). *Ma-wang-tui po-shu Lao-tzu shih-t'an.* Taipei: Ho Lo t'u-shu.

Yi Fu. (555-639 AD). *See: Fu Yi.*

Yi Zhang. (1992). *Modern Chinese transcription of Laozi.* China Bookshop, Beijing, China.

Yuanzhi Ding. (1998). *See: Ding Yuanzhi.*

Yu-lan Fung. (1983). *See: Fung Yu-lan.*

Yusan Lu. (1987). *Laozi Shiyi. Annotation of Laozi.* Tianjin People Press, Tianjin, China.

Zhan Jianfeng. (1982). *Laozi: the Person, the Book and the Theory of Dao.* Hubei People Press, Hubei, China.

Zhang Song-ru. (1981). *Correct Readings of Laozi.* Jinlin People Press, Jinlin, China.

Zhang Yi. (1992). *See: Yi Zhang.*

Zhu Chen. (1929). *Laozi.* Shanghai, Shangwu Yinshuguan, Zhonghua Minguo 18 nian 10 yue.

Zuo-xin Xu. (1981). *See: Xu Zuo-xin.*

Zuqian Lu. (1965). *Yin zhu he shang gong lao zi dao de jing.* Tai bei shi: Yi wen yin shu guan.

SECULAR VERSUS SACRED

The chapters 40 and 42 contain the core of the *Dao* section of Lao Zi's *Dao De Jing—The world's things originate from Existence. Existence originates from Non-existence [40.03-04]. The One generated the Two. The Two generated the Three. The Three generated All-things [42.02-04]*. Those sections support the notion that *Dao De Jing* is a secular manuscript about physics, rather than a sacred manuscript about divine entities (Schade, Stunning Revelations about Lao Zi's Dao De Jing, 2017). Nevertheless, Lao Zi's manuscript contains several pictographs that have both secular and sacred meanings. The correct interpretation of those pictographs is important for the translation and understanding of *Dao De Jing*. Although we will never know for sure whether Lao Zi favoured the secular or sacred interpretations, it is the aim of this section to evaluate these ambiguities within the context of *Dao De Jing*.

Sky versus Heaven

Although the pictograph 天 is used colloquially as *Heaven*, the formal pictographs for *Heaven* are 天堂 (Schade, Dictionary Lao Zi's Dao De Jing, 2018). Hence, this supports the notion that in Lao Zi's philosophy the meaning of 天 is *Sky*, rather than *Heaven*.

Chapter 32[179]—the pictograph 天 could mean indeed *Sky* or *Heaven*. However, the choice is here inconsequential. In all other relevant chapters, the context suggests that 天 means *Sky*, rather than *Heaven*. Therefore, based on the principles of consistency and simplicity, the meaning of 天 in this chapter was determined to be *Sky*, rather than *Heaven*.

Chapters 5[180] and 23[181]—the rain mentioned in line 23.03 refers to clouds in the *Sky*, rather than in *Heaven*. The rain falling from the *Sky* and the nutrients of the *Earth* keep all things alive. Hence, the *Sky*, rather than *Heaven* is the complementary opposite of the *Earth*. Therefore, the simplest explanation is that 天 means *Sky*, rather than *Heaven*.

Chapters 6[182] and 25[183]—Lao Zi refers here to the origin of 天. In religious terminology, *Heaven* was the first in existence and, therefore, it could be the origin of the *Sky*. However, *Heaven* itself is second to none and could not have another entity as its origin. Furthermore, in line 25.10b, Lao Zi points out that 天 follows the Way. Again, *Heaven* would not follow anything else than itself, while the *Sky* would inevitably follow the *Way of Nature*. Hence, the context supports the notion that 天 means *Sky*, rather than *Heaven*.

Chapter 7[184]—Lao Zi explains that 天 is not fostering itself. In accord, the *Sky* is fostered by the *Way of Nature*. In contrast, *Heaven* would foster itself in a sacred context. Consequently, 天 means here *Sky*, rather than *Heaven*.

Chapter 39[185]—Lao Zi predicts that 天 would become clear if it obtains the *One*. However, by definition, *Heaven* would already have the *One* and would be clear since the creation. This supports the notion that 天 means *Sky*, rather than *Heaven*.

Nature versus Heaven

Chapter 67,[186] the pictograph 天 could mean either *Nature* or *Heaven* (Schade, Dictionary Lao Zi's Dao De Jing, 2018). The choice is here inconsequential. Furthermore, in all other relevant chapters, the context suggests that 天 means *Nature*, rather than *Heaven*.

Chapter 9 [187] — 天 is associated with withdrawing. Furthermore, in chapter 16,[188] withdrawing or returning is associated with *All-things* and *Nature*, rather than *Heaven*. This suggests that 天 means in both chapters *Nature*, rather than *Heaven*.

Chapter 10[189]—Lao Zi mentions that females open and close the gates of 天. However, it is unlikely that any mortal, male or female, could literally open the sacred gates of *Heaven*. Instead, opening and closing the gates refers more likely to birth and death. This suggests that 天 means here *Nature*, rather than *Heaven*.

Chapter 47[190]—Lao Zi warns us not to look through a window to learn about the *Way of* 天. Anyone looking out a window would see *Nature* rather than *Heaven*. This supports the notion that 天 means *Nature*, rather than *Heaven*.

Chapter 59[191]—frugality is associated with the pictograph 天. *Heaven* would provide unlimited affluence, while *Nature* is associated with seasonal shortages. This suggests that frugality is related to *Nature* and, therefore, the pictograph 天 means *Nature*, rather than *Heaven*.

Chapter 68[192]—Lao Zi calls employing people *Matching with* 天. However, employing people is associated with the allocation of natural resources, rather than heavenly ones. This suggests that the pictograph 天 means *Nature*, rather than *Heaven*.

Chapter 73[193]—Lao Zi points out that 天 takes a low place. In religion, *Heaven* does not take a low place, because the devotees are expected to pay homage to the exalted *Heaven*. Therefore, 天 means *Nature*, rather than *Heaven*.

Way of Nature versus Way of Heaven

Chapter 77[194] and 81[195]—the combined pictographs 天之道 could mean either secular *Way of Nature* or sacred *Way of*

Heaven (Schade, Dictionary Lao Zi's Dao De Jing, 2018). This ambiguity is removed in chapter 79,[196] because Lao Zi points out that the 天之道 is with the competent 善 *people*, rather than the devoted ones. Competent people are successful in the secular world—*They obtain what they seek and escape what they suffer here and now [62.09b]*. Nowhere, does Lao Zi advices people to pray or pay homage to divine powers. Hence, the combined pictographs 天 之 道 should be translated as the secular *Way of Nature*, rather than the sacred *Way of Heaven*.

World, State, and Country

The combined pictographs 天 下 could be literally translated as either *below Sky* or *below Heaven* (Schade, Dictionary Lao Zi's Dao De Jing, 2018). However, in the context of *Dao De Jing*, both expressions refer either to the secular *World,*[197] *State,*[198] or *Country.*[199] In case the pictograph 天 would have sacred connotations, the meaning of the term 天下 remains secular.

There is no reason to assume that Lao Zi used different meanings for the pictograph 天 across chapters. Therefore, the principles of consistency and simplicity suggest that 天 should be translated throughout the entire text as a secular entity, rather than a sacred one.

Emperor versus God

The pictograph 帝 could mean either secular *Emperor* or sacred *God* (Schade, Dictionary Lao Zi's Dao De Jing, 2018). Lao Zi wrote—吾不知其谁之子也象**帝**之先 [04.04a-b]. This could mean—*I do not know whose child it is, but it seems to predate the* **_Emperor_** *[04.04a-b]*. Alternatively, it could mean—*I do not know whose child it is, but it seems to predate* **_God_** *[04.04a-b]*. However, if 帝 would mean *God,* then nothing could predate 帝. God would be the first in existence as the creator of everything.   Instead, Lao Zi insists that something predated 帝. This suggests that 帝 means secular *Emperor,* rather than sacred *God.*

The combined pictographs 天子 could mean either secular *Rightful Emperor* or sacred *Son of Heaven* (Schade, Dictionary Lao Zi's Dao De Jing, 2018).   Lao Zi wrote—故立**天子** ...[62.07a].   This could mean—*Therefore, when the* **_Emperor_** *is crowned...[62.07a]*. Alternatively, it could mean—*Therefore, when the* **_Son of Heaven_** *is crowned...[62.07a]*. The title *Son of Heaven* implies that the Emperor is the *Son of God.* However, a *God* could not be raised in status through the crowning by mere mortals. This supports the notion that 天子 is an honorary and illustrious title for the mortal Emperor, rather than an objective description of reality. This suggests that 天子 means secular *Emperor*, rather than sacred *God*.

Gravity versus Spiritual Force

Chapter 6—Lao Zi uses the pictograph 神 *spirit* in the phrase 谷神不死 *Immortal Valley* **Spirit** *[06.01]*. Superficially, this poetic phrase seems to refer to a divine, sacred, or spiritual entity. In addition, he calls that spirit the 玄牝 *Mysterious Female* and points out that she is the *origin of the Sky and the Earth [06.02]*. Following that line of thought, our world would have a divine, sacred, or spiritual origin. However, 神 means also *secular power, force, or energy* (Schade, Dictionary Lao Zi's Dao De Jing, 2018).

Taking into account both the secular and sacred meanings, 神 could be described as an entity that is hidden from our awareness in the same way as a non-physical spirit. Nevertheless, that apparently non-physical entity affects reality with physical power, force, and energy. Such an intertwined sensory and extrasensory entity could be scientific, rather than spiritual. After all, physicists know many extrasensory forces that affect the secular reality such as gravity, electro-magnetic, and nuclear forces. It cannot be excluded that Lao Zi would have used 神 to describe such extrasensory physical forces, rather than extrasensory spiritual forces.

In Lao Zi's philosophy, valley is a metaphor for a downwards movement of water. He points out that the invisible *Immortal Valley Spirit* forces water down the valley into the low river and subsequently into the even lower sea. As the river and the sea receive all the water from the valleys, Lao Zi calls them—*Kings of a hundred valleys [66.01-03]*. This suggests that Lao Zi used the pictograph 谷 *valley* as a metaphor for the *downward* movement of water. His *Valley Spirit* could be conceptualized as an extrasensory entity that wields enormous downwards physical powers, which are able to pull all the water of the entire world to the lowest point.

The combined pictographs 不死 could mean either *immortal* or *eternal.* Substituting *eternal* for *immortal,* changes Lao Zi's phrase *Immortal Valley Spirit* into *Eternal Valley Spirit.* The pictograph 谷 means *valley,* which is Lao Zi's metaphor for *downwards.* Substituting *downwards* for *valley,* changes *Eternal Valley Spirit* into *Eternal Downward Spirit.* The pictograph 神 means either *spirit* or *force.* Substituting *force* for *spirit,* changes *Eternal Downward Spirit* into *Eternal Downward Force.* Therefore, Lao Zi's *Immortal Valley Spirit* could be called in modern terms the *Eternal Downward Force.* This is a very good description of the extrasensory secular force that physicists call nowadays *Gravity.* Lao Zi's concepts of 牝 *female,* 下 *low,* 江 *river,* 海 *sea,* 神 *force,* 溪 *stream,* 谷 *valley,* 水

water, and 阴 *Yin* are all associated with his 谷神不死 *Eternal Downward Force* (Schade, Lao Zi's Dao De Jing Demystified, 2017).[200]

Lao Zi's poetic description of gravity predates Sir Isaac Newton's scientific description with more than 2,000 years. Lao Zi used water in order to explain gravity, while Newton used his famous apple. Furthermore, Lao Zi surpasses Newton, because Lao Zi points out that the *Eternal Downward Force* or *Gravity* is the *origin of the Sky and Earth [06.02]*. In accord, modern theoretical physicists hypothesize that billions of years ago, gravity has turned the gases of the universe into fluids and solid matter.

The concept of gravity was crucial for Albert Einstein's theories about relativity and the subsequent discovery of black holes. Compared to the rapidly developing sciences during the last few hundred years, that stagnation of two thousand years is a very long time. One can only wonder how far physics could have been if Lao Zi's contemporaries would have understood the enormous implications of his *Eternal Downward Force.*

Lao Zi points out that nature is so powerful, because it aligns with the *Eternal Downward Force* by taking a low position. [201] Therefore, he counsels sages, leaders, and countries to become the *stream of the world*[202] by occupying the low positions. [203] See also the Endnotes and (Schade, Stunning Revelations about Lao Zi's Dao De Jing, 2017).

Secular Entities versus Spiritual Ones

As mentioned in the previous section, 神 could mean sacred *spirit* or secular *energy* (Schade, Dictionary Lao Zi's Dao De Jing, 2018).

Chapter 29—Lao Zi points out that the world is a *container of* 神. [204] Lao Zi must have known that no mortal could control a container of non-physical sacred spirits with secular physical 为 *actions* and 执 *holds*. Therefore, his advice refers to the attempt of incompetent people to control the container of energy comprising the secular world. Hence, it makes sense to translate 神 as *energy*, rather than *spirit*.

Chapter 39—Lao Zi wrote: ...*the* 神 *obtained the One through effectiveness...* *[39.04]* [205] . The pictograph 灵 *effectiveness* is associated with the secular human mind, rather than sacred spirits. Furthermore, the rest of that chapter is about secular entities such as the *Sky, Earth, Valley, and All-things.* Hence, the context suggests that 神 is about one's extrasensory secular mental spirit or energy, rather than extrasensory sacred spirits.

Chapter 60—Lao Zi wrote: *Use the Way to attend to the world, then the* 鬼 *will have no power [60.02]* [206] . The pictograph 鬼

could mean either sacred *spirit* or secular *underhanded person* (Schade, Dictionary Lao Zi's Dao De Jing, 2018). However, the world is a secular entity. This suggests that 鬼 refers to a secular *underhanded person*, rather than a sacred *spirit*.

Sage versus Saint

The combined pictographs 圣人 could mean either secular *Sage* or sacred *Saint* (Schade, Dictionary Lao Zi's Dao De Jing, 2018).

Chapter 62—The core of Lao Zi's *De* section of Lao Zi's *Dao De Jing* is success, which he defines as: *...obtain what you seek and escape what you suffer [62.09b]. Succeed without boasting. Succeed without attacking. Succeed without arrogance. Succeed without excess. That is called succeeding without force [30.07-11].* That success is about the secular here and now of daily life. In Lao Zi's philosophy, success is maximized by aligning with the *Way of Nature,* or in modern terminology, with the laws of physics.

During the creation of our universe, the forever permanent *Nothingness* was divided into the equal but opposite polarities called *Existence* and *Non-existence*. Together, they will always recreate *Nothingness,* which cannot be increased or decreased. Therefore, the eternal balance of *Existence* and *Non-existence* forces the *Way of Nature,* in its manifestation of 气 *Qi,* to destroy all extremes. Consequently, extremes are places of misfortune that should be avoided (Schade, Stunning Revelations about Lao Zi's Dao De Jing, 2017).

Laozian sages align with the *Way of Nature*, because it is unstoppable and cannot be opposed. Therefore, they avoid extremes[207] by fostering 德 *virtues*[208] such as: 慈 *compassion*[209]; 啬 *frugality*[210]; 曰不敢为天下先 *humbleness*[211]; 退 *retreat*[212]; 朴 *simplicity*[213]; 时 *timing*[214]; and 静 *tranquillity*[215]. For the same reason, they inhibit: 为 *action*[216]; 骄 *arrogance*[217]; 事 *effort*[218]; 欲 *desire*[219]; 见 *display*[220]; 强 *force*[221]; 藏 *hoarding*[222]; 敌 *resistance*[223]; 争 *strive*[224]; and 富 *wealth*[225].

The previous paragraphs show that Lao Zi mentions many secular virtues in his *Dao De Jing*. However, he does not mention any sacred ritual, devotion, worship, or prayer as a virtue. Therefore, the context of his manuscript supports the notion that the pictographs 圣人 mean secular *Sage,* rather than sacred *Saint.* Laozian sages are concerned with the sensory reality of the 'here and now', rather than with the extrasensory reality (Schade, Think Smarter with Nemonik Thinking, 2016) and (Schade, Glossary Nemonik Thinking, 2016). Sages are practical, efficient, and competent people, rather than religious, pious, and spiritual devotees. They align with the balancing forces of the *Way of Nature* by simply avoiding dangerous extremes in daily life. Despite their practical approach to life, they have high moral standards, because it is in their own interest to help and protect other people. Therefore, their morality will last.

Lao Zi's Tenet

As shown previously in this section, it is very unlikely that any of Lao Zi's pictographs was intended to mean spiritual or sacred phenomena such as *God, Heaven, or Spirits*. Nevertheless, even such a sacred interpretation would not make much difference to the secular meaning of *Dao De Jing*.

Information about Lao Zi as a person is covered by the dust of time. Indeed, he might have been a religious scientist. No one knows. However, Lao Zi's *Dao De Jing* shows that he was a true theoretical physicist. He remained objective and neither advocated nor rejected spiritual or sacred phenomenon. The essence of his manuscript is about the sciences of physics and psychology, rather than religion. In his philosophy, *Dao* is the secular origin, principle, substance, and force of the universe (Schade, Stunning Revelations about Lao Zi's Dao De Jing, 2017). His secular tenet was the guiding light for the meta-translation of *Dao De Jing* (Schade, Meta-translation Lao Zi's Dao De Jing (1-37), 2018) and (Schade, Meta-translation Lao Zi's Dao De Jing (38-81), 2018).

THE WAYS OF DAO

Understanding the context is crucial for the proper interpretation of Chinese pictographs. Even professional translators might find it difficult to translate books about physics and psychology if they do not understand those topics. Therefore, it is important to examine the *Way of Nature* and the *Way of People* by contrasting the ideas of the Chinese philosophers Lao Zi (570-490 BC) and Confucius, K'ung Ch'iu, or K'ung Chung-ni (551-479 BC).

The pictograph 道 *Dao* means literally *road, path, way, or pathway*. Both, Lao Zi and Confucius used 道 as the core of their philosophies. However, it would be incorrect to conclude that therefore their philosophies are similar. Lao Zi interpreted 道 as the *Way of Nature*, while Confucius used that same pictograph to refer to his entirely different *Way of Gentlemen*. As evident from the title 道德經 *Dao De Jing*, Lao Zi made a clear distinction between 道 *Way of Nature* and 德 *Way of People*. Consequently, Confucius' 道 *Way of Gentlemen* is not an antithesis of Lao Zi's 道 *Way of Nature*. Instead, it is an antithesis concerning Lao Zi's 德 *Way of People*. In Confucius' philosophy, 道 *Dao* is comparable to Lao Zi's 德 *De*.

It is obvious that nature can exist without people, but that people cannot exist without the rest of nature. In accord, Lao Zi points out that people are the lowest category in the hierarchy of the universe—*People follow the Earth, the Earth follows the Sky, the Sky follows the Way, and the Way follows nature [25.09-10c]*. Therefore, people have to align with nature in order to maximize their success—*Use the Way of Nature to obtain what you seek and use it to escape what you suffer [62.09b]*.

Laozian virtue is the competence to align with the *Way of Nature*. In contrast, Confucian virtue is the competence to align with the artificial *Way of Gentlemen*. Lao Zi's *Way of People* is based on *'what is'*, while Confucius' *Way of Gentlemen* is based on *'what ought to be'*. Hence, Lao Zi's natural *Way of People* is eternal, unchangeable, and objective, while Confucius' artificial *Way of Gentlemen* is temporary, changeable, and subjective. Therefore, Lao Zi's *Way of People* is superior to Confucius' *Way of Gentlemen*.

To align with the artificial *Way of Gentlemen*, Confucians foster virtues such as 仁 *benevolence*, 义 *justice*, and 礼 *propriety*. However, those virtues are not spontaneous. A complex set of artificial rules replaces natural behaviour creating artificial social privileges and obligations.

In Confucian philosophy, benevolence is based on the love for one's fellow men. To be benevolent, it is essential that we do not impose on others what we do not want others to impose on us. However, Confucian virtues were fostered by social elite who called themselves *gentlemen*. The distinction between that elite and common people creates an artificial division of society. To maintain that division, Confucians are forced to support law and order, control, and social hierarchy. In turn, their effort nurtures the seed of rebellion.

In contrast to Lao Zi's immutable *Way of Nature*, the changeable *Way of Gentlemen* is corruptible. That allows the privileged to take advantage of it in order to foster their socio-economic status. They have no intention to address society's real problems. In contrast, they use the *Way of Gentlemen* to justify and maintain socio-economic imbalances—*It is the Way of Nature to take from what is plenty and give to what is not enough. However, the Way of People is different. They take from what is not enough and give to what is plenty [77.04a-06b].*

Reality shows that the socio-economic privileged are benevolent because it is their aim is to be seen as *gentlemen*. They pursue virtue for the sake of virtue—*Inferior virtue pursues virtue. Therefore, it is no virtue [38.02a-b].* Their inferior virtues evoke actions that maintain the malignant status quo— *Superior benevolence acts and yet there is no use in those actions. Superior justice acts and there is purpose in those actions. Superior propriety acts and if there is no agreement, then the arms are bared.*

Therefore, after the Way is lost there will be virtue [38.04a-07]. As a result, Confucian virtues become a toxic cloak that conceals the malice that is hidden behind artificial and ritualistic behaviour. By corrupting the *Way of Gentlemen*, the privileged reject the core of Confucius philosophy by imposing on others what they do not want others to impose on themselves.

The Greek philosopher Socrates (470-399 BC) pointed out that justice is a subjective concept that is hard to define. History shows that extreme imbalances in the distribution of wealth, status, privilege, and power will ultimately lead to rebellion and violent social struggles. When that happens, the privileged call for '*Justice*' in order to protect the imbalances that support them. Their kind of justice often results in maintaining the status quo by increasing law and order. Under the pretence of stabilising society, they will act to defend the socio-economic inequalities and maintain their advantageous positions—*Superior justice acts and there is purpose in those actions [38.05a-b].* The only purpose of their justice is to preserve their privileges with more injustice.

Propriety is an analgesic for common people that fosters their conformity to the set of artificial rules and beliefs regulating society. The privileged forge propriety into a lethal weapon to maintain social imbalances. Peer pressure, cognitive dissonance, indoctrination, and institutions such as education and religion will condition the common people to behave and think 'properly'. Propriety explains with subjective arguments why it is proper to have differences in society and why the common people should accept those inequalities. For instance, the myth that the rich work harder than the poor explains the differences in wealth. For some of us that myth might be hard to swallow. We see the rich having fine lunches in expensive restaurants, while at the same time Joe Average breaks his back digging a drain for their sewage system.

Propriety is hidden so deeply in the soul of the conditioned people that only the young rebels dare question it. Lao Zi warns us that if there is no sufficient reaction to the persuasive powers of society then those rebels will be either forced to conform or they will be destroyed—*Superior propriety acts and if there is no agreement, then the arms are bared [38.06a-d]*. We only have to watch the six o'clock news to see the truth of Lao Zi's statement.

Artificial virtues carry the seed of their own destruction by creating and maintaining social-economic differences—*If the great Way is rejected, then there will be benevolence and justice. Knowledge and cleverness will appear and then there is great hypocrisy. Family relationships will be disharmonious and then there is animal dirt everywhere. The state's household will be a confused disorder and then there is bureaucracy [18.01a-04b]. Those who have propriety possess only a thin layer of loyalty and sincerity, which is the beginning of disorder [38.11a-c].*

In Lao Zi's philosophy, the appearance of Confucian virtues is a clear sign that society has lost the *Way of Nature*— *After the Way of Nature is lost there will be virtue. After virtue is lost, there will be benevolence. After benevolence is lost, there will be justice. After justice is lost, there will be propriety. Those who have propriety possess only a thin layer of loyalty and sincerity, which is the beginning of disorder [38.07-11c].* Therefore, Lao Zi rejects the artificial virtues that Confucius advocates—*Discard adoration and reject knowledge and the people will benefit a hundred times. Discard benevolence and reject righteousness and the people will return to filial piety and compassion [19.01a-02b].* Artificial virtue offers no solution to our modern problems. Instead, it is an ominous sign that we have a huge problem, because the *Way of Nature* is lost.

Lao Zi's *Way of People* is natural and, therefore, it does not have to be enforced. For example, everyone and everything is subject to heat, gravity, wind, and lightening. In contrast, Confucius' *Way of Gentlemen* is artificial and, therefore, it has to be enforced by people. Criminals have to be penalized by other people. Hence, someone's demand for freedom is likely to restrict someone else's freedom. That Confucian force to control society will evoke a chain of reactions fostering endless conflicts—*When effort is needed, then there is never enough to take the world* [48.06a-b].

Most of our current global problems are the result of ignoring the crucial differences between Lao Zi's *Way of People* and Confucius' *Way of Gentlemen*. The vast majority still believes that the Viking King Canute the Great could make Confucian laws in order to drive back the tides of the oceans.

In the context of nemonik thinking; Lao Zi's *Way of Nature* is associated with the *objective mindmode*, while Confucius' *Way of Gentlemen* is associated with the *collective mindmode*. The objective mindmode is concerned with the unchangeable laws of physics, while the collective mindmode is concerned with the forever changing laws made by people for people (Schade, Think Smarter with Nemonik Thinking, 2016).

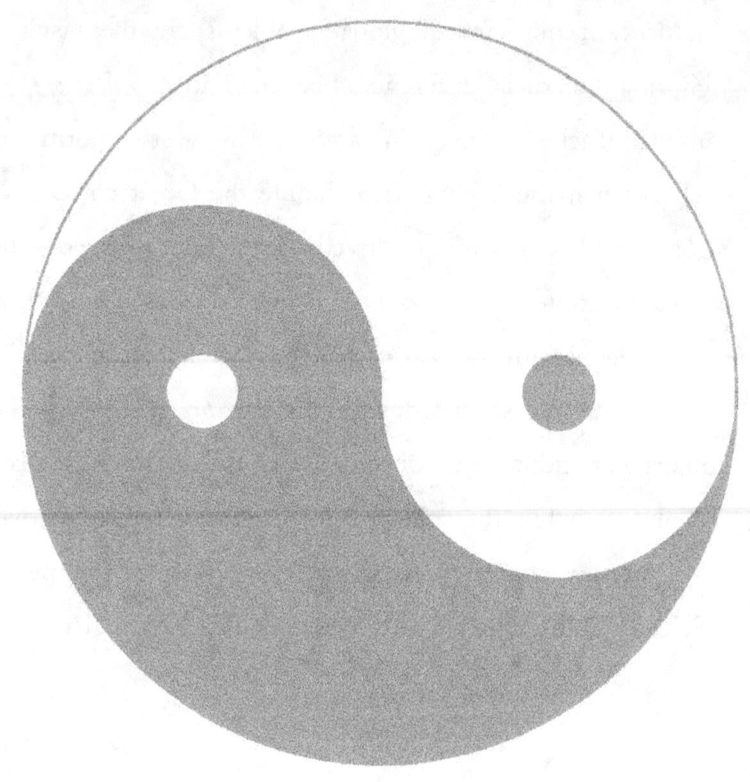

Yin-Yang

CHINESE VERSIONS OF *DAO DE JING*

Wang Bi version (226-249 AD)

The Wang Bi (王弼) version of Lao Zi's *Dao De Jing* (老子之道德經) is named after the famous Chinese philosopher Wang Bi (226–249 AD). Although Wang Bi died young, he compiled the standard version of *Dao De Jing* comprising two sections and 81 chapters. Wang Bi was a member of the *Xuanxue or Profound Learning School* (玄學). In his comments, he advocates the cosmological and metaphysical aspects of *Dao De Jing*, rather than the alternative religious interpretation. For almost 2,000 years, Wang Bi's version has been widely used in China and has been the basis for many English translations. Several Wang Bi versions of *Dao De Jing* are in *Existence*, but their differences are considered to be minor. The Wang Bi version presented in this study was created by integrating the following references and electronic copies.

References

(Feng Wu, 2012); (Lau, D. C., 1989); (Lin, J. P., 1977);
(Lizhen Lin, 2008); and (Rump, A. and Wing-tsit Chan,
1979).

http://en.wikipedia.org/wiki/Tao_Te_Ching

http://plato.stanford.edu/entries/laozi/

http://www.*Dao*isopen.com/downloads/About%20the%20
Charts.pdf

http://www.*Dao*istcenter.org/*Dao*dejing.html

http://www.iep.utm.edu/*Dao*ism/#H4

http://www.reference.com/browse/Tao_Te_Ching

He-Shang Gong version (179-157 BC)

The He-Shang Gong (河上公) version of Lao Zi's *Dao De Jing* (老子之道德經) is named after the legendary Chinese *Dao*ist philosopher He-Shang Gong (179-157 BC). He-Shang Gong is also known as the River Sage, because he lived along the banks of the Yellow River. Allegedly, he discovered a copy of *Dao De Jing* dated about 579 BC, which contained the 81 chapters as known to date. However, there is no proof of the *Existence* of that manuscript. Legend holds that He-Shang Gong imparted his knowledge about *Dao De Jing* to the Emperor Wen of the Han dynasty (202-157 BC). However, his version of *Dao De Jing* was only generally accepted during the reign of the Emperor Xuanzong (r. 712-755). The He-Shang Gong version has been used predominantly by scholars to evaluate textual differences with the Wang Bi version. Several He-Shang Gong versions of *Dao De Jing* are in *Existence*, but their differences are considered to be minor. The He-Shang Gong version presented in this study was created by integrating the following references and electronic copies.

References

(Donglaixiansheng, 1965); (Luzuqian; Yanlingfeng, 1966); (Xu Kangsheng, 1985); and (Zuqian Lu, 1965).

http://plato.stanford.edu/entries/laozi/

http://www.*Dao*isopen.com/downloads/About%20the%20 Charts.pdf

http://www.nlc.gov.cn/zxfw/jiangzuozhanlan/zhanlan/*Dao* dejing/html/03.htm

http://www.reference.com/browse/Tao_Te_Ching

Fu Yi version (555-639 AD)

The Fu Yi (傅奕) version of Lao Zi's *Dao De Jing* (老子之道德經) is named after the Chinese court astrologer and *Dao*ist Fu Yi (555-639 AD). In 574 AD, a copy of *Dao De Jing* was recovered allegedly from a tomb near the Grand Canal town of Xuchou.   From that manuscript, Fu Yi compiled the *Chiao-ting Gupen Laozi or Ancient Text of Laozi Collated*. The tomb was allegedly sealed around 200 BC and, therefore, the Fu Yi version dates from the same period as the Mawangdui versions. Several Fu Yi versions of *Dao De Jing* are in *Existence*, but their differences are considered to be minor. The Fu Yi version presented in this study was created by integrating the following references and electronic copies.

References

(Xu Kangsheng, 1985).

http://home.pages.at/onkellotus/TTK/Chinese_Uni-FY_TTK.html

http://plato.stanford.edu/entries/laozi/

http://www.*Dao*isopen.com/downloads/About%20the%20Charts.pdf

http://www.nlc.gov.cn/zxfw/jiangzuozhanlan/zhanlan/*Dao*dejing/html/03.htm

Mawangdui version-A (~200 BC)

The Mawangdui-A (马王堆) version of Lao Zi's *Dao De Jing* (老子之道德經) is named after the town Mawangdui near Changsha in the Hunan province of China. In 1973, archaeologists opened there a tomb that contained the remains of a nobleman named Li Tsang who died in 168 BC. The archaeologists recovered several manuscripts including two silk versions of *Dao De Jing* that are now known as the Mawangdui-A and-B versions. The A and B versions were apparently written by different scribes and in different styles. Similar to the Wang Bi versions, both Mawangdui versions comprise 81 chapters. However, a comparison of the chapter sequence of the Mawangdui version expressed in Wang Bi's chapter numbers shows many differences—38, 39, 41, 40, 42-66, 80, 81, 67-79, 1-21, 24, 22, 23, 25-37. Furthermore, the A-version does not avoid the pictograph Bang 邦, which would have been taboo during the reign of the first Han emperor Liu Bang 劉邦 (r. 206–194 BC). Based on the calligraphic styles and imperial taboo avoidances, some scholars believe that A and B can be dated to the 2nd century BC. Several Mawangdui versions of *Dao De Jing* are in *Existence*, but their differences are considered to be minor. The Mawangdui version presented in this study was created by integrating the following references and electronic copies.

References

(Henricks, 1993); (Lau, D. C., 1989); (Mawangdui Han mu bo shu zheng li xiao zu, 1976); (Ma-wang-tui Han mu po-shu Lao-tzu, 1976); (Xu Kangsheng, 1985); and (Yeng Ling-feng, 1976).

http://en.wikipedia.org/wiki/Tao_Te_Ching

http://plato.stanford.edu/entries/laozi/

http://station7.kgw.tu-berlin.de/Arbeitsstelle/Laozi/MWD.html

http://www.*Dao*isopen.com/downloads/About%20the%20Charts.pdf

http://www.*Dao*istcenter.org/*Dao*dejing.html

http://www.iep.utm.edu/*Dao*ism/#H4

http://www.nlc.gov.cn/zxfw/jiangzuozhanlan/zhanlan/*Dao*dejing/html/03.htm

http://www.reference.com/browse/Tao_Te_Ching

Mawangdui version-B (~200 BC)

The Mawangdui-B (马王堆) version of Lao Zi's *Dao De Jing* (老子之道德經) is named after the town Mawangdui near Changsha in the Hunan province of China. In 1973, archaeologists opened there a tomb that contained the remains of a nobleman named Li Tsang who died in 168 BC. The archaeologists recovered several manuscripts including two silk versions of *Dao De Jing* that are now known as the Mawangdui-A and-B versions. The A and B versions were apparently written by different scribes and in different styles. Similar to the Wang Bi versions, both Mawangdui versions comprise 81 chapters. However, a comparison of the chapter sequence of the Mawangdui version expressed in Wang Bi's chapter numbers shows many differences—38, 39, 41, 40, 42-66, 80, 81, 67-79, 1-21, 24, 22, 23, 25-37. In contrast to the A-version, the B-version seems to avoid the pictograph Bang 邦, which would have been taboo during the reign of the first Han emperor Liu Bang 劉邦 (r. 206–194 BC). Based on the calligraphic styles and imperial taboo avoidances, some scholars believe that A and B can be dated to the 2nd century BC. Several Mawangdui versions of *Dao De Jing* are in *Existence*, but their differences are considered to be minor. The Mawangdui version presented in this study was created by integrating the following references and electronic copies.

References

(Henricks, 1993); (Lau, D. C., 1989); (Mawangdui Han mu bo shu zheng li xiao zu, 1976); (Ma-wang-tui Han mu po-shu Lao-tzu, 1976); (Xu Kangsheng, 1985); and (Yeng Ling-feng, 1976).

http://en.wikipedia.org/wiki/Tao_Te_Ching

http://plato.stanford.edu/entries/laozi/

http://station7.kgw.tu-berlin.de/Arbeitsstelle/Laozi/MWD.html

http://www.*Dao*isopen.com/downloads/About%20the%20Charts.pdf

http://www.*Dao*istcenter.org/*Dao*dejing.html

http://www.iep.utm.edu/*Dao*ism/#H4

http://www.nlc.gov.cn/zxfw/jiangzuozhanlan/zhanlan/*Dao*dejing/html/03.htm

http://www.reference.com/browse/Tao_Te_Ching

Guodian version (~300 BC)

The Guodian (郭店) version of Lao Zi's *Dao De Jing* (老子之道德經) is named after the village Guodian located near Jingmen in the Hubei province of China. In 1993, archaeologists opened there a small tomb that possibly belonged to a tutor or a prince. The tomb contained about 800 slips of bamboo including parts of Lao Zi's *Dao De Jing*. Based on the shape of the bamboo slips and the calligraphy, the *Dao De Jing* material was divided into *Three* groups known as the Guodian A, B, and C. However, the Guodian version was not divided in 道 *Dao* and 德 *De* sections. Furthermore, a comparison of the chapter sequence of the Guodian version expressed in Wang Bi's chapter numbers shows no connection at all—19, 66, 46, 29, 15, 64, 37, 63, 2, 32, 24, 5, 16, 64, 56, 57, 55, 44, 40, 9, 59, 48, 20, 13, 41, 52, 45, 54, 17, 18, 35, and 31. This suggests that the chapter sequence and division of Lao Zi's *Dao De Jing* is unreliable. In addition, the Guodian version supports the claim that *Existence originates from Non-existence*] *[40.04]*. That phrase is crucial, because it explains the origin, formation, and working of the universe. However, the Guodian version does not contain the second part of the key to the secrets of *Dao De Jing.—The One generated the Two [42.02]*. The Guodian version has been dated as early as 300 BC, which makes it the oldest known version of Lao Zi's manuscript. Several Guodian versions of *Dao De Jing* are in *Existence*, but their differences are considered to be minor. The Guodian version presented in this study was created by integrating the following mentioned references and electronic copies.

References

(Ding Yuanzhi, 1998); (Guanghui Jiang, 1999); (Hao Peng, 1998); (Henricks, R. G., 2000); (Holloway, 2009); (Hubeisheng Jingmenshi bowuguan, 1998); (Jingmen shi bo wu guan, 1998); and (Wen Xing, 2005).

http://en.wikipedia.org/wiki/Tao_Te_Ching#Mawangdui_and_Guodian_texts

http://plato.stanford.edu/entries/laozi/

http://www.archaeology.org/9811/newsbriefs/laozi.html

http://www.*Dao*isopen.com/downloads/About%20the%20Charts.pdf

http://www.iep.utm.edu/*Dao*ism/#H4

http://www.nlc.gov.cn/zxfw/jiangzuozhanlan/zhanlan/*Dao*dejing/html/03.htm

http://www.reference.com/browse/Tao_Te_Ching

Yin-Yang

MY OTHER BOOKS

Dictionary Nemonik Thinking [1 of 3]

We need clear definitions to communicate. However, definitions associated with the mind and reality are inherently hypothetical, fuzzy, and intertwined. Therefore, the first part of this dictionary translates nemonik concepts into common keywords (e.g. *advance* into attack, bypass, etc.). In contrast, the second part translates common keywords into nemonik concepts (e.g. attack, bypass, etc. into *advance*). Nemonik thinking will improve your life. It accelerates your thinking; improves your memory; mobilizes your subconscious genius; strengthens your weaknesses; and reveals opportunities and threats. It helps you to pursue your goals in the right state of mind; at the right place, at the right time, with the right resources; and the right information. Nemonik thinking will assist you to think on your feet and become panic resistant during emergencies. Nemonik thinking is simple to learn, but it so sophisticated that it will make you a superior problem solver. Nemonik thinkers evaluate a checklist of seventeen nemoniks for each situation. Nemoniks are memorized keywords describing all aspects of your mind, reality, and their interaction (Schade, Think Smarter with Nemonik Thinking, 2016).

Free eBook @
nemonik-thinking.org

We need clear definitions to communicate.   However, definitions associated with the mind and reality are inherently hypothetical, fuzzy, and intertwined. Therefore, this glossary attempts to provide definitions of the main concepts associated with nemonik thinking. Nemonik thinking will improve your life. It accelerates your thinking; improves your memory; mobilizes your subconscious genius; strengthens your weaknesses; and reveals opportunities and threats. It helps you to pursue your goals in the right state of mind; at the right place, at the right time, with the right resources; and the right information. Nemonik thinking will assist you to think on your feet and become panic resistant during emergencies. Nemonik thinking is simple to learn, but it so sophisticated that it will make you a superior problem solver. Nemonik thinkers evaluate a checklist of seventeen nemoniks for each situation.   Nemoniks are memorized keywords describing all aspects of your mind, reality, and their interaction (Schade, Think Smarter with Nemonik Thinking, 2016).

Think Smarter with Nemonik Thinking [3 of 3]

Nemonik thinking will improve your life. It accelerates your thinking; improves your memory; mobilizes your subconscious genius; strengthens your weaknesses; and reveals opportunities and threats. It helps you to pursue your goals in the right state of mind; at the right place, at the right time, with the right resources; and the right information. Nemonik thinking will assist you to think on your feet and become panic resistant during emergencies. Nemonik thinking is simple to learn, but it so sophisticated that it will make you a superior problem solver. Nemonik thinkers evaluate a checklist of seventeen nemoniks for each situation. Nemoniks are memorized keywords describing all aspects of your mind, reality, and their interaction. Nemonik thinking is like playing a musical keyboard with seventeen keys producing an infinite repertoire of practical strategies. Nemonik thinking provides the strategic options for any possible situation, while Lao Zi's *Dao De Jing* provides the principle that identifies which of those options will fit the actual situation (Schade, Stunning Revelations about Lao Zi's Dao De Jing, 2017). The resulting strategies will maximize your success, which is to obtain what you seek and escape what you suffer. You might be the best thinker in the world, but only nemonik thinking could make you the smartest thinker you can be.

Free eBook @
nemonik-thinking.org

The Basics of Nemonik Mindpower

This is a crucial shortcut to a significant increase in your mindpower. You only have to memorize seventeen simple keywords called nemoniks that describe the mind, reality, and their interaction. Although simple, those nemoniks create a butterfly effect that will keep improving your mind forever. Without effort, they will accelerate your thinking, improve your memory, mobilize your hidden genius, turn your weaknesses into strengths, reveal opportunities and threats, and prepare you for emergencies. Pursue your goals in the right frame of mind. Nemonik thinking will make you the best thinker you can be.

Free eBook @
nemonik-thinking.org

Dictionary Lao Zi's *Dao De Jing* [1 of 5].

This Chinese-English and English-Chinese dictionary is especially compiled for the translation of Lao Zi's ancient book *Dao De Jing* (Schade, Meta-translation Lao Zi's Dao De Jing (1-37), 2018) and (Schade, Meta-translation Lao Zi's Dao De Jing (38-81), 2018). *Dao De Jing* means literally—*A Classic about the Way of Nature and the Way of People*. It aims to maximize your success, which is to obtain what you seek and escape what you suffer. Success is maximized by aligning the *Way of People* with the *Way of Nature* (Schade, Stunning Revelations about Lao Zi's Dao De Jing, 2017). The Chinese versions used in this study include— (Wang Bi, 226-249 AD); (He-Shang Gong, 179-157 BC); (Fu Yi, 555-639 AD); (Mawangdui-A, ~200 BC); (Mawangdui-B, ~200 BC); and (Guodian, ~300 BC). Together, those versions contain about 1,600 different pictographs. Every language changes over time and, therefore, some of Lao Zi's ancient pictographs are not used anymore, while the meaning of others has changed. In addition, most modern Chinese pictographs have several English meanings that foster ambiguity. Therefore, the exhaustive English meanings for each pictograph were extracted from reputable sources. Furthermore, a system of *Digital Index for Pictographs (DIP)* is introduced that simplifies the digital classification of Chinese pictographs.

Free eBook @
nemonik-thinking.org

The title of Lao Zi's ancient book *Dao De Jing* means literally—*A Classic about the Way of Nature and the Way of People*. *Dao De Jing* aims to maximize your success, which is to obtain what you seek and escape what you suffer. Success is maximized by aligning the *Way of People* with the *Way of Nature* (Schade, Stunning Revelations about Lao Zi's Dao De Jing, 2017). Despite the great efforts, previous translations of *Dao De Jing* do not present an adequate understanding of that mysterious manuscript. In order to take optimal advantage of the expertise accumulated in such earlier studies, this meta-translation is based on an English meta-analysis and a Chinese meta-analysis. The English meta-analysis is based on the following English translations— (Chan Wing-Tsit, 1988); (Cheng Gia-Fu and English, J, 1972); (Henricks, 1993); (Land, 1990); (Lau, 1985); (Lin, J. P., 1977); (Man-ho Kwok; Palmer, M.; & Ramsay, J., 1997); (Waley, 1968); and (Wing, 1986). The Chinese meta-analysis is based on the following Chinese versions of *Dao De Jing*— (Wang Bi, 226-249 AD); (He-Shang Gong, 179-157 BC); (Fu Yi, 555-639 AD); (Mawangdui-A, ~200 BC); (Mawangdui-B, ~200 BC); and (Guodian, ~300 BC). This meta-translation of Dao (Chapters 1-37) is based on a special dictionary (Schade, Dictionary Lao Zi's Dao De Jing, 2018), while it is the foundation for (Schade, Lao Zi's Dao De Jing Demystified, 2017).

Free eBook @
nemonik-thinking.org

Meta-translation Lao Zi's *Dao...* [3 of 5]

The title of Lao Zi's ancient book *Dao De Jing* means literally—*A Classic about the Way of Nature and the Way of People*. *Dao De Jing* aims to maximize your success, which is to obtain what you seek and escape what you suffer. Success is maximized by aligning the *Way of People* with the *Way of Nature* (Schade, Stunning Revelations about Lao Zi's Dao De Jing, 2017). Despite the great efforts, previous translations of *Dao De Jing* do not present an adequate understanding of that mysterious manuscript. In order to take optimal advantage of the expertise accumulated in such earlier studies, this meta-translation is based on an English meta-analysis and a Chinese meta-analysis. The English meta-analysis is based on the following English translations— (Chan Wing-Tsit, 1988); (Cheng Gia-Fu and English, J, 1972); (Henricks, 1993); (Land, 1990); (Lau, 1985); (Lin, J. P., 1977); (Man-ho Kwok; Palmer, M.; & Ramsay, J., 1997); (Waley, 1968); and (Wing, 1986). The Chinese meta-analysis is based on the following Chinese versions of *Dao De Jing*— (Wang Bi, 226-249 AD); (He-Shang Gong, 179-157 BC); (Fu Yi, 555-639 AD); (Mawangdui-A, ~200 BC); (Mawangdui-B, ~200 BC); and (Guodian, ~300 BC). This meta-translation of De (Chapters 38-81) is based on a special dictionary (Schade, Dictionary Lao Zi's Dao De Jing, 2018), while it is the foundation for (Schade, Lao Zi's Dao De Jing Demystified, 2017).

Free eBook @
nemonik-thinking.org

Lao Zi's *Dao De Jing* Demystified [4 of 5]

The title of Lao Zi's ancient book *Dao De Jing* means literally—*A Classic about the Way of Nature and the Way of People.* It aims to maximize your success, which is to obtain what you seek and escape what you suffer. Success is maximized by aligning the *Way of People* with the *Way of Nature.* The current study presents four English versions of increasing demystification. The first one is the *Meta-translation* version as developed in (Schade, Meta-translation Lao Zi's Dao De Jing (1-37), 2018) and (Schade, Meta-translation Lao Zi's Dao De Jing (38-81), 2018). However, Lao Zi's poetic style, mysticism, metaphors, and synonyms are still inhibiting a clear understanding. The second one is the *Clarification* version, which is presented in parallel with the *Meta-translation.* That clarification increased the consistency of Lao Zi's terminology, but significant chapters about *Dao* are still located in the *De* section and vice versa. Therefore, the third one is the *Chapters Reorganized* version in which the chapters are relocated to the *Dao* and *De* sections. Nevertheless, the text remains fuzzy, because several chapters relate to both sections. Therefore, the fourth one is the *Sentences Reorganized* version in which the sentences are sorted by topic. That version is the foundation for (Schade, Stunning Revelations about Lao Zi's Dao De Jing, 2017).

Free eBook @
nemonik-thinking.org

Stunning Revelations about Lao Zi... [5 of 5]

The title of Lao Zi's ancient book *Dao De Jing* means in modern terminology—*A Classic about the Physics of Psychology.* *Dao De Jing* is a significant contribution of the Chinese literature to the contemporary sciences of physics and psychology. Lao Zi presents a sophisticated theory concerning the origin, formation, and working of the universe. Although that theory is at the cutting edge of modern physics, it provides a simple and practical principle. That principle holds that the unstoppable force *Qi* will always maintain the multitude of *Yin-Yang* balances comprising our universe. Therefore, Lao Zi's theory of psychology predicts that people can only maximize their success by aligning with *Qi.* Success is to obtain what you seek and escape what you suffer. Unfortunately, humanity has ignored Lao Zi's principles for two-and-halve thousand years. As a result, we are now facing manmade problems such as climate change, continuous warfare, dwindling resources, environmental pollution, and overpopulation. Those problems threaten your personal success and they cannot be solved with the same way of thinking that has created them. Therefore, Lao Zi's *Dao De Jing* is more relevant than ever. His way of dynamic thinking fosters solutions that reach peacefully across the fault-lines created by race, religion, and ideology. This book is based on (Schade, Lao Zi's Dao De Jing Demystified, 2017).

Free eBook @
nemonik-thinking.org

Lao Zi's *Dao De Jing* (Chinese-English)

Lao Zi's *Dao De Jing* or Lao Tzu's *Tao Te Ching* is a beautiful example of ancient Chinese literature. *Dao De Jing* means literally—*A Classic about the Way of Nature and the Way of People*. It aims to maximize your success, which is to obtain what you seek and escape what you suffer. Success is maximized by aligning the *Way of People* with the *Way of Nature*. After two-and-halve thousand years, Lao Zi's wisdom is still ahead of time and outshines intellectual giants such as Confucius, Sun Zi, Socrates, Plato, and Aristotle. Lao Zi's deep understanding of nature and people is your guiding light to a better future, because his way of dynamic thinking reaches peacefully across the fault-lines created by race, religion, and ideology. Therefore, *Dao De Jing* is more relevant than ever. This book comprises Chinese and English versions of *Dao De Jing*, which are extracted from (Schade, Lao Zi's Dao De Jing Demystified, 2017). Furthermore, Lao Zi's amazing secrets are revealed in (Schade, Stunning Revelations about Lao Zi's Dao De Jing, 2017).

Free eBook @
nemonik-thinking.org

Lao Tzu's *Tao Te Ching* (English)

Lao Tzu's *Tao Te Ching* or Lao Zi's *Dao De Jing* is a beautiful example of ancient Chinese literature. *Tao Te Ching* means literally—*A Classic about the Way of Nature and the Way of People.* It aims to maximize your success, which is to obtain what you seek and escape what you suffer. Success is maximized by aligning the *Way of People* with the *Way of Nature.* After two-and-halve thousand years, Lao Tzu's wisdom is still ahead of time and outshines intellectual giants such as Confucius, Sun Zi, Socrates, Plato, and Aristotle. Lao Tzu's deep understanding of nature and people is your guiding light to a better future, because his way of dynamic thinking reaches peacefully across the fault-lines created by race, religion, and ideology. Therefore, *Tao Te Ching* is more relevant than ever. This book comprises an English version of *Tao Te Ching,* which is extracted from (Schade, Lao Zi's Dao De Jing Demystified, 2017). Furthermore, Lao Tzu's amazing secrets are revealed in (Schade, Stunning Revelations about Lao Zi's Dao De Jing, 2017).

Free eBook @
nemonik-thinking.org

Lao Zi for Nemonik Thinkers

Lao Zi's *Dao De Jing* is the most significant contribution from ancient China to contemporary psychology. *Dao De Jing* means in modern terminology—*A Classic about the Physics of Psychology.* It aims to maximize your success, which is to obtain what you seek and escape what you suffer. Success is maximized by aligning psychology with the laws of physics. In accord, nemonik thinking aims to maximize your success by evaluating a checklist of seventeen nemoniks for each situation. Nemoniks are memorized keywords describing all aspects of your mind, reality, and their interaction (Schade, Think Smarter with Nemonik Thinking, 2016). Nemonik thinking provides the exhaustive strategic options for any possible situation, while *Dao De Jing* provides the principle that identifies which of those options will fit the actual situation. Although Lao Zi's holistic format enhances the mystery and poetic beauty of his amazing manuscript, it also reduces the effectiveness of *Dao De Jing* as a rational teaching tool. Therefore, I have used the nemonik template to restructure *Dao De Jing* for nemonik thinkers. Furthermore, Lao Zi's amazing secrets are revealed in (Schade, Stunning Revelations about Lao Zi's Dao De Jing, 2017).

Free eBook @
nemonik-thinking.org

Education Kills Humanity

The aim of this study is to evaluate the educational system with nemonik thinking (Schade, Think Smarter with Nemonik Thinking, 2016). The system conditions students with certificates to maximize their probability of winning the educational competition. The winners are rewarded with advantageous positions in society, while the losers are doomed to serve the winners. Therefore, conventional thinking is conflict oriented, which fosters aggression, control, effort, and force. The conditioned compulsion to win arguments inhibits also the truth and, therefore, it corrupts conventional thinking. As a result, the educational system produces incompetent leaders and rebellious followers. That counterproductive combination fosters manmade problems such as climate change, continuous warfare, dwindling resources, environmental pollution, and overpopulation. Those problems cannot be solved with the same way of conventional thinking that has created them. In contrast, nemonik thinking aims for success, rather than winning. Success is to obtain what you seek and to escape what you suffer. Therefore, nemonik thinking is goal oriented, which fosters freedom, alignment, compassion, allies, and win-win strategies. You might be the best thinker in the world, but only nemonik thinking could make you the smartest thinker you can be. This book contains extracts from (Schade, Think Smarter with Nemonik Thinking, 2016).

Free eBook @
nemonik-thinking.org

Global Warming is the Solution

The aim of this study is to accelerate the development of climatology with nemonik thinking (Schade, Think Smarter with Nemonik Thinking, 2016). About 400,000 years of data, extracted from the Antarctic Vostok ice-core, were subjected to statistical analyses. The results suggest that the duration and thermal stability of the current interglacial are significantly larger than those of the four previous ones are. Hence, the results could not be contributed to natural variables. This supports the hypothesis that the current interglacial period changed some time ago into a glacial period, while artificial global warming has compensated for that natural global cooling. During a glacial period, the average global atmospheric temperature could decrease with about 10.0 °C. This would reduce the global food supply; threaten the global infrastructure; and force billions of people to migrate back towards the equator. Therefore, artificial global warming could be the solution for natural glacial cooling. Further research of this topic is crucial.

Free eBook @
nemonik-thinking.org

The Threat of Bilateral Climate Change

The aim of this study is to accelerate the development of climatology with nemonik thinking (Schade, Think Smarter with Nemonik Thinking, 2016). During the industrial period, the atmospheric CO2 concentration has increased about 120 ppm, while the average global atmospheric temperature increased about 1.4 °C. However, the Vostok thermal function of CO2 during the last 400,000 years predicts that the increase of 120 ppm of CO2 would increase the temperature with 11.6 °C. Hence, there is a thermal gap of 10.2 °C between the observed and predicted temperature. This gap could be explained by the proposed bilateral hypothesis of climate change. This hypothesis holds that the observed increase in average global atmospheric temperature of 1.4 °C is the balance of an artificial global warming of 11.6 °C and a natural global cooling of 10.2 °C. Those large opposing thermal phenomena could explain the recent climatological instability. Furthermore, the bilateral hypothesis predicts that an uncontrolled decrease of atmospheric CO2 could trigger glacial conditions threatening humanity. Therefore, further research of this topic is crucial. This book contains extracts of (Schade, Global Warming is the Solution, 2016).

Free eBook @
nemonik-thinking.org

Sun Zi's The Art of War (planned)

Sun Zi (554-496 BC) was a Chinese warrior-philosopher who wrote the military classic *Bing Fa* or *The Art of War*. Sun Zi applied Lao Zi's philosophy to the art of warfare (Schade, Stunning Revelations about Lao Zi's Dao De Jing, 2017). Similar to Lao Zi, the aim of Sun Zi is to maximize your success by constant positioning. Incompetent warriors will be forced to fight, because they fail to position themselves adequately. As a result, they will destroy their own resources and their potential spoils of war. Hence, a third party might take advantage of their weaknesses and defeat both opponents. Therefore, Sun Zi concludes that superior warriors do not fight. They will pursue the right goals, and are in the right place, at the right time, with the right resources and information, and in the right state of mind. Although Sun Zi's book is about war, his strategies apply to every facet of daily life. He addresses the questions raised by nemonik thinking of where, what, and when to advance, stay, retreat, accumulate, preserve, dispose, act, wait, prepare, accept, reject, reveal, and conceal (Schade, Think Smarter with Nemonik Thinking, 2016). Therefore, maximize your success by incorporating Sun Zi's strategies in your daily thinking.

Free eBook @
nemonik-thinking.org

WEBSITE

It is the aim of my website to provide interactive on-line information about nemonik thinking. This includes discussions, books, blog, videos, exercises, updates, activities, web links, and tests. Join the nemonik thinkers and receive the latest updates. It is a work in progress. Check it out and have your say. I look forward to your feedback at:

http://nemonik-thinking.org

ENDNOTES

1 Factorials: 20 x 22 x 3 x 10 = 13.200.

2 The *Dao* chapters 40 and 42 are incorrectly included in the *De* section, which might indicate changes in the original text (Schade, Lao Zi's Dao De Jing Demystified, 2017).

3 The *De* chapter 30 is incorrectly included in the *Dao* section, which might indicate changes in the original text (Schade, Lao Zi's Dao De Jing Demystified, 2017).

4 [01.00] In the traditional Chinese versions of *Dao De Jing*, *Dao or the Way of Nature* is the first part, while *De or the Way of People* is the second one. In the older Mawangdui versions A and B, the sequence is the other way around. Therefore, the line numbers of the traditional versions differ from the Mawangdui versions. Nevertheless, the present meta-translation follows the chapter sequence of the traditional versions, because one has to understand *Dao or the Way of Nature*, before one could understand *De or the Way of People*.

5 Appendix—Chinese versions *Dao De Jing*

6 Appendix—Chinese versions *Dao De Jing*

7 Appendix—Chinese versions *Dao De Jing*

8 Appendix—Chinese versions *Dao De Jing*

9 Appendix—Chinese versions *Dao De Jing*

10 Appendix—Chinese versions *Dao De Jing*

11 Appendix—Chinese versions *Dao De Jing*

12 Appendix—Chinese versions *Dao De Jing*

13 Appendix—Chinese versions *Dao De Jing*

14 [01.03] — **(a)** secular *All-things*, rather than sacred *Heaven*. The Wang Bi version mentions (天地) *sky and earth,* which could be interpreted as the sacred *Heaven* and the secular *earth*. However, the older Mawangdui versions mention the secular (万物) All-things. For the secular versus the sacred see [04.04b, 05.01a, and 06.02]. — **(b)** (Yang Ju-chou, 1987) translated 无名 as *non-being denotes* and (Land, 1990) as *non-existent.* However, Yang and Land are

inconsistent and translate 无名 also as *Nameless* [32.01, 37.01, 37.03, 37.04, & 41.18]. Lao Zi used elsewhere 无 and 有 as a pair of polarities meaning *Non-existence* and *Existence* [02.03, 11.04 & 40.04]. — **(c)** Lin translated 无名 as *Nameless (non-being)* (Lin, J. P., 1977). This suggests that *Nameless* is the same as *non-being*. In support of this idea, Chan points out that in *Dao*ism, Nameless is equivalent to *Non*-being (Chan Wing-Tsit, 1988, p. 97). However, this idea seems to be incorrect. The undivided *Way* or the *One* needs no names, because there are no parts that need names. Therefore, the *One* is Nameless. Nameless means undivided. The *One* was divided into two parts that are named 无 *Non-being* or *Non-existence* and 有 *Being* or *Existence* [40.03, 42.02]. Thus, *Non*-being has been given a name and by definition, it cannot be equivalent to Nameless. — **(d)** Some scholars have translated 无名 as: *no name, un-named, or nameless* (Waley, 1968), (Cheng Gia-Fu and English, J, 1972), (Wing, 1986), (Chan Wing-Tsit, 1988), (Willemsens, 1990), and (Henricks, 1993). Accordingly, translating 无名 consistently as *Nameless* throughout the entire text poses no problems. — **(e)** There seems to be agreement in the literature that 无名 *Nameless* is the opposite of 有名. This suggests that 有名 should be translated as *having a name* or *being named*.

[15] [01.04] 有名 *being named*. See note 01.03.

[16] [01.05a] Many translators have followed Wang Bi and Ho-shang Kung who punctuated after 无欲 [01.05a] and 有欲 [01.06]. Meaning respectively *having no desires* and *having desires* (Chan Wing-Tsit, 1988, p. 99).

[17] [01.05b] The Mawangdui (A-version) mentions 眇 meaning *negligible, paltry, little, tiny, or minute*. The literature seems to be inconsistent in the translation of 眇 and mentions: *secret essences* (Waley, 1968); *mystery* (Cheng Gia-Fu and English, J, 1972), (Willemsens, 1990); *subtlety* (Lin, J. P., 1977),

(Wing, 1986), (Chan Wing-Tsit, 1988), (Henricks, 1993); *secrets* (Lau, 1985); and *indiscernible point of origin* (Land, 1990). I have interpreted 眇 as *detail*. This interpretation is maintained consistently throughout my version [01.08 & 15.01b].

[18] [01.06a] 有欲 *having desires*. See note 01.05a.

[19] [01.07] The Nameless is the undivided oneness of the *Way*. If we have different objects, we use names to differentiate between them. The Named refers to the divided *Way* into concrete objects or things. However, that division does not increase or decrease the *Way*. The Nameless and Named are just different labels for different manifestations of the same *Way*. The Nameless and the Named might produce different names, but they are derived from the same *Way*. Ultimately, they have the same title.

[20] [01.08] 眇 *detail*. See note 01.05b.

[21] [02.01a] 天下 Secular *Sky below* or sacred *Heaven below* means secular *World*. This is an observation of beauty in the secular *World*, rather than in the sacred *Heaven*. Therefore, 天下 is translated as secular *World*. For the secular versus the sacred see [04.04b, 05.01a, and 06.02].

[22] [02.03] The *One* was divided into two parts 无 *Non-existence* and 有 *Existence* [40.03, 42.02].

[23] [02.06] — Lao Zi's concepts of 牝 *female*, 下 *low*, 江 *river*, 海 *sea*, 神 *force*, 溪 *stream*, 谷 *valley*, 水 *water*, and 阴 *Yin* are associated with the 谷神不死 *Immortal Valley Spirit* or in modern terminology the *Eternal Downward Force or Gravity* [06.02].

[24] [02.09a] 圣人 sages are secular people, rather than sacred devotees [02.09a]. Sages maximize their success by aligning with the secular *Way of Nature*, rather than with the sacred *Way of Heaven*. In accord, Lao Zi defines success as—To obtain what you seek and to escape what you suffer [62.09]. The *Way of Nature* destroys extremes

and cannot be opposed [9, 50, 77]. Therefore, Laozian sages foster 德 virtues that avoid extremes and reduce action such as: 啬 frugality [59, 67]; 慈 compassion [19, 67]; 卑 humbleness [67]; 静 tranquillity [16, 21, 26, 37, 45, 57, 61]; 朴 simplicity [15, 19, 28, 32, 37, 57, 65, 73]; and 退 retreat [7, 9, 69]. On the other hand, they inhibit: 极 extremes [16, 29, 46, 50]; 欲 desire [1, 3, 15, 19, 24, 29, 34, 37, 39, 46, 57. 64, 66, 67]; 藏 hoarding [9, 44, 81]; 贵富 admiring wealth [9, 22, 30, 44, 46, 81]; 见 displaying [3, 19, 22, 24, 36, 69, 72, 77, 80]; 骄 arrogance [9, 16, 22, 24, 30]; 为 action [2, 3, 5, 8, 10, 29, 30, 34, 38, 43, 47, 48, 51, 53, 57, 63, 64, 69, 74, 75, 77, 81]; 事 effort [3, 12, 48, 57, 63, 64, 65]; 强 force [30, 38, 42, and 72]; 敌 resistance [69]; and 争 strive [3, 8, 22, 66, 68, 73, 81]. In contrast, Lao Zi does not mention any sacred rituals, devotion, worship, or praying as virtues. Laozian virtues do not have to be enforced, because they foster personal success in the here and now. Therefore, Laozian sages are secular, efficient, and competent, rather than sacred, religious, and spiritual. They have high moral standards, because it is in their own interest to help and protect other people. Therefore, their morality will last.

[25] [02.09b] 无为 *Non-action.*

[26] [02.11] — **(a)** 生而不有 *generate but not possess.* Same phrase 02.11, 10.08, and 51.11. — **(b)** This phrase is not part of the Mawangdui and Guodian texts. This might have been added later.

[27] [02.12] 为而弗恃 *act but not rely.* Same phrase 02.12, 10.09, 51.12, and 77.09.

[28] [03.02a] 难得之货 *difficult obtain their goods.* Same phrase 03.02a, 12.05 & 64.16b.

[29] [03.04] 圣人 *sages* are secular people, rather than sacred devotees [02.09a].

[30] [03.05] 无欲 *having no desires.* See note 01.05a.

[31] [03.07] 无为 *Non-action.*

[32] [04.02c] — **(a)** In the traditional texts, the sequence of the phrases 04.02c to 04.02e is the same as the sequence of the phrases 56.05 to 56.07. However, the sequence of those phrases in the Mawangdui text is different. This increased order might be a beautification from a later date. — **(b)** 解其纷 *untangle their disorder.* Same phrase 04.02c and 56.05.

[33] [04.02d] 和其光 *soft their glare.* Same phrase 04.02d and 56.06.

[34] [04.02e] 同其尘 *merge their dust.* Same phrase 04.02e and 56.07.

[35] [04.04a] 吾 or 我 *I.* Lao Zi writes in the first person [04.04a, 13.07-13.09, 16.02, 20.08a, 20.10b, 20.11, 20.12b, 20.13b, 20.17, 20.18a, 20.12, 25.04, 25.05, 29.01, 37.03, 42.12, 43.03, 54.14, 57.04, 57.10, 57.11-57.14, 67.05a, 67.05b, 69.02, 69.03, 70.05, and 74.02c]. This suggests that indeed one author wrote *Dao De Jing,* rather than a number of authors over time.

[36] [04.04b] 帝 secular *Emperor,* rather than sacred *God. Dao De Jing* mentions— 道 *Way* [04.01a] and 象帝之先 *seem Emperor ('s) predate* [04.04b]. Together, this means—*The Way … seems to predate the Emperor.* On the other hand, every religion adheres to the dogma that God is the creator of everything and, therefore, God must have been the first in existence. However, in Lao Zi's philosophy 道 *Way* is the first in existence and, therefore, 帝 cannot mean God. Lao Zi does not mean that the *Way predates God,* but that the *Way predates the Emperor.* Hence, 帝 means secular Emperor, rather than sacred God. In ancient China the 天子 Emperor might have been worshipped as 帝 God. Although the Emperor might have been called God, as a human he could not have

created the universe. The Emperor remained a human being with all the limitations of our species. In addition, we may understand *Emperor* as a metaphor for 人 *People*. Similarly, Lao Zi interchanges 王 *King* and 人 *People* [25.08-09]. Furthermore, Lao Zi does not mention God as one of the four *Greatnesses*, which are—*the King, the Earth, the Sky and the Way [25.07-25.10]*. If *Dao De Jing* was about religion, we would also expect to find references to worshipping and serving God. However, such references are missing. Moreover, if *Dao De Jing* was a sacred manuscript, then Lao Zi would portray a sage more as a holy saint, rather than as a competent person. Furthermore, the Guodian version is the oldest version of *Dao De Jing*. This version is entirely secular because it does not mention the concept of God or Emperor. This suggests that *Dao De Jing* is about the physical origin, formation, and working of the universe. It is about the sciences of astrophysics and psychology, rather than religion. *Dao De Jing* is a secular manuscript, rather than a sacred one. For the secular versus the sacred see [04.04b, 05.01a, and 06.02].

[37] [05.01a] 天 secular *Sky* or sacred *Heaven*. Colloquially, 天 could be interpreted as *Heaven* (Waley, 1968), (Cheng Gia-Fu and English, J, 1972), (Lin, J. P., 1977), (Chan Wing-Tsit, 1988), (Lau, 1985), (Wing, 1986), (Land, 1990), (Willemsens, 1990), (Henricks, 1993), (Man-ho Kwok; Palmer, M.; & Ramsay, J., 1997). However, the formal pictographs for *Heaven* are 天堂 *sky hall*, while Lao Zi mentions only 天 *sky*. Furthermore, Lao Zi used 天 as *Sky* in a secular meaning in the phrases—*Violent rains do not drum all day. Who serves them? The Sky and the Earth [23]*. The clouds of the 天 *Sky*, rather than 天堂 *Heaven* provide the *Earth* with rain. In addition, he points out that you do not learn the 天道 *Way of Nature* by looking through a window [47.02]. If you look through a window you see

the secular 天 *sky or nature*, but not the sacred 天堂 *Heaven*. In addition, Lao Zi did not mention God as a *Greatness* in the hierarchy of the universe [25.07-25.10]. Hence, the interpretation of Lao Zi's 天 should be *Sky*, rather than *Heaven*. In accord, other translators have translated 天 as secular *sky* (Griffith, S. B., 1971, p. 65); or secular *Nature* (Yang Ju-chou, 1987), (Wing, 1986), and (Chan Wing-Tsit, 1988). Following that thought, *Dao De Jing* is about the physical origin, formation, and working of the universe. It is about physics and psychology, rather than religion. *Dao De Jing* is a secular manuscript, rather than a sacred one. For the secular versus the sacred see [04.04b, 05.01a, and 06.02].

[38] [05.01b] 刍狗 *straw dog*. Chan points out that in ancient China people used straw dogs as sacrifices (Chan Wing-Tsit, 1988, p. 108). In accord, Yang mentions *sacrifices* rather than *straw dogs* (Yang Ju-chou, 1987, p. 31). The term *straw dog* is confusing. It seems to be uncaring, while Lao Zi considers compassion as the first one of his *Three* treasures—*The first one is called compassion [67]*. In Lao Zi's philosophy, straw dogs have also excellent qualities, because they do not act. If people act as straw dogs, they do not act at all. In that case, they align with the *Way* and follow Lao Zi's crucial principle of *Non-action—Sages will use Non-action. Therefore, they will not fail [64]*. Hence, straw dog might be Lao Zi's metaphor for *Non-action*.

[39] [05.02a] 圣人 sages are secular people, rather than sacred devotees [02.09a].

[40] [05.02b] 刍狗 *straw dog*. See note [05.01b].

[41] [05.03] 天 secular *Sky* or sacred *Heaven*. For the secular versus the sacred see [04.04b, 05.01a, and 06.02].

[42] [05.06b] 中 *middle, inside* or *centre*. Lao Zi uses 中 as an antonym for 闻, which we may translate as *listening or learning*. Lao Zi associates 闻 with Confucian knowledge

and rational thinking. The opposite would be intuitive thinking, which is thinking without conscious thought. Intuitive thinking is following your centre, your inner-self or your heart. Hence, 中 is translated as *heart*.

[43] [06.01] 神 secular *gravity*, rather than sacred *spirit* [06.02]. Lao Zi's concepts of 牝 *female*, 下 *low*, 江 *river*, 海 *sea*, 神 *force*, 溪 *stream*, 谷 *valley*, 水 *water*, and 阴 *Yin* are associated with the 谷神不死 *Immortal Valley Spirit* or in modern terminology the *Eternal Downward Force or Gravity* [06.02].

[44] [06.02] — **(a)** 神 secular *gravity*, rather than sacred *spirit* [06.02]. Lao Zi uses 神 in the term 谷神不死 *valley spirit (immortal)* or *Immortal Valley Spirit* [06.01]. This poetic title seems to refer to a divine, sacred, or spiritual entity. In addition, he calls that spirit the 玄牝 *Mysterious Female* and points out that this female is the origin of the *Sky* and the *Earth* [06.02]. Following that line of thought, our world would then have a divine, sacred, or spiritual origin. However, 神 means also secular *energy and power*. Taking into account both meanings, 神 could be described as an entity that is normally hidden from our awareness in the same way as a *Non*-physical spirit. Nevertheless, that *Non*-physical entity affects reality with physical force and energy. Such an intertwined *Non*-physical and physical entity could be scientific, rather than divine. For example, Lao Zi points out that the invisible *Immortal Valley Spirit* forces water down the valley into the low river and subsequently into the even lower sea. As the river and the sea receive all the water from the valleys, Lao Zi calls them—*Kings of a hundred valleys* [66.01-3]. He points out that nature is so powerful, because it takes a low position [73.04]. Therefore, the *Mysterious Female* has great powers, because females are associated with that powerful low position of nature [61.04-5]. Hence, Lao Zi's *Immortal*

Valley Spirit or *Mysterious Female* could be conceptualized as an invisible entity that wields enormous physical powers able to pull all the water in the world to the lowest point. Therefore, Lao Zi's *Immortal Valley Spirit* could be called in modern terms the *Eternal Gravity Force*, which is secular, rather than sacred. Lao Zi's concepts of 牝 *female*, 下 *low*, 江 *river*, 海 *sea*, 神 *force*, 溪 *stream*, 谷 *valley*, 水 *water*, and 阴 *Yin* are associated with the 谷神不死 *Immortal Valley Spirit* or in modern terminology the *Eternal Downward Force or Gravity* [06.02]. — **(b)** Lao Zi's poetic description of gravity predates Sir Isaac Newton scientific description with more than 2,000 years. The importance of Lao Zi's idea can hardly be overestimated. Gravity is one of the major forces for the formation and working of the universe. The concept of gravity was crucial for Albert Einstein's theories about relativity and the subsequent discovery of black holes. Two thousand years is a long time. One wonders how far physics would have been developed today if Lao Zi's contemporaries would have understood his concept of gravity. — **(c)** In accord with his theory of the *Eternal Gravity Force*, Lao Zi points out that nature is powerful, because it aligns with that force by taking a low position [73.04]. Therefore, he counsels sages, leaders, and countries to become the stream of the world [28.01b and 28.02a] by occupying the low positions [28.07b, 28.08a, 41.090, 61.01, 61.06-11, and 68.04]. — **(d)** Lao Zi is correct, because gravity is the origin of the *Sky* and *Earth*, because it turned gas into fluids and solid matter. — **(e)** Within the secular context of gravity, 天 is translated as secular *Sky*, rather than sacred *Heaven*. For the secular versus the sacred see [04.04b, 05.01a, and 06.02]. (Every time that I initially disagreed with Lao Zi, I discovered later that I did not understand him. Date of this endnote 21-12-2016).

---

[45] [07.01] 天 secular *Sky*, rather than sacred *Heaven*. *Heaven* would foster itself 07.03. Therefore, 天 is translated as *Sky*. For the secular versus the sacred see [04.04b, 05.01a, and 06.02].

[46] [07.02] 天 secular *Sky*, rather than sacred *Heaven*. *Heaven* would foster itself 07.03. Therefore, 天 is translated as *Sky*. For the secular versus the sacred see [04.04b, 05.01a, and 06.02].

[47] [07.03] 天 secular *Sky*, rather than sacred *Heaven*. *Heaven* would foster itself 07.03. Therefore, 07.01 and 07.02 are about the secular *Sky* and *Earth*. For the secular versus the sacred see [04.04b, 05.01a, and 06.02].

[48] [07.05a] 圣人 sages are secular people, rather than sacred devotees [02.09a].

[49] [07.05b] In the Mawangdui B-version, this line is preceded by an additional six pictographs (而身先外元身). Those pictographs are ignored in the present version, because they seem to be redundant and do not appear in the other Chinese versions. It might be a comment added at a later date, suggesting that the Mawangdui B-version is a copy of the A-version.

[50] [08.01] Lao Zi's concepts of 牝 *female*, 下 *low*, 江 *river*, 海 *sea*, 神 *force*, 溪 *stream*, 谷 *valley*, 水 *water*, and 阴 *Yin* are associated with the 谷神不死 *Immortal Valley Spirit* or in modern terminology the *Eternal Downward Force or Gravity* [06.02].

[51] [08.02] Lao Zi's concepts of 牝 *female*, 下 *low*, 江 *river*, 海 *sea*, 神 *force*, 溪 *stream*, 谷 *valley*, 水 *water*, and 阴 *Yin* are associated with the 谷神不死 *Immortal Valley Spirit* or in modern terminology the *Eternal Downward Force or Gravity* [06.02].

[52] [08.07] 天 secular *Sky*, rather than sacred *Heaven*. Only the Mawangdui B version mentions 天 *sky or Heaven* (人仁信

天). The meanings of the pictographs in the other versions are secular. This suggests that 天 in the Mawangdui B version means secular *Sky*, rather than sacred *Heaven*. For the secular versus the sacred see [04.04b, 05.01a, and 06.02].

[53] [09.05b] 天 secular *Nature*, rather than sacred *Heaven*. Withdrawing seems to be related to the nature of tides, plants, storms, day and night, and seasons etc. that withdraw after their extreme is reached. This reference to nature suggests that 天之道 means the secular *Nature's Way*, rather than the sacred *Heaven's Way*. For the secular versus the sacred see [04.04b, 05.01a, and 06.02].

[54] [10.01a] 营魄 *corps de esprit*.

[55] [10.04a] 国 *country, state, nation, realm or region*. See note 25.08.

[56] [10.05] 天 secular *Nature*, rather than sacred *Heaven*. A mortal cannot open and close the gates of *Heaven*. Lao Zi's sentence refers to the role of mortals in the secular cycle of life (opening the gate of nature) and death (closing the gate of nature). Therefore, 天 is translated as secular *Nature*. For the secular versus the sacred see [04.04b, 05.01a, and 06.02].

[57] [10.08] 生而不有 *generate but not possess*. Same phrase 02.11, 10.08, and 51.11.

[58] [10.09] — **(a)** 为而弗恃 *act but not rely*. Same phrase 02.12, 10.09, 51.12, and 77.09. — **(b)** This phrase is not part of the Mawangdui and Guodian texts. This might have been added later.

[59] [10.10] 长而弗宰 *develop but not exploit*. Same phrase 10.10 and 51.13.

[60] [10.11] 谓玄德 *call profound virtue*. Same phrase 10.11 and 51.14.

[61] [11.01b] — **(a)** 当其 (无有) ⎯⎯之用也 *is its (Non-existence) ⎯⎯ ('s) use—* Same phrase 11.01b, 11.02b, and

11.03b. — **(b)** 无 *Non-existence* and 有 *Existence*. See note 02.03.

[62] [11.02b] 当其 (无有) ‗‗‗‗之用也 *is its (Non-existence)* ‗‗‗‗ *('s) use*— Same phrase 11.01b, 11.02b, and 11.03b.

[63] [11.03b] 当其 (无有) ‗‗‗‗之用也 *is its (Non-existence)* ‗‗‗‗ *('s) use*— Same phrase 11.01b, 11.02b, and 11.03b.

[64] [11.04] See note 01.03.

[65] [12.01] In the traditional texts, the phrases that contain the pictograph 五 *five* continue uninterrupted [12.01-12.03]. Hence, it might be that the traditional texts were beautified.

[66] [12.06a] 圣人 sages are secular people, rather than sacred devotees [02.09a].

[67] [12.07] 故去罢耳此 *therefore reject that accept this*. Similar phrase 12.07, 38.15, and 72.07.

[68] [13.07] 吾 or 我 *I*. See note 04.04a.

[69] [13.10a] 天下 Secular *Sky below* or sacred *Heaven below* means secular *World*. Only God can be trusted with *Heaven*. A mortal cannot be trusted with the purpose of *Heaven* [13.10b]. Therefore, the meaning of 天下 is secular, rather than sacred. For the secular versus the sacred see [04.04b, 05.01a, and 06.02].

[70] [13.10b] 天下 Secular *Sky below* or sacred *Heaven below* means secular *World*. Only God can be trusted with *Heaven*. A mortal cannot be trusted with the purpose of *Heaven* [13.10b]. Therefore, the meaning of 天下 is secular, rather than sacred. For the secular versus the sacred see [04.04b, 05.01a, and 06.02].

[71] [13.11a] 天下 Secular *Sky below* or sacred *Heaven below* means secular *World*. Only God can be trusted with *Heaven*. A mortal cannot be trusted with the purpose of *Heaven* [13.10b]. Therefore, the meaning of 天下 is secular, rather than sacred. For the secular versus the sacred see [04.04b, 05.01a, and 06.02].

[72] [13.11c] 天下 Secular *Sky below* or sacred *Heaven below* means secular *World*. Only God can be trusted with *Heaven*. A mortal cannot be trusted with the purpose of *Heaven* [13.10b]. Therefore, the meaning of 天下 is secular, rather than sacred. For the secular versus the sacred see [04.04b, 05.01a, and 06.02].

[73] [14.05] As we cannot examine the *Way* by seeing, hearing or feeling, it makes common sense that the faint image obtained with our senses are merged into one image called the *One*.

[74] [14.10] 惚 *dim* and 恍 *elusive*. Also in 14.10, 21.02, 21.03, and 21.05.

[75] [14.13] 无 *Non-existence* and 有 *Existence*. See note 02.03.

[76] [15.01b] 眇 *detail*. See note 01.05b.

[77] [15.10] Lao Zi's concepts of 牝 *female*, 下 *low*, 江 *river*, 海 *sea*, 神 *force*, 溪 *stream*, 谷 *valley*, 水 *water*, and 阴 *Yin* are associated with the 谷神不死 *Immortal Valley Spirit* or in modern terminology the *Eternal Downward Force or Gravity* [06.02].

[78] [15.11] In the traditional texts, Lao Zi's argument about 浊 *mud* continues [15.11-15.13]. It might be that these texts were beautified.

[79] [16.02b] 吾 or 我 *I*. See note 04.04a.

[80] [16.13] 天 secular *Nature*, rather than sacred *Heaven*. If Honourable is Kingly [16.12] and Kingly is natural [16.13], then honourable is natural (Aristotelian logic). Lao Zi advises sages to be honourable or natural in this secular *World*, rather than in the sacred *Heaven*. Whether 天 is secular or sacred, to be honourable in *Heaven* would be too late. Therefore, 天 is translated as secular *Nature*. For the secular versus the sacred see [04.04b, 05.01a, and 06.02].

[81] [16.14] 天 secular *Nature*, rather than sacred *Heaven*. See [16.13]. For the secular versus the sacred see [04.04b, 05.01a, and 06.02].

[82] [16.15b] 没身不殆 *produce life without danger.* Same phrase 16.15b and 52.03c.

[83] [18.01a] This chapter starts with 故 *Therefore* .... It seems to be a continuation of the previous chapter. Alternatively, the sequence of the text might have been disrupted.

[84] [18.04a] 国 *country, state, nation, realm or region.* See note 25.08.

[85] [19.06] 朴 *pure, plain, simple, honest, or unadorned.* Some translators mention here the *uncarved block* (Waley, 1968), and (Lau, 1985), which is a metaphor for the simplicity and oneness of the *Way*. Similarly, other translators mention *simplicity* (Cheng Gia-Fu and English, J, 1972), (Lin, J. P., 1977), (Wing, 1986), (Chan Wing-Tsit, 1988), (Land, 1990), (Man-ho Kwok; Palmer, M.; & Ramsay, J., 1997); or *genuine* (Henricks, 1993). Hence, it seems appropriate to translate 朴 as *simplicity.*

[86] [20.01] In the traditional texts, this is the first sentence of chapter 20. However, in the Mawangdui texts, this sentence is part of the previous chapter. Lao Zi concludes what sages should do [19.05-20.01]. Therefore, it would make sense to move this sentence to finish chapter 19.

[87] [20.02b] 其相去几何 *they (each other) difference (how much).* Similar phrase as 20.03b.

[88] [20.03b] 其 相 去 何 若 *they (each other) different how seem.* *Similar* phrase as 20.02b.

[89] [20.07b] 登 *step on, tread, press down with foot, mount, ascend, publish, record, and climbing.* In addition, 台 *means table, stage and platform.* Thus, 登台 is related to stepping on a stage for entertainment to celebrate 春 *spring.*

[90] [20.08a] 吾 or 我 *I.* See note 04.04a.

[91] [20.10b] *lack* is selected as the antonym for 余 *surplus* in phrase 20.10a, rather than 遗 *loss.*

[92] [20.12b] 胃 The meaning of this pictograph is unclear.

[93] [20.13a] (察察, 祭祭, or 蔡蔡) versus [20.13b] (闷闷, 闵闵, or 闽闽) are ambiguous antonyms, which are interpreted as *very certain* [20.13a] and *very uncertain* [20.13b].

[94] [20.13a] — **(a)** (察察, 祭祭, or 蔡蔡) versus [20.13b] (闷闷, 闵闵, or 闽闽) are ambiguous antonyms, which are interpreted as *very certain* [20.13a] and *very uncertain* [20.13b]. — **(b)** [20.13b] 闽闽 The meaning of these pictographs remained unclear.

[95] [21.02] 惚 *dim* and 恍 *elusive.* Also in 14.10, 21.02, 21.03, and 21.05.

[96] [21.03] 惚 *dim* and 恍 *elusive.* Also in 14.10, 21.02, 21.03, and 21.05.

[97] [21.05] 惚 *dim* and 恍 *elusive.* Also in 14.10, 21.02, 21.03, and 21.05.

[98] [21.11] 父 *father.*

[99] [21.12] — **(a)** 吾 or 我 *I.* See note 04.04a. — **(b)** 吾何以知 *I how consider know...* Same phrase 21.12, 54.14, and 57.04.

[100] [22.07a] 圣人 sages are secular people, rather than sacred devotees [02.09a].

[101] [22.07b] 天下 Secular *Sky below* or sacred *Heaven below* means secular *World.* God is the shepherd of *Heaven.* Mortals can be the shepherds of the *World* but not *Heaven.* Therefore, the meaning of 天下 is secular, rather than sacred. For the secular versus the sacred see [04.04b, 05.01a, and 06.02].

[102] [23.04] 天 secular *Sky,* rather than sacred *Heaven.* 雨 *rain* [23.03] is produced by the secular *Sky* [23.04], rather than the sacred *Heaven.* Therefore, 天 is translated as secular *Sky.* For the secular versus the sacred see [04.04b, 05.01a, and 06.02].

[103] [23.06] 有兄人于乎 *have brother people.* The meaning of the pictographs is unclear within the context.

[104] [23.10] 德 means 'virtue or favour', which should be the antonym of 失 'lose' in [23.11]. Therefore, 得 'gain', as used in the other Chinese versions than Mawangdui, is a better interpretation of 德 than 'virtue' as used in Mawangdui.

[105] [23.12] 同于失者失亦乐得之 *merge to lose those lose also happy obtain their.* This phrase is not part of the Mawangdui and Guodian texts. This might have been added later.

[106] [23.13] 信不足焉有 (不信) 焉 truth *not enough then have (no trust) how.* This phrase is not part of the Mawangdui and Guodian texts. This might have been added later.

[107] [24.01] In the Mawangdui texts, this chapter follows chapter 21. The traditional sequence makes more sense. Chapters 23 and 24 are both about over-extension. However, it might be that the traditional texts were beautified.

[108] [24.02] 跨者不行 *stride those not move.* This phrase is not part of the Mawangdui and Guodian texts. This might have been added later.

[109] [24.08] 物或恶之 *thing (may be) disgust ('s).* Same phrase 24.08 and 31.02.

[110] [24.09] 有欲 *having desires.* See note 01.05a.

[111] [25.01] — **(a)** 天 secular *Sky*, rather than sacred *Heaven*. In religion, *God* and *Heaven* predate everything else. Therefore, 天 is translated as secular *Sky*, rather than sacred *Heaven*. For the secular versus the sacred see [04.04b, 05.01a, and 06.02]. — **(b)** Some translators mentioned the word *chaos* in this phrase (Lin, J. P., 1977) and (Henricks, 1993). However, the words *desolate* and *empty* (25.02) contradict that interpretation. Chaos is by definition associated with Existence. The origin would have been either chaotic or empty. A chaotic emptiness is a contradiction in terms.

[112] [25.03b] 周行而不殆 *thorough act and not danger.* This phrase is not part of the Mawangdui and Guodian texts. This might have been added later.

[113] [25.03c] 天下 Secular *Sky below* or sacred *Heaven below* means secular *World.* Nothing could be the origin of *Heaven.* Therefore, the meaning of 天下 is secular, rather than sacred. For the secular versus the sacred see [04.04b, 05.01a, and 06.02].

[114] [25.04] 吾 or 我 *I.* See note 04.04a.

[115] [25.07b] 天 secular *Sky*, rather than sacred *Heaven.* In other lines of chapter 25, 天 is the secular *Sky* [25.01, 25.10a-c]. For the secular versus the sacred see [04.04b, 05.01a, and 06.02].

[116] [25.08] — **(a)** 国 *country, state, nation, realm or region.* In accord, Lao Zi used that meaning of 国 [10.4, 18.04, 36.08, 54.07, 54.12, 59.06, 59.07, 60.01, 61.01, 61.01, 61.06, 61.07, 61.09, 61.10, 65.03, 65.04, 78.08, 78.09, 80.01, and 80.10]. However, Chan mentions that Wang Bi and Ho-shang Kung explain that 国 also means *without name* or *unlimited space* (Chan Wing-Tsit, 1988, pp. 145, note 2). In accord, several translators mention here *universe* (Cheng Gia-Fu and English, J, 1972), (Lin, J. P., 1977), (Wing, 1986), and (Chan Wing-Tsit, 1988). The *Way* and the *Sky* are concepts that are not restricted to any one country. The *Way* is not restricted to our planet. Therefore, *universe* seems to be indeed a more appropriate translation of 国 than *country.* — **(b)** 王 *King.* Comparison of the lines 25.08 and 25.09 shows that Lao Zi replaces 王 *King* by 人 *people* in his argument. This suggests that Lao Zi used King as a symbol for People. Chan mentions that the Fu I and Fan *Ying*-yuan versions have *man* instead of *King* (Chan Wing-Tsit, 1988, p. 145). This supports the notion that King is a metaphor for People.

[117] [25.10a] 天 secular *Sky*, rather than sacred *Heaven*. The sacred *Heaven* would follow the *Way* [25.10b] or nature [25.10c]. Therefore, 天 is translated as secular *Sky*. For the secular versus the sacred see [04.04b, 05.01a, and 06.02].

[118] [25.10b] 天 secular *Sky*, rather than sacred *Heaven*. The secular *Sky* would follow the *Way*, but the sacred *Heaven* would follow neither the *Way* [25.10b] nor nature [25.10c]. For the secular versus the sacred see [04.04b, 05.01a, and 06.02].

[119] [26.05b] 天下 Secular *Sky below* or sacred *Heaven below* means secular *State*. All lords who are believers in *Heaven* would believe that they are less important than *Heaven*. Hence, Lao Zi would state the obvious. Therefore, 天下 is translated as secular *State*. A ruler who considers himself less important than the state he is ruling might be a good ruler. For the secular versus the sacred see [04.04b, 05.01a, and 06.02].

[120] [27.06a] 圣人 sages are secular people, rather than sacred devotees [02.09a].

[121] [27.07] 常善救物 *always competent save thing*. This phrase is not part of the Mawangdui and Guodian texts. This might have been added later.

[122] [27.14] 眇 *detail*. See note 01.05b.

[123] [28.01a] — **(a)** Lao Zi's concepts of 牝 *female*, 下 *low*, 江 *river*, 海 *sea*, 神 *force*, 溪 *stream*, 谷 *valley*, 水 *water*, and 阴 *Yin* are associated with the 谷神不死 *Immortal Valley Spirit* or in modern terminology the *Eternal Downward Force or Gravity* [06.02]. — **(b)** The phrases 28.01a, 28.04a, and 28.07a seem to be related to chapter 42 about *Yin* and *Yang* [42.05 and 42.06].

[124] [28.01b] — **(a)** 天下 Secular *Sky below* or sacred *Heaven below* means secular *World*. Stream seems to be related to the secular *World*. Therefore, 天下 is translated as secular

World. For the secular versus the sacred see [04.04b, 05.01a, and 06.02]. — **(b)** Lao Zi's concepts of 牝 *female*, 下 *low*, 江 *river*, 海 *sea*, 神 *force*, 溪 *stream*, 谷 *valley*, 水 *water*, and 阴 *Yin* are associated with the 谷神不死 *Immortal Valley Spirit* or in modern terminology the *Eternal Downward Force or Gravity* [06.02].

[125] [28.02a] — **(a)** 天下 Secular *Sky below* or sacred *Heaven below* means secular *World.* Stream seems to be related to the secular *World.* Therefore, 天下 is translated as secular *World.* For the secular versus the sacred see [04.04b, 05.01a, and 06.02]. — **(b)** Lao Zi's concepts of 牝 *female*, 下 *low*, 江 *river*, 海 *sea*, 神 *force*, 溪 *stream*, 谷 *valley*, 水 *water*, and 阴 *Yin* are associated with the 谷神不死 *Immortal Valley Spirit* or in modern terminology the *Eternal Downward Force or Gravity* [06.02].

[126] [28.04a] — **(a)** The phrases 28.01a, 28.04a, and 28.07a seem to be related to chapter 42 about *Yin* and *Yang* [42.05 and 42.06]. — **(b)** The Mawangdui phrases 72.07 to 72.09 appear immediately after the Mawangdui phrase 72.03. This sequence interrupts the argument about 朴 *simplicity.* Although the traditional sequence seems to be more appropriate, it might be that the order of the traditional texts was beautified. — **(c)** The first pictographs 知其白守其 *know its ... observe its* are exactly the same as the first pictographs of line 28.07. In addition, 白 means *pure and white,* which is here the opposite of 黑 *black.* Therefore, 白 is interpreted here as *white.*

[127] [28.04b] 天下 Secular *Sky below* or sacred *Heaven below* means secular *World.* No mortal could be the example of *Heaven.* Therefore, 天下 is translated as secular *World.* For the secular versus the sacred see [04.04b, 05.01a, and 06.02].

[128] [28.05a] — **(a)** 天下 Secular *Sky below* or sacred *Heaven below* means secular *World*. No mortal could be the example of *Heaven*. Therefore, 天下 is translated as secular *World*. For the secular versus the sacred see [04.04b, 05.01a, and 06.02]. — **(b)** The Mawangdui phrases 72.07 to 72.09 appear immediately after the Mawangdui phrase 72.03. This sequence interrupts the argument about 朴 *simplicity*. Although the traditional sequence seems to be more appropriate, it might be that the order of the traditional texts was beautified.

[129] [28.06a] The Mawangdui phrases 72.07 to 72.09 appear immediately after the Mawangdui phrase 72.03. This sequence interrupts the argument about 朴 *simplicity*. Although the traditional sequence seems to be more appropriate, it might be that the order of the traditional texts was beautified.

[130] [28.07a] — **(a)** The phrases 28.01a, 28.04a, and 28.07a seem to be related to chapter 42 about *Yin* and *Yang* [42.05 and 42.06]. — **(b)** The first pictographs 知其白守其 *know its ... observe its* are exactly the same as the first pictographs of line 28.04. In addition, 白 means *pure and white*, which is here the opposite of 辱 *impure* or *disgraced*. Therefore, 白 is interpreted here as *pure*.

[131] [28.07b] — **(a)** 天下 Secular *Sky below* or sacred *Heaven below* means secular *World*. Valleys are associated with the secular *World*. Therefore, 天下 is translated as secular World. For the secular versus the sacred see [04.04b, 05.01a, and 06.02]. — **(b)** Lao Zi's concepts of 牝 *female*, 下 *low*, 江 *river*, 海 *sea*, 神 *force*, 溪 *stream*, 谷 *valley*, 水 *water*, and 阴 *Yin* are associated with the 谷神不死 *Immortal Valley Spirit* or in modern terminology the *Eternal Downward Force or Gravity* [06.02].

[132] [28.08a] — **(a)** 天下 Secular *Sky below* or sacred *Heaven below* means secular *World*. Valleys are associated with the

secular *World*. Therefore, 天下 is translated as secular World. For the secular versus the sacred see [04.04b, 05.01a, and 06.02]. — **(b)** Lao Zi's concepts of 牝 *female,* 下 *low,* 江 *river,* 海 *sea,* 神 *force,* 溪 *stream,* 谷 *valley,* 水 *water,* and 阴 *Yin* are associated with the 谷神不死 *Immortal Valley Spirit* or in modern terminology the *Eternal Downward Force or Gravity* [06.02].

133 [28.10] 器 *tool, utensil,* etc. Chan argues that 器 has also a more general meaning and could be interpreted as *concrete things* (Chan Wing-Tsit, 1988, pp. 150, note 3).

134 [28.11a] 圣人 sages are secular people, rather than sacred devotees [02.09a].

135 [29.01a] — **(a)** 天下 Secular *Sky below* or sacred *Heaven below* means secular *World.* No mortal could interfere with *Heaven.* Therefore, 天下 is translated as secular *World.* For the secular versus the sacred see [04.04b, 05.01a, and 06.02]. — **(b)** Chapter 29 seems to be a logical extension of chapter 28.

136 [29.01b] 吾 or 我 *I.* See note 04.04a.

137 [29.02a] — **(a)** 天下 Secular *Sky below* or sacred *Heaven below* means secular *World.* Continues from [29.01a]—no mortal could interfere with *Heaven.* Therefore, 天下 is translated as secular *World.* For the secular versus the sacred see [04.04b, 05.01a, and 06.02]. — **(b)** 神 secular *amazing, clever, energy, and power,* rather than sacred *divine, God, and spirit.* Within the context of 天下 secular *World,* 神 is interpreted as secular *energy.* — **(c)** Chapter 29 seems to be a logical extension of chapter 28.

138 [29.03a] 为之者败之 *act ('s) those fail ('s).* Same phrase 29.03a and 64.10a.

139 [29.03b] 执之者失之 *hold ('s) those lose ('s).* Same phrase 29.03b and 64.10b.

140 [29.05] 吹 or 坐 *blow or subside*. The meaning of the pictographs is unclear within the context. However, *cold* is the antonym for 热 *hot*.

141 [29.08a] 圣人 sages are secular people, rather than sacred devotees [02.09a].

142 [30.01b] 天下 Secular *Sky below* or sacred *Heaven below* means secular *World*. One cannot use soldiers to force the sacred *Heaven*. Therefore, 天下 is translated as secular *World*. For the secular versus the sacred see [04.04b, 05.01a, and 06.02].

143 [30.03] 所居 *place stay*. Interpreted as *camped*.

144 [30.04] 大军之后必有凶年 *big army ('s) behind certainly happen bad harvest*. This phrase is not part of the Mawangdui and Guodian texts. This might have been added later.

145 [30.12] 物壮而老 *thing strong yet weak* . Similar phrases 30.12 and 55.16.

146 [30.13] 谓之不道 *call their not Way*. Same phrase 30.13 and 55.17.

147 [30.14] 不道早已 *not Way early perish*. Same phrase 30.14 and 55.18.

148 [31.02] 物或恶之 *thing (may be) disgust ('s)*. Same phrase 24.07 and 31.02.

149 [31.03] 有道 *possess Way* makes more sense in this context than 有欲 *possess desire*.

150 [31.10b] 天下 Secular *Sky below* or sacred *Heaven below* means secular *State*. In religion, only God can understand and achieve the goals of *Heaven*. Therefore, 天下 is translated as *State*. Those rulers who like to kill people will evoke reactions that will destroy their *State*. For the secular versus the sacred see [04.04b, 05.01a, and 06.02].

151 [31.11] 左 *left* is associated with the unorthodox.

152 [31.12] 右 *right* is associated with the orthodox.

153 [32.01] — **(a)** 无名 *Nameless.* See note 01.03. — **(b)** 道恒 （无名） *Way forever (nameless).* Same phrase 32.01 and 37.01a.

154 [32.02b] 天下 Secular *Sky below* or sacred *Heaven below* means secular *World.* The sacred *Heaven* could control whatever it wants to control. Therefore, 天下 is translated as secular *World.* For the secular versus the sacred see [04.04b, 05.01a, and 06.02].

155 [32.03a] 侯王若能守之 *marquise king if can follow its.* Same phrase 32.03a and 37.02a.

156 [32.04] 天 secular *Sky* or sacred *Heaven.* For the secular versus the sacred see [04.04b, 05.01a, and 06.02].

157 [32.09] 知止 / (所以) 不殆 *know stop / (why) not danger.* Same phrase 32.09 and 44.07.

158 [32.10a] 天下 Secular *Sky below* or sacred *Heaven below* means secular *World.* Indeed, the secular *World* is lower than the *Way.* However, the sacred *Heaven* could not be lower than anything. Therefore, 天下 is translated as secular *World.* For the secular versus the sacred see [04.04b, 05.01a, and 06.02].

159 [32.10b] Lao Zi's concepts of 牝 *female,* 下 *low,* 江 *river,* 海 *sea,* 神 *force,* 溪 *stream,* 谷 *valley,* 水 *water,* and 阴 *Yin* are associated with the 谷神不死 *Immortal Valley Spirit* or in modern terminology the *Eternal Downward Force or Gravity* [06.02].

160 [32.10b] Lao Zi's concepts of 牝 *female,* 下 *low,* 江 *river,* 海 *sea,* 神 *force,* 溪 *stream,* 谷 *valley,* 水 *water,* and 阴 *Yin* are associated with the 谷神不死 *Immortal Valley Spirit* or in modern terminology the *Eternal Downward Force or Gravity* [06.02].

161 [33.05] 知足 *...know enough ...* Similar warnings 33.05 and 44.06.

[162] [34.05a] (万物) 归焉 *(All-things) return then.* Same phrase 34.05a and 34.08a.

[163] [34.05b] 而弗为主 *yet not act master.* Same phrase 34.05b and 34.08b.

[164] [34.06] 无欲 *having no desires.* See note 01.05a.

[165] [34.08a] (万物) 归焉 *(All-things) return then.* Same phrase 34.05a and 34.08a.

[166] [34.08b] 而弗为主 *yet not act master.* Same phrase 34.05b and 34.08b.

[167] [34.10a] — **(a)** 圣人 sages are secular people, rather than sacred devotees [02.09a]. — **(b)** 能成大 ... *can achieve great.* Same phrase 34.10a and 63.11. — **(b)** Same meaning 34.10a and 63.11.

[168] [35.01] 天下 Secular *Sky below* or sacred *Heaven below* means secular *World.* Mortals might go to the sacred *Heaven,* but *Heaven* will not come to them. Therefore, 天下 is translated as secular *World.* For the secular versus the sacred see [04.04b, 05.01a, and 06.02].

[169] [35.07] 既 *already.* The context suggests that 既 should be interpreted as *finished or depleted.*

[170] [36.01b] 古 *ancient.* Interpreted as *before.*

[171] [36.02b] 古 *ancient.* Interpreted as *before.*

[172] [36.08] 国 *country, state, nation, realm or region.* See note 25.08.

[173] [37.01] — **(a)** 无名 *Nameless.* See note 01.03. — **(b)** 道恒 (无名) *Way forever (nameless).* Same phrase 32.01 and 37.01a.

[174] [37.01b] 而无 (不为) *and Non-existent (Non-action).* This phrase is not part of the Mawangdui and Guodian texts. This might have been added later.

[175] [37.02a] 侯王若能守之 *marquise king if can follow its.* Same phrase 32.03a and 37.02a.

[176] [37.03b] — **(a)** 无名 *Nameless.* See note 01.03. — **(b)** 吾 or 我 *I.* See note 04.04a.

[177] [37.04a] — **(a)** 无名 *Nameless.* See note 01.03

[178] [37.05b] 天下 Secular *Sky below* or sacred *Heaven below* means secular *World.* The sacred *Heaven* is perfect and does not need any regulation. Therefore, 天下 is translated as secular *World.* For the secular versus the sacred see [04.04b, 05.01a, and 06.02].

[179] [32.04-05] If the 天 and the Earth would unite with each other, then it would rain sweet dew.

[180] [05.01a & 03] The Sky and the Earth do not have to be benevolent, if All-things would act as straw dogs... What is between the Sky and the Earth is like a pair of bellows.

[181] [23.03-04] Violent rains do not drum all day. Who serves them? The Sky and the Earth.

[182] [06.02] The home of this Mysterious Female is called the origin of the Sky and the Earth.

[183] [25.01 & 07 & 09-10] There was a thing Undivided and complete before the Sky and the Earth were born... Therefore, the Way is great, the Sky is great, the Earth is great, and the King is also great... Therefore, people follow the Earth, the Earth follows the Sky, the Sky follows the Way, and the Way follows nature.

[184] [07.01-03] The Sky endures and the Earth last long. Why do the Sky and the Earth last long and endure? That is, because they do not foster themselves.

[185] [39.02 & 09] the Sky obtained the One through pureness; ... if the Sky is not clear yet,

[186] [67.18] 天 will protect them with a wall of compassion.

[187] [09.05b] withdrawing yourself is the Way of Nature.

[188] [16.02a-04] All-things around us rise, and I watch them return. Those things are numerous and each one returns to its roots. Returning to the roots is called tranquillity.

[189] [10.05] Open and close the gates of nature as a female.

[190] [47.02] Do not look through the window in order to learn about the Way of Nature.

[191] [59.01] In ruling people and working with nature there is nothing like frugality.

[192] [68.06-7] That is called employing people. That is called matching with nature.

[193] 73.04a & 10-11] Nature takes a low place... The net of nature is very extensive. It dredges and nothing escapes.

[194] [77.01-04] The Way of Nature is like flexing a bow. High things are lowered. Low things are raised. It takes from those who have plenty. It gives to those who have not enough. Therefore, it is the Way of Nature to take from what is plenty and give to what is not enough.

[195] [81.10] Therefore, the Way of Nature is beneficial and without harm.

[196] [79.06] The Way of Nature has no favourites. It is always with the competent people.

[197] 天下 World—02.01a, 13.10, 13.11a & c, 22.07b, 25.03c, 28.01b, 28.02a, 28.04b, 28.05a, 28.07b, 28.08a, 29.01a, 29.02a, 30.01b, 31.10b, 32.02b, 32.10a, 35.01, 39.07, 40.03, 43.01, 43.04c, 45.11b, 46.01a, 46.02a, 47.01b, 48.05a, 48.06b, 49.09, 49.10b, 52.01, 54.08, 54.13-14, 56.15, 57.03-4, 57.05b, 60.02a, 61.02-3, 62.10, 63.08-9, 66.08-9, 67.01, 67.08, 67.11, 77.07b, 78.01, 78.05, and 78.09b.

[198] 天下 State—26.05b.

[199] 天下 Country—61.01.

[200] Sentences related to Lao Zi's 谷神不死 *Immortal Valley Spirit [06.01]* or in modern terminology the *Eternal Downward Force or Gravity* [06.01-2, 08.01-2, 15.10, 28.01a-02a, 28.07b, 28.08a, 32.10a-c, 39.05, 39.12a, 41.09, 42.05a, 61.01, 61.03-04, 61.05b, 61.06a, 61.07a, 61.08, 61.11b, 66.01-3, 68.04, 73.04a, 77.02, 78.01]. For the secular versus the sacred see [04.04b, 05.01a, and 06.02].

[201] Nature takes a low position [73.04].

[202] Stream of the world [28.01b, 28.02a].

[203] Sages should take a low position [28.07b, 28.08a, 41.09, 61.01, 61.06-11, and 68.04].

[204] [29.01-03b] If people desire to take the world and interfere with it, I see that they have no alternative. The world is a container of energy that cannot be interfered with. Those who act will fail. Those who hold will lose.

[205] [39.01-06] Of those in the past that obtained the One: the Sky obtained the One through pureness; the Earth obtained the One through quietness; the mind obtained the One through effectiveness; the valley obtained the One through filling; All-things obtain the One by growing.

[206] [60.02a-03b] Use the Way to attend to the world, then the underhanded will have no power. It is not that the underhanded have no power, but their power will not harm people.

[207] Avoid 极 *extremes*—[16.01] Concentrate on removing extremes. Nurture tranquillity diligently. [29.08a] Therefore, sages reject extremes. [46.03] No greater suffering than having extreme desires. [50.04a-06] Three in ten people live extremely and move into the realm of death. What is the reason? That is because they live extremely.

[208] Foster 德 *virtue*—[10.01-05] Carry the team spirit and unite it inseparable with the One. Concentrate vital energy and be as flexible as an infant. Study and eliminate problems. Inspect them competently without flaws. Love the people and rule the country without using knowledge. Open and close the gates of nature as a female. Understand the surroundings without using knowledge. Generate them and raise them. Generate, but do not possess. Act, but do not rely on it. Develop but do not exploit. This is called profound virtue. [21.01] The greatest virtue is following only the Way. [23.08-10] Those who submit their affairs to virtue will merge with virtue. Those who submit their affairs to loss will merge with loss.

Those who merge with virtue will also gain the Way. [28.02a-03b] Be the stream of the world and the eternal virtue never leaves. If the eternal virtue never leaves, then you will return to infancy. [28.05a-06b] Be the example for the world and the eternal virtue never errs. If the eternal virtue never errs, then it returns to moderation. [28.08a-09b] Be the valley of the world and the eternal virtue will be always enough. If the eternal virtue is always enough, then you will return to simplicity. [38.01a-03b] Superior virtue pursues no virtue. Therefore, it is virtue. Inferior virtue pursues virtue. Therefore, it is no virtue. Superior virtue uses Non-action and there is no action used. [38.07-08] Therefore, after the Way is lost, there will be virtue. After virtue is lost, there will be benevolence. [41.09] Superior virtue is just like a valley. [41.11-12] Extensive virtue seems to be insufficient. Established virtue seems to drift along. [51.01-02] The Way generates them and virtue raises them. [51.05-06] Therefore, All-things respect the Way and admire virtue. Respecting the Way and admiring virtue is not done to obtain a noble position, but it is always done to be natural. [51.11-14] Generate, but do not possess. Act, but do not rely on it. Develop but do not exploit. This is called profound virtue. [54.04-08] Cultivate it in yourself and it will be genuine. Cultivate it in your household and it will be plenty. Cultivate it in your village and its virtue will last long. Cultivate it in your country and its virtue will be abundant. Cultivate it in the world and its virtue will be extensive. [55.01] Those who have substantial virtue could be compared to new-born babies. [59.03-04] Prepare for the call to serve early by a significant accumulation of virtue. If there is a significant accumulation of virtue, then nothing is impossible. [60.07] Therefore, virtue unites and returns. [65.05-08] Examine also the principle. Always remembering to examine the principle is called profound virtue. Profound virtue is deep. Even far away things return to it. [68.04-05] Competent leaders will take a low position. That is called the virtue of not striving. [79.04-05] Therefore, those with virtue will uphold the agreement. Those without virtue will uphold the details.

209 Foster 慈 *compassion*—[19.02] Discard benevolence and reject righteousness and the people will return to filial piety and compassion. [67.05-06] I have always three treasures that I keep and protect. The first one is called compassion. [67.09] Those who are compassionate can be courageous. [67.12 & 15] Now, those who abandon compassion and are yet courageous; they will certainly die. [67.16-18] Those who use compassion to attack will triumph. Those who use it to defend will stand firm. Nature will protect them with a wall of compassion.

210 Foster 嗇 or 俭 *frugality*—[59.01-02] In ruling people and working with nature there is nothing like frugality. Only those who are frugal are called to early service. [67.05] I have always three treasures that I keep and protect. [67.07] The second one is called frugality. [67.10] Those who are frugal can be generous. [67.13] abandon their frugality and are yet generous; [67.15] they will certainly die.

211 Foster 日不敢为天下先 *humbleness*—[67.05] I have always three treasures that I keep and protect. [67.08] The third one is called humbleness.

212 Foster 退 *retreat or withdrawal*—[07.05a] Accordingly, sages withdraw themselves. [09.05a] When merit is achieved, withdrawing yourself is the Way of Nature. [69.01-03] Warriors have a saying that states: "I do not dare to act as a host, but act as a guest. I do not dare to advance an inch, but retreat a foot."

213 Foster 朴 *simplicity*—[15.01] Those Ancients who practised the Way competently, understood profoundly the smallest details. [15.09] Vague, like they were simple. [19.06] Show modesty and embrace simplicity. [28.09-10] If the eternal

virtue is always enough, then you will return to simplicity. Simplicity breaks up and then it becomes tools. [37.03-04] If this transformation would cause desire, then I would suppress it by using the simplicity of the Nameless. Suppressing it by using the simplicity of the Nameless will not disgrace them. [57.13] I desire not to desire and the people will become simple by themselves.

214 Foster 时 *timing or proactivity*—[08.11] In action, the goodness is timing. [63.07-15] Act large, while it is still small. The world's most difficult things arise from the easiest.   The world's largest things arise from the smallest.   Therefore, all sages will avoid great actions. Hence, they can achieve greatness. Those who make rash promises are certainly difficult to trust. Those who regard everything as easy will have certainly many difficulties. Therefore, sages regard everything as difficult.   Hence, they have no difficulties in the end. [64.01-09] That what is at rest is easy to hold. That what is not manifest is easy to plan. That what is fragile is easy to break. That what is small is easy to scatter. Act when it has not happened yet. Control it when it is not chaotic yet. A tree that takes both arms to embrace grows from a little cutting. Nine-tenth of a tower rises from a simple basket of earth. A thousand meters height starts from under your feet.

215 Foster 静 *tranquillity*—[16.01b] Nurture tranquillity diligently.   [16.04-05] Returning to the roots is called tranquillity.   Tranquillity is called returning to order. [26.02] Tranquillity is the sovereign of rashness. [37.05] Use tranquillity without disgrace and the world will regulate itself. [45.10-11] Tranquillity overcomes the heat. Hence, pure tranquillity can be used to regulate the world. [57.11] I am tranquil and the people will perfect themselves.   [61.04-05b] The female always uses tranquillity to overcome the male.   She is tranquil. Therefore, she is better in a low position.

[216] Inhibit 为 *action*—[02.09] Therefore, sages manage their affairs with Non-action. [02.12] Act, but do not rely on it. [03.06-07] Let those who know, not dare to act but stop. Act with Non-action, then there will be no anarchy. [05.02] Sages do not have to be benevolent, if common people would act as straw dogs. [10.09] Act, but do not rely on it. [29.03a] Those who act will fail. [34.10] Therefore, sages can achieve greatness, because they do not act great. [38.03] Superior virtue uses Non-action and there is no action used. [43.03-04] Therefore, I know that there is benefit in Non-action. Teaching without speaking and Non-action will benefit the whole world. [47.06] They do not act and yet they achieve. [48.03-04] Contract and contract until there is Non-action left. There is no action and yet there is action. [51.12] Act, but do not rely on it. [53.01b-02] When walking on the Great Road, the only thing scary is action. [57.10] I practice Non-action and the people will transform themselves. [63.01] Act with Non-action. [63.10] Therefore, all sages will avoid great actions. [64.05] Act when it has not happened yet. [64.10a] Those who act will fail. [64.11a] Therefore, sages will use Non-action. [64.18] Sages complement the nature of all All-things, but they do not dare to act. [65.01a] Therefore, the Ancients said: "Do not use the Way of Action to enlighten people." [77.09] Therefore, sages act, but do not rely on it.

[217] Inhibit 骄 or 妄 *arrogance*—[09.04a-09] Admiring wealth and arrogance brings personal loss and misfortune. When merit is achieved, withdrawing yourself is the Way of Nature. Returning to order is a constant. Knowing this constant is brilliant. Not acknowledging this constant is arrogant. Arrogance causes misfortune. [22.11] They are not arrogant. Therefore, they will develop. [24.06] Those who are arrogant are without development. [30.09] Succeed without arrogance.

[218] Inhibit 事 *effort*—[48.05-06] If one wants to take the world, then one should always use no effort. When effort is needed, then there is never enough to take the world. Use no effort when taking the world. [57.12] I use no effort and the people will become wealthy by themselves. [63.02] Work without effort.

[219] Inhibit 欲 *desire*—[01.05-06] Therefore, be always without desire and see its details. Have always desires and see its limits. [03.03] Do not display what is desirable and the people will not revolt. [03.05] Let the people always be without knowledge and without desire. [15.14-15] Those who keep the Way do not desire fullness. Only those who desire no fullness are therefore able to exhaust themselves without renewal. [19.07] Lack selfishness and restrain desires. [20.18] I desire only to differ from other people and value the nourishment from the Mother. [24.09] Therefore, those who have desires will not succeed. [29.01a] If people desire to take the world and interfere with it, I see that they have no alternative. [34.06] It is always without desire. [37.03] If this transformation would cause desire, then I would suppress it by using the simplicity of the Nameless. [39.20] Hence, do not desire the great splendour of jade, but the grace of natural rock. [46.03-06] No greater suffering than having extreme desires. No greater misfortune than not knowing what is enough. No misfortune is more disastrous than the desire to accumulate. Therefore, know that enough is enough and there will be always enough. [57.13] I desire not to desire and the people will become simple by themselves. [64.16] Therefore, sages desire not to desire and do not admire goods that are difficult to obtain. [66.04-05] Therefore, sages who desire to be above the people must place themselves below them. Those who desire to lead people must place themselves behind them. [77.11] They do not desire to display their knowledge.

220 Inhibit 见 *display*—[03.03] Do not display what is desirable and the people will not revolt. [19.06] Show modesty and embrace simplicity. [22.08] They do not display themselves. Therefore, they are brilliant. [24.03] Those who display themselves are without brilliance. [72.05] Therefore, sages know themselves, but do not display themselves. [77.11] They do not desire to display their knowledge.

221 Inhibit 强 *force, power*; 师 *army*; and 兵 *soldier*—[30.01b-03] Do not use soldiers to force the world. Such actions are likely to rebound. Where armies have camped only thorny bushes will grow. [30.06-11] Do not dare to take power. Succeed without boasting. Succeed without attacking. Succeed without arrogance. Succeed without excess. That is called succeeding without force. [36.06] The soft and weak will overcome the strong. [42.10a-11] Therefore, the teachers of humanity discus and teach people that violent people will achieve nothing but death. [68.01] Competent warriors do not like war. [72.02-04] Do not take their dwellings by force. Do not reject them a place to live. Only, if they are not rejected, they will not reject you. [76.05-07] Therefore, the hard and strong are called companions of death. The soft and weak are the companions of life. Hence, a strong army will not win. A strong tree will be broken. [78.04] The softest will overcome the hardest. The weakest will overcome the strongest.

222 Inhibit 藏 *hoarding*; 积, 持, 得 *accumulate*; and 富 *wealth*—[09.01] Accumulating and filling up are not as good as stopping in time. [44.04-07] Most people love to spend a lot. The larger their hoard the more they have to lose. Therefore, know what is enough and there will be no disgrace. Know when to stop and there will be no danger. [46.05-06] No misfortune is more disastrous than the desire to accumulate. Therefore, know that enough is

enough and there will be always enough. [81.07] Sages do not hoard.

223 Inhibit 敌 *resistance*—[69.01-03] Warriors have a saying that states: "I do not dare to act as a host, but act as a guest. I do not dare to advance an inch, but retreat a foot." [69.06-09] Be without resistance. Hold without weapons. No greater misfortune than meeting no resistance. Meeting no resistance is close to losing my treasures.

224 Inhibit 争 *strive*—[03.01] Do not value knowledge and the people will not strive. [08.02] The goodness of water benefits All-things and it does not strive. [08.12] Only those who do not strive will therefore not fail. [22.12-13] They do not strive. Therefore, no one can strive with them. The ones called the 'Ancients' said: "Those who bend will be preserved." [66.09] Having no purpose, they do not strive. Therefore the world cannot strive with them. [68.01-05] Competent warriors do not like war. Competent chiefs will not get angry. Competent conquerors will not engage. Competent leaders will take a low position. That is called the virtue of not striving. [73.06] The Way of Nature is not to strive, but to overcome through competence. [81.11] Accordingly, the Way of People should be action without strive.

225 Inhibit 富 *wealth*—[09.04] Admiring wealth and arrogance brings personal loss and misfortune. [22.06] Have surplus then be confused. [30.10] Succeed without excess. [81.05-06] Those who are competent have not much. Those who have much are not competent. [44.02-03] Life or wealth? What is worth more? Gain or loss? What hurts more?